FIRMS, MARKETS AND ECONOMIC CHANGE

Innovating successfully is one of the key challenges facing modern managers, firms and governments. The rise to prominence of Japanese *keiretsu* in recent years has called into question the effectiveness of traditional Western forms of corporate organization. Will the future favor networks of small innovative firms, as in California's Silicon Valley, or will giant integrated firms dominate? Should governments play a role in directing the innovation process or should decisions be left to private enterprise?

Firms, Markets and Economic Change draws on industrial economics, business strategy, and economic history to illuminate these topics. The authors develop a dynamic theory of organizational boundaries that draws on both transaction-cost economics and the dynamic-capabilities or resource-based approach to strategy. They use this theory to propose an alternative explanation for vertical integration, and they emphasize the interplay of organizational form and product design, putting forward the theory of modular systems. In addition to offering detailed case studies of the early American automobile industry, the stereo-components industry, and the microcomputer industry, the book also turns its attention to the causes of industrial inertia and to the normative questions of organizational form and innovation.

The authors argue that innovation is a complex process whose organizational and institutional implications defy neat categorization. Different organizational forms may be appropriate depending on the specific circumstances of technology, organizational competence and consumer knowledge. As a result, government policy needs to facilitate change in a broad way rather than prescribe organizational forms or attempt to direct innovation.

Richard N. Langlois is Professor of Economics at the University of Connecticut, Storrs. His research interests include the economics of organization, the economics of technology, and economic history. He is the editor of *Economics as a Process: Essays in the New Institutional Economics* (1986) and the lead author of *Microelectronics: An Industry in Transition* (1988).

Paul L. Robertson is a Senior Lecturer in the Department of Economics and Management at University College, University of New South Wales. In recent years, he has taught strategic and project management as well as economic history. In addition to many articles, he is the co-author, with Sidney Pollard, of *The British Shipbuilding Industry, 1870–1914* (1979).

FIRMS, MARKETS AND ECONOMIC CHANGE

A Dynamic Theory of Business Institutions

Richard N. Langlois and Paul L. Robertson

London and New York

First published 1995
by Routledge
11 New Fetter Lane, London EC4P 4EE
Simultaneously published in the USA and Canada
by Routledge
29 West 35th Street, New York, NY 10001

© 1995 Richard N. Langlois and Paul L. Robertson

Typeset in Garamond by
J&L Composition Ltd, Filey, North Yorkshire
Printed and bound in Great Britain by
Biddles Ltd, Guildford and King's Lynn

British Library Cataloguing in Publication Data
A catalogue record for this book is available from the British
Library

ISBN 0–415–12119–1 (hbk)
ISBN 0–415–12385–2 (pbk)

Library of Congress Cataloguing in Publication Data
Firms, markets and economic change.
p.   cm.
ISBN 0–415–12119–1 (hbk) — ISBN 0–415–12385–2 (pbk)
1. Industries. 2. Marketing. 3. Product life cycle.
4. Business enterprises—Case studies. 5. Product
management—Case studies.
HD2326.F547   1995
338.5–dc20   94–23752
CIP

To our parents

Normand Richard Langlois
Loretta Ann Langlois
John Richards Robertson
and the memory of Geraldine Geering Robertson (1913–1993)

CONTENTS

CONTENTS

FIGURES AND TABLES

FIGURES

FIGURES AND TABLES

TABLES

ACKNOWLEDGMENTS

Over the years, we have benefited from the help and encouragement from many people. Steve Jones and Craig Freedman were kind enough to read and comment on an earlier draft of the entire manuscript. A number of individuals have at various stages contributed critical readings, comments, and discussions useful in writing the individual chapters and the papers from which they emerged. These include: Lee Alston, Lou Cain, Rondo Cameron, Bo Carlsson, Fred Carstensen, Wes Cohen, Metin Cosgel, Bernard Elbaum, Gunnar Eliasson, Peter Hall, Paul Hallwood, Tim Hatton, Ken-ichi Imai, Paul Johnson, Colin Kirkpatrick, Eric Lampard, Dan Landau, William Lazonick, Brian Loasby, John Lyons, Don McCloskey, Stefan Markowski, Scott Masten, Stan Metcalfe, Lanse Minkler, Dick Nelson, Dan Raff, John Duncan Robertson II, John Richards Robertson, Deborah Savage, John Singleton, L. G. Thomas, Art Wright, and Tony Yu. We have very much appreciated their helpful advice, although we have not always taken it. In addition, parts of the book have been presented as conference and seminar papers at many venues in the United States, Australia, and Europe. Again, we received useful comments from people too numerous to name. Responsibility for all interpretations and errors remains, of course, our own.

Richard Langlois would like to thank Fadi Abusamra, László Csontos, Michael Everett, and Donald Vandegrift for research assistance on the history of the microcomputer industry. Paul Robertson would like to thank University College, University of New South Wales for financial help. Special thanks also goes to the University of Manchester for granting him a Hallsworth Research Fellowship that allowed him to spend the autumn term of 1992 at the University. In addition, he wishes to thank Professor Graeme Snooks and the Department of Economic History, Research School of the Social Sciences at the Australian National University for a research fellowship and office facilities during the first half of 1993. Parts of the manuscript were typed and diagrams prepared by Jean Considine, Joan Fenwick, and Jill Kenna of the Department of Economics and Management, University College. We wish to thank them for their patience and technical advice.

The greatest thanks is owed to our wives, Deborah Savage and Ellen Robertson, and to our children, Zachary Langlois and Emily, James, and Sarah Robertson. They have remained supportive throughout despite the occasional disruptions to their lives that our preoccupations have caused.

As is typical of a work that reflects a long period of collaboration, this book makes use of pieces of our writings that have already appeared in print: "Creating External Capabilities: Innovation and Vertical Disintegration in the Microcomputer Industry," *Business and Economic History* 19: 93–102 (1990) and "Business Organization as a Coordination Problem: Toward a Dynamic Theory of the Boundaries of the Firm," *Business and Economic History* 22(1): 31–41 (Fall 1993), reprinted with the permission of the Business History Conference; "Economic Change and the Boundaries of the Firm," *Journal of Institutional and Theoretical Economics* 144(4): 635-657 (1988), reprinted with the permission of J. C. B. Mohr (Paul Siebeck); "Transaction-Cost Economics in Real Time," *Industrial and Corporate Change* 1(1): 99–127 (1992) and "Institutions, Inertia, and Changing Industrial Leadership," *Industrial and Corporate Change* 3(2): 359–378 (1994), reprinted with the permission of Oxford University Press; "Explaining Vertical Integration: Lessons from the American Automobile Industry," *Journal of Economic History* 49(2): 361–375 (June 1989), reprinted with the permission of Cambridge University Press; "Networks and Innovation in a Modular System: Lessons from the Microcomputer and Stereo Component Industries," *Research Policy* 21(4): 297–313 (1992) and "Innovation, Networks, and Vertical Integration," *Research Policy*, in press, reprinted with kind permission from Elsevier Science B. V., Amsterdam, The Netherlands; "Modularity, Innovation, and the Firm: the Case of Audio Components," in Frederick M. Scherer and Mark Perlman (eds) *Entrepreneurship, Technological Innovation, and Economic Growth: Studies in the Schumpeterian Tradition*, Ann Arbor: University of Michigan Press, 1992, reprinted with the permission of the University of Michigan Press; and "External Economies and Economic Progress: The Case of the Microcomputer Industry," *Business History Review* 66(1): 1–50 (Spring 1992), copyright © 1992 by the President and Fellows of Harvard College, reprinted by permission of Harvard Business School.

1

INTRODUCTION

ON BUSINESS INSTITUTIONS

The recent awards of Nobel Prizes to Ronald Coase and Douglass North are but one indication of a growing theoretical interest within economics in the nature and role of social institutions. Indeed, there has already appeared a large body of literature bearing the flag of the New Institutional Economics (Langlois 1986a, 1993). This book is intended as a contribution in this developing tradition, albeit a contribution with a focus on one specific set of social institutions: what we call business institutions.

By using the term business *institutions*, we intend to stress that our concern extends beyond business *organization* – which connotes the idea of the business firm – to encompass a wide variety of structures, including those institutions generally described as markets. Business institutions are, of course, in part a matter of legal institutions, and we certainly find occasion to discuss the notion of property-rights. But by business institutions we mean more than an explicit (or even implicit) legal framework. In the broader theory of social institutions, the fundamental concept of an institution ultimately boils down to the idea of recurrent patterns of behavior – habits, conventions, and routines. In this book, we take a similar perspective, in that the most elemental form of a business institution for us is a productive *routine*, a habitual pattern of behavior embodying knowledge that is often tacit and skill-like. Nelson and Winter (1982) used the idea of routines as the basis of their evolutionary theory of industry structure and economic growth. But to the extent that the New Institutional Economics has focused on issues of organizational form, it has done so through the lens of the transaction-cost economics pioneered by Coase (1937) and honed today by Williamson (1985) and others. One way to understand our project in this volume is to see it as an attempt to carry evolutionary economics more forcefully into the traditional bailiwicks of transaction-cost theory by presenting and applying an evolutionary theory of economic capabilities.[1]

Business institutions are more than just a theoretical concern. Much of

1

the present-day debate over industrial policy is implicitly a debate over organizational patterns and structures. Although the discussion often turns to issues of legal regime and government policy, much of it also centers on business institutions in our sense: What are the patterns of organization most conducive to innovation and economic growth? Are large vertically integrated firms superior to networks of "flexibly specialized" firms – or vice-versa? Do the patterns of organization in Japan, for example, confer advantages over patterns of institutions elsewhere? We offer this book as a step toward creating the kind of conceptual apparatus necessary for clarifying these and similar issues.

The approach we take has strong antecedents. We consider ourselves within the broad current of economics that runs from Adam Smith to Alfred Marshall and Joseph Schumpeter.[2] The reader will encounter those names frequently in what follows. We are also indebted to a number of present-day writers, including but not limited to G. B. Richardson, Edith Penrose, Alfred Chandler, Richard Nelson and Sidney Winter, Brian Loasby, David Teece, and Morris Silver. But, although this rather unusual practice of giving credit to the past denies us some of the rhetoric of novelty, we do not thereby wish to renounce all claims to originality.

OVERVIEW OF THE THEORY

Present-day transaction-cost economics tends to see business institutions – and the firm in particular – as optimal responses to incentive problems.[3] The importance of coordinating resources is recognized in such concepts as "asset specificity," but the principal focus of transaction-cost theory is on aspects of behavior that inhibit markets from providing effective coordination. In terms of the game-theoretic imagery of the New Institutional Economics (Langlois 1986a, 1993), we might say that mainstream transaction-cost theory explains the firm as the solution of a prisoner's-dilemma-like game. In a prisoner's dilemma, the fundamental problem the players face is less one of information than one of incentives. And the measure of a governance structure (to use Williamson's terminology) lies in its ability to align incentives and overcome "opportunism." In this formulation, the *raison d'être* of the firm does not lie in coordination as such, but in its ability to provide coordination when divergent incentives between buyers and sellers and between agents and principals impede the smooth operation of markets.

Transaction-costs theorists, however, do not give close consideration to why coordination is necessary. The efficient coordination of resources not only permits operational efficiency in the production and distribution of goods and services along existing lines, but it is also vital for strategic uses that require new, and not always readily evident, combinations of resources. The value of business institutions – firms prominently among them – is

2

that they can supply this coordination function as well as (or perhaps rather than) merely an incentive-alignment function. To put it another way, business institutions may also arise as solutions to *coordination* games. In a world of fundamental uncertainty, in which capabilities and knowledge differ among actors, this, rather than incentive questions, may be the central role of such institutions.

To see why this may be so, let us return to the idea of productive routines. The repertoire of routines of an organization (or network of organizations) constitutes the *capabilities* that organization (or network) possesses. Those business institutions that can create and utilize superior capabilities tend to perform better. As Schumpeter (1950) maintained, this process in which new capabilities emerge and are tested *is* the competitive process.[4] Such a process is necessarily complex and historically contingent, but there are a few theoretical generalizations one can make about which types of business institutions will be most likely to succeed under various circumstances.

One of the principal determinants of the appropriate form of business institution is the nature of the economic change that the institution must confront. The second critical factor is the existing structure of relevant capabilities, including both the substantive content of those capabilities and the organizational structure under which they are deployed in the economy.

One pattern typical in the history of business institutions emerges when a *systemic* innovation offers the potential to create new value through, for example, an improvement in the non-price characteristics of a product (which may sometimes mean a "new" product); a reduction in price; or an increase in the return to the input suppliers. To be successful, such a systemic innovation requires simultaneous change in several stages of production.[5] But this may render some existing assets obsolete and, at the same time, call for the use of capabilities not previously applied in the production of the product. If, in addition, the existing capabilities are under separate ownership – or, to put it loosely and somewhat inaccurately, the existing production system is coordinated through market mechanisms – then we arrive at one important rationale for the institution of the business firm. Under this scenario, the business firm arises because it can more cheaply redirect, coordinate, and where necessary create the capabilities necessary to make the innovation work. Because control of the necessary capabilities in the firm would be relatively more concentrated than in a market-based organizational structure, such a firm could overcome not only the recalcitrance of asset-holders whose capital would be the victim of creative destruction, but also the "dynamic" transaction costs[6] of informing and persuading new input-holders with necessary capabilities.

This scenario accurately describes the situation surrounding the creation and growth of many of the enterprises Alfred Chandler chronicled in *The Visible Hand* (1977). With the lowering of transportation and communications costs in the America of the nineteenth century, there arose profit opportunities for those who could create mass markets and take advantage of economies of scale in mass production. Examples range from steel and farm machinery to cigarettes and branded goods. In all these cases, profitable improvements in product attributes and costs[7] required the creative destruction of existing decentralized systems of production and distribution in favor of systems involving significantly different capabilities. Gustavus Swift's creation of the system of refrigerated meat-packing (Chandler 1977, pp. 299–302) was a systemic innovation that rendered obsolete the older network of live-animal distribution. Swift was forced to integrate into both refrigerated railroad cars and wholesale distribution in order to overcome the opposition of vested interests and to persuade others in the chain of production of the value of his innovation (Silver 1984, pp. 28–29).

This picture of the rationale for the firm is what we might legitimately call a strategic, entrepreneurial, or Schumpeterian theory of vertical integration. The superiority of centralized control of capabilities lies in the ability to redeploy those capabilities in the service of an entrepreneurial opportunity when such redeployment would otherwise be costly. The firm overcomes the "dynamic" transaction costs of economic change. It is in this sense that we may say the firm solves a coordination problem: it enables complementary input-holders to agree on the basic nature of the system of production and distribution of the product. It provides the structure in a situation of structural uncertainty.

A number of writers, with Schumpeter himself in the lead, have taken this picture of the firm to imply the superiority of the firm – especially the large vertically integrated firm – in most if not all times and places. In fact, however, the scenario we just depicted is by no means the only important one, let alone the only possible one. In the Swift example, the superiority of the firm rested on its ability cheaply to redeploy, coordinate, and create necessary capabilities in a situation in which (1) the entrepreneurial opportunity involved required systemic change and (2) the necessary new capabilities were not cheaply available from an existing decentralized or market network. In situations, however, in which one or both of these conditions is missing, the benefits of the firm are attenuated, and its rationale slips away. This in fact is the expected outcome in a dynamic situation. Both the levels of transaction costs and the relative value of capabilities held by firms may be expected to decrease over time because they are underpinned by knowledge. People may find ways of eliminating impediments to the smooth operation of markets, and other firms can acquire once-tacit capabilities and routines through trial-and-error experimentation. Thus, while we can expect to find capabilities clustered within firms during the early stages of a systemic innovation, specialization of functions may increase as the innovation matures.

4

Moreover, in many circumstances change – even sometimes rapid change – may proceed in an autonomous rather than a systemic fashion. A prime example of this occurs when the attributes buyers desire can be provided in the form not of a preset package but of a *modular system*. Stereo systems and IBM-compatible personal computers are prominent examples, and we examine these in detail below; but there are many others as well, including cases in the realm of process technology (Langlois 1992c). For present purposes, the key feature of a modular system is that the connections or "interfaces" among components of an otherwise systemic product are fixed and publicly known. Such standardization creates what we might call *external economies of scope* that substitute in large part for centralized coordination among the wielders of complementary capabilities. This allows the makers of components to concentrate their capabilities narrowly and deeply and thus to improve their piece of the system independently of others.

Moreover, in highly developed economies, a wide variety of capabilities may be available for purchase on ordinary markets, in the form either of contract inputs or finished products. At the same time, it may also be the case that the existing network of capabilities that must be creatively destroyed (at least in part) by entrepreneurial change is not in the hands of decentralized input-suppliers but is in fact concentrated in existing large firms. The unavoidable flip-side of seeing firms as possessed of capabilities – and therefore as accretions of habits and routines – is that such firms are quite as susceptible to institutional inertia as is a system of decentralized economic capabilities. Even though firms may have a strategic decision-making function, they may yet be unable to reorient themselves in the face of rapid change. Economic change has in many circumstances come from small innovative firms relying on the capabilities available in the market rather than existing firms with ill-adapted internal capabilities.

PLAN OF THE BOOK

In what follows, we develop the ideas touched on here. Our approach is to mix together theory, economic history, and applications to policy, as we believe there is more to gain from a conversation among these modalities than there is from their strict separation. Nonetheless, some chapters are clearly mostly theory; others are heavily economic history; and others address the debate over industrial policy quite centrally.

In Chapters 2 and 3 we develop an evolutionary theory of the firm. Chapter 2 develops the theory of economic capabilities alluded to above. Although influenced by the work of economists, the capabilities approach finds a more welcome home in the literature of strategic management. Chapter 2 spends a considerable amount of time addressing that literature and connecting our ideas to it. Chapter 3 is the central theoretical chapter of the book. It sets out the theory of dynamic transaction costs and shows how they, and the changing value of capabilities, provide an explanation of the changing value of vertical integration.

Chapters 4 and 5 are the most deeply historical. Chapter 4 enlarges upon the dynamic theory of the firm in Chapter 3 by confronting it with a detailed history of integration and disintegration in the pre-war American automobile industry. One of the claims of Chapter 3 is that transaction costs are fundamentally a short-run phenomenon. By looking at the automobile industry over a number of decades, Chapter 4 is able to follow the ebb and flow of transaction costs and to examine how historical sequences of events – rather than just transaction costs seen *ex visu* of a given point of time[8] – shape the organizational structures of an industry. Chapter 5 is a mix of history and theory. It develops the theory of modular systems, and then applies that theory through detailed case studies of the early stereo-components industry and the microcomputer industry. Chapters 3 and 4 concentrate heavily, but by no means exclusively, on the causes of vertical integration and thus on the firm as a business institution. Chapter 5 is a kind of counterpoint, focusing in a complementary way on the nature and role of "external" rather than internal capabilities in economic growth.

Chapters 6 and 7 introduce industrial-policy issues into the mix. Chapter 6 uses both theory and history to examine the nature and causes of institutional inertia. Building on the institutional theory developed earlier, this chapter draws on such ideas as punctuated equilibria and population dynamics to explain the sources of inertia, and it adduces four hypotheses about when particular types of organizational structures will be able to appropriate the gains from innovation.

Finally, Chapter 7 turns directly to the industrial-policy debate. As we suggested above, a central aspect of that debate is that between proponents of large vertically integrated firms on the one hand and advocates of networks of small specialized producers on the other. This chapter argues that neither institutional structure is the panacea its enthusiasts claim. The menu of institutional alternatives is in fact quite large, and both firms and networks – of which there is more than one kind – can be successful, growth-promoting adaptations to the competitive environment. Industrial structures vary in their ability to coordinate information flows necessary for innovation and to overcome power relationships adverse to innovation. The relative desirability of the various structures depends on the nature and scope of technological change in the industry and on the effects of various product life-cycle patterns. The principal policy conclusion of this analysis is that the government's role ought to be facilitating rather than narrow and prescriptive, allowing scope for firms to develop organizational forms that are best adapted to their particular environments.

2

CAPABILITIES, STRATEGY AND THE FIRM

Holmstrom and Tirole (1989, p. 65) have recently outlined criteria that a theory of the firm must meet, criteria that apply to other types of organizations as well. In their view, such theories need to address two main questions. First, the theory must account for the purpose of organizations, or why they exist at all. Second, the theory must explain the boundaries of the organization – its scale and scope. In Chapters 2 and 3, we develop a dynamic evolutionary model to address these questions.

Our basic argument is that firms and other types of organizations consist of two distinct but changing parts. The first part, the *intrinsic core*, comprises elements that are idiosyncratically synergistic, inimitable, and noncontestable. That is, the capabilities in the intrinsic core cannot be duplicated, bought, or sold, and they combine to generate unique outcomes that are more valuable than the outcomes that the core elements could produce separately. The remainder of the organization consists of *ancillary capabilities* that are contestable and may not be unique.

The boundaries of the organization – the extent to which ancillary capabilities will be internalized or bought through the market – depend (1) on the strength of the organization's own capabilities relative to those that can be purchased, i.e., on relative production costs and (2) on the respective transaction and governance costs involved in making or buying the capabilities. In any case, however, both the intrinsic core and the ancillary capabilities that comprise an organization, and the prevailing levels of transaction costs, may be expected to change over time because they are underpinned by knowledge. Thus in the long run, the boundaries of the firm may alter as the organization itself, and other organizations, learn in ways that change the relative values of ancillary capabilities and levels of transaction and governance costs. Moreover, the instrinsic core capabilities of an organization may erode in the long run as other firms acquire through trial-and-error search knowlege that was formerly tacit or proprietary.

As our principal focus is on privately owned, for-profit organizations, we will generally use the word "firm." Much of the discussion that follows, however, is equally applicable to organizations in general.

CLASSICAL AND NEOCLASSICAL THEORIES

Many writers have noted that the main thrust of economic theory long ago shifted away from the concerns of Adam Smith and the classicals.[9] The "marginalist" or neoclassical theory that emerged after 1873 was designed not to understand the springs of economic growth and the sources of wealth but rather to analyze the allocation of known and given resources. In his *Theory of Political Economy* (1911, p. 267), William Stanley Jevons put the matter starkly. "The problem of economics," he wrote, "may, as it seems to me, be stated thus: – Given, a certain population, with various needs and powers of production, in possession of certain lands and other sources of material: required, the mode of employing their labour which will maximize the utility of the produce." Of course, marginalist theory is, and always was (Jaffé 1976), far from homogeneous in its concerns, and neoclassical economics grew to encompass a number of distinct variations, each arguably pointing at a different set of concerns. The Walrasian system poses an answer to an abstract logical problem whose general relevance one may question. "Marshallian" comparative statics – itself only one aspect of Marshall's opus – was designed to answer an important set of questions: how in the short run do exogenous changes in boundary conditions affect the direction of change in price and quantity (both supplied and demanded) in relatively isolated markets? (Langlois and Koppl 1991). And both the Marshallian and Austrian strands did retain important aspects of the classical tradition, albeit in different ways.

Is Jevons's formulation of the economic problem the one that best illuminates the activities of economic institutions, and in particular of firms and markets? Arguably, these activities are motivated at least as much by the sorts of issues that animated Smith: what are the sources of economic growth and industrial competitiveness? How do the organization of production and the institutions of society affect economic growth and competitiveness? To the extent that firms and other business organizations have been concerned by such issues, mainstream theory has been of limited usefulness. Indeed, in the areas in which the concerns of entrepreneurs and managers and those of economic theorists have overlapped – namely so-called Industrial Organization theory – neoclassical models have been strained well beyond their limits, leading to inappropriate applications of theory and, as in the area of antitrust policy, often absurd and harmful policy conclusions.[10]

We might say that, in a fundamental sense, the traditional neoclassical theory of the firm "takes the firm as the unit of analysis."[11] That is to say, the formal neoclassical theory of the firm takes the "firm" as a fundamental building block in the construction of a theory of the industry. This building block is a simplified and anthropomorphized ideal type – a "monobrain," as Fritz Machlup (1967) put it. Especially in its true Marshallian formulation, such an approach has proven extremely valuable for the questions of partial-equilibrium comparative statics for which it was intended.[12] But, not surprisingly, that theory has not proven very useful in analyzing what goes on inside the firm or, more importantly, how production is actually organized within the economy. In Axel Leijonhufvud's (1986, p. 203) irreverent image, the formal neoclassical conception of the firm "is more like a recipe for bouillabaisse where all the ingredients are dumped in a pot, (K, L), heated up, f(•), and the output, X, is ready." It provides no insight into organizational structure or the sequencing of tasks.

Attacks on mainstream theory are in abundant supply these days, and such a blanket criticism is not our goal here. Rather, we want to suggest that discussions of the appropriate boundaries of firms in a market context ought to be informed by the questions with which entrepreneurs and managers concern themselves. These are questions, not only of allocation and welfare, but also very importantly of growth and development: how is new value created? They are, moreover, institutional questions: how do social institutions and forms of business organization lead to growth and competitiveness? And how are these institutions shaped in turn by growth and competition? Confronting such questions analytically may not mean abandoning mainstream ideas so much as abandoning those assumptions that were designed for other purposes and are inappropriate to the study of firm behavior.

THE "WHY" OF FIRMS

From the standpoint of any particular firm, all of the activities undertaken in the course of producing and distributing any given good or service must be performed either by that firm or by some other unit from which the firm buys or to which it sells.[13] Thus one way of classifying productive processes is according to their degree of formal articulation. When examined in this way, they range along a spectrum from market-based systems, with each transaction between components being conducted separately, to unified concerns that, as far as possible, internalize their activities through common ownership and control of the functions of supply, research, operations, and marketing. This way of casting the spectrum from "market" to "firm" goes back at least to Coase (1937) and is implicit (and sometimes explicit) in most of the modern transaction-cost literature.[14] Although useful for many purposes, however, this unidimensional characterization lacks much of the subtlety needed to think carefully about firm/market relationships. There are in fact many dimensions along which various forms of industrial organization differ from one another. For the moment, we suggest that expansion from one dimension to two will yield a high marginal increase in explanatory power.[15]

There is something of a debate in the present-day economics of organization between the nexus-of-contracts view of the firm (Cheung 1983) and the property-rights view (Hart 1989; Moore 1992). The former holds that organization within a firm is no less a contractual matter than organization through markets, and a "firm" is nothing more than a particularly dense intersection of contracts. What differs between market and firm is the nature of the contracts involved, with contracts within the firm having an ongoing and more open-ended character (Ben-Porath 1980). Such contracts require various degrees of conscious, ongoing administrative coordination among the parties. We might say, then, that the essence of the firm in this view is the nature of the coordination involved. In the property rights view, by contrast, ownership is the issue. The boundaries of the firm, rather fuzzy under the "nexus" view, are here brightly illuminated by the title to ownable assets, and two stages of production are held to be vertically integrated when the assets involved are under common ownership. We thus have two dimensions along which to analyze organizational forms.[16] One dimension is the degree of ownership integration; the other is the degree of coordination integration (see Figure 2.1). We can use this construct to revisit various kinds of actually existing relationships.

For our purposes, these views are complementary rather than mutually exclusive, and each captures an important aspect of what internal and external organization means. Moreover, these two aspects are potentially separable. A major automobile firm can be integrated into the production of a particular part in the sense that it owns a company producing such parts, even if the parent deals with the subsidiary largely through the market on a more-or-less equal footing with other suppliers. At the same time, two

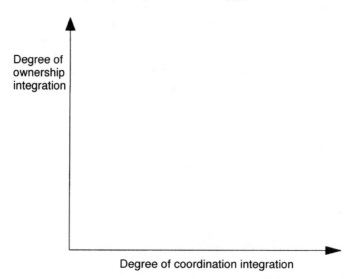

Figure 2.1 The two dimensions of integration

distinct legal entities may be engaged in an ongoing development project that involves exclusive dealing, significant exchange of information, and administrative coordination.

Although useful for our analysis, however, the discussion so far still neglects important aspects of firm behavior. One basic assumption that proponents of both the nexus-of-contracts view and the property-rights view have taken over from neoclassical economics is that firms are a second-best alternative that persist as a result of "market failure." In addition, all of these schools of thought center their theories around the premise that the primary behavioral goal of firms is to provide profits for their owners. In this view, the organizational form that a firm adopts is (consciously?) chosen because it will deliver a return on investment at least as great as any alternative form of organization. This assumption holds both for the relationship of the firm to its external environment – what the firm chooses to do itself and what it purchases and sells to others – and for the internal organization of the firm – how it goes about producing whatever goods or services it has decided belong within its proper sphere of activity.

From the perspective of real-world firm behavior and the boundaries of the firm, these assumptions ignore some of the most important factors that determine firm organization and underpin the relationship between firms and markets. They essentially relegate to second place, or even assume away altogether, the activities that the people working for the firm are actually engaged in. These include deciding what to produce and how to produce it and then actually producing it in the way that best rewards the firm's owners. Hence, success derives from the firm providing goods and services that meet the needs of potential customers in a way that generates the highest possible returns to its owners. In short, the behavior of firms is determined with an eye on both blades of the Marshallian scissors (Langlois and Robertson 1992).[17]

If this is true (and we think it is), then we should conceive of firms as organizations that need to tackle a variety of goals. These goals are interdependent in the sense that, while all must be addressed in some form if the desired product is to eventuate, some may conflict with others if they are not coordinated or "managed." This holds even if we leave aside questions of opportunism and shirking. If the firm is to survive, let alone prosper, it must make sure that it produces something that customers desire, which means that it must acquire and accurately use information, or knowledge, about products and production processes. In fact, a firm must be organized to undertake one, several, or all of the following activities associated with the profitable production of a good or service: conception, design and development, manufacturing, provision of inputs, marketing and distribution, and many others. A design that is outstanding in the sense that it meets the performance attributes (Lancaster 1971)

11

potential purchasers desire, however, may for that very reason cost more to produce than those same purchasers are willing to pay; or it may be impossible to produce at all. Thus one reason for organizing such diverse activities is to provide coordination between aspects of production so that a plausible outcome results in the form of a good or service that can be produced: (a) with non-cost attributes attractive to potential buyers; (b) at a price that is also acceptable to those buyers; and (c) that allows for an acceptable return on the productive resources involved.

It is a separate question whether the proper vehicle for generating such a plausible outcome is a vertically integrated firm, or several firms specializing in different links in the productive chain, or a group of independent and unattached workers. The answer depends in part, of course, on levels of transaction costs, but it also depends on the nature of the activities to be performed and on the types and distribution of resources that are needed, especially in the form of human skills or talents.

Williamson (1985) indicates that transactions can occur only across a "technologically separable interface." If it is technically impossible to perform two of more stages in a production process separately, then there can be no transactions as the product proceeds along these stages, and the activities must remain within a single organization. Otherwise, in Williamson's view, the movement from one stage to another does constitute a transaction that firms may either internalize or handle through market-based exchange. But technical considerations are not the only factors that determine the size of a firm's irreducible core. There are other types of interrelationships that provide organizational bonding, many of which are behavioral or cognitive in nature. When there is a low degree of interdependence among activities, the outcome of their operations is "additive" in the sense that the total result is the sum of the output of the individual operations. However, when the performance of particular operations cannot proceed without the completion of other operations, the resulting high degree of interdependence may lead to "superadditive" results. In this case, the outcome from the combined performance of the operations is greater than (and frequently different from) the outcome of the operations being undertaken separately (Cheung 1983).

Interdependence, therefore, leads by definition to certain types of operational inseparability or indivisibility. In itself, however, this does not mean that the possibility of transactions between components is ruled out. Although the coordinated efforts of several workers may be required to lift a slab, the workers can be hired and replaced individually. Similarly, in theory (and occasionally in practice) the machines in a factory may have varied ownership even though the production of a particular good depends on their coordinated use.

The real factor that can rule out transactions in the course of a productive process is not inseparability *per se* but a combination of interdependence of activities *and* the costliness of transferring knowledge about or imitating one or more of the components of a process. (In the next chapter, we explore the economics of these "dynamic" transaction costs in much greater detail.) The extreme case here, of course, is when various components of a process are *inimitable*. Mahoney and Pandian (1992) capture this latter idea by distinguishing between "contestable synergy" and "idiosyncratic synergy."[18] When there is contestability, as in the example of the lifting of the slab, there is "a combination of resources that create value but are competitively available" (Mahoney and Pandian 1992, p. 368). Idiosyncratic synergy, on the other hand, occurs when the enhanced outcome is specific to the particular resources that are being combined and substitutes are not available.[19] In general, we should expect that the irreducible, or *intrinsic*, core of any organization would be the coordinated set of resources that is idiosyncratically synergistic and vital to the goals of the organization.

What are examples of idiosyncratically synergistic resources? Although it is possible to conceive of a mineral that has only one use and a production process that cannot function without that mineral, one can usually purchase both minerals and processes. Similarly, although a group of people may have a higher total output when working together than when in other combinations, under most circumstances the people are legally free to move eventually even though they may be under contract for the time being.

The idiosyncratically synergistic resources that bind organizations together are, in fact, most frequently forms of knowledge that are difficult both to acquire and to communicate to others. This knowledge is often expressed in the form of the individual and collective behavior of members of the organization. As Prescott and Visscher put it, the "firm is a structure within which agents have the incentive to acquire and reveal information in a manner that is less costly than in possible alternative institutions" (1980, p. 460). Through working together, people learn to behave in institutionally specific ways that are efficient but cannot be easily, cheaply, or quickly taught to others. Therefore, these firms develop ways of acting that are competitively valuable but, because they have evolved within a particular context, are likely to vary from those of other firms. This variance increases as the industrial context of firms differs, but will be present to a degree even among firms in the same or similar industries. To the extent that this behavior is efficient and hard to replicate, it provides an advantage to the firm that would be lost if the firm were split up or dispersed.

ROUTINES, CAPABILITIES, AND ORGANIZATION

In sum, we are arguing that idiosyncratic knowledge and ways of acting are at the heart of the firm as organization. This is a notion that animates a developing school of thought that cuts across economics and strategic

CAPABILITIES, STRATEGY AND THE FIRM

management – what we can call the capabilities, or resources, view of the firm.[20]

Although one can find versions of the idea in Smith, Marshall, and elsewhere, the modern discussion of the capabilities of organizations probably begins with Edith Penrose (1959), who suggested viewing the firm as a "pool of resources." In what is arguably still the richest treatment of the subject, Penrose outlined a number of conditions that might induce a firm to undertake a strategy of diversification. These conditions can be extended to cover innovation as well. According to Penrose, firms have a tendency to acquire surplus quantities of both material and human resources. First, because of indivisibilities, firms may obtain excess amounts of one or more inputs. Resources must often be purchased in bundles and, except in the relatively rare situations in which the inputs needed for the amount produced happen to coincide with the "least common multiple" of the bundles, there will be surpluses. Secondly, the efficiency of human resources tends to increase over time as personnel become more knowledgeable and more adept at dealing both with the external environment and with the administration of the firm itself.

The firm has a clear incentive to make good use of these excess resources. The way in which it employs its surpluses, however, will vary according to the firm's strengths. Not only will the varieties of resources differ among firms, but many of the most important types of resources are heterogeneous. In particular, human resources involving entrepreneurship, management, or research are not standardized, rendering each firm unique because it has kinds and combinations of resources different from those of other firms.

Penrose believes that this heterogeneity of resources will have a strong endogenous influence on the strategy adopted, since each firm should attempt to make the best use of its surpluses given the qualitative nature of its own strengths. While there may be a range of uses to which a particular combination of excess resources can be put, the firm will tend to choose those that fit most closely with the types of knowledge and scope of operations that have evolved from earlier experience because these are likely to prove most profitable.

Although her terminology differs, Penrose anticipated many of the most important ideas later elaborated by Richardson, Teece, and Nelson and Winter. To all these authors, the firm is a pool not of tangible but of intangible resources. In particular, it was Richardson who introduced the useful term *capabilities* to refer to the skills, experience, and knowledge that a firm possesses. Drawing on Penrose, he notes that, just as a technological stage of production may be an "antibottleneck" with excess capacity, so may an organization have excess capacity in its organizational capabilities. In both cases, the result is the taking on of additional work. But in the case of organizational capabilities, the new activity need not be linked

14

Figure 2.2 A theory of specialization
Source: Shoe/By Jeff MacNelly
(Reprinted by permission: Tribune Media Services)

technologically to what the firm had previously been doing; rather, the new activity need only require a similar set of capabilities. In Richardson's terminology, the activities need not be *complementary*, that is synergistically related; rather, they must be *similar*. The converse of a theory of diversification, of course, is a theory of non-diversification – a theory of specialization (see Figure 2.2). Such a theory would explain, as Coase once put it, "why General Motors was not a dominant factor in the coal industry, and why A&P did not manufacture airplanes" (Coase 1972, p. 67). And the basic answer is that capabilities have their limits. There are diminishing returns to spreading one's capabilities over more activities. This is so not merely for the reasons emanating from traditional span-of-control arguments (e.g., Robinson 1934), but also because each new activity the firm could consider diversifying into will often be increasingly dissimilar to – will require capabilities slightly different from – those the firm started out with. Richardson therefore concludes that firms "would find it expedient, for the most part, to concentrate on similar activities" when choosing a strategy (1972, p. 895).

What gives this observation its salience is that what is similar need not be what is complementary. That is, the various activities in the chain of production may – or may not – each require skills that are quite distinct. The manufacture of silicon wafers, from which integrated circuits begin, requires capabilities quite different from the fabrication of the semiconductors; as a result, the wafers are supplied by chemical companies, like Wacker Chemie, whose other activities are similar. The manufacture of the optical steppers used in the photolithography of the semiconductors is also unlike the fabrication of chips; but it is quite like the making of other precision optical equipment, which is why Nikon and Canon are among the suppliers of these devices (Langlois *et al.* 1988).

Ansoff (1965) and Panzar and Willig (1981) have employed a wider definition than Richardson of the attributes that firms may build on in choosing the scope of their activities. These include excess capacity in

15

marketing, production, raw material procurement, and finance, as well as managerial or entrepreneurial knowledge, skills, and experience. For convenience, however, we will follow Teece (1980) in using "capabilities" to refer to all of these attributes.

Another aspect of capabilities that has recently received a great deal of attention is organizational culture. In practice, not all organizations may be equally able to cope with change, as existing patterns of behavior involving both executives and subordinates may be resistant to change. Organizations develop collective habits or ways of thinking that can be altered only gradually. When a given culture is either flexible or consistent with a proposed change in product or process technology, the transition to the new regime will be relatively easy. If, however, the culture is incompatible with the needs posed by the change and is inflexible, the viability of the change will be threatened (Robertson 1990; Camerer and Vepsalainen 1988).

More recently, David Teece (1980, 1982) has developed a similar account of the scope of the firm. Teece explicitly draws on the evolutionary theory of Nelson and Winter, who have formulated a more microanalytic account of the nature of capabilities: namely, the habits and routines that individuals and organizations acquire through practice. "Routines," as Nelson and Winter put it (1982, p. 124), "are the skills of an organization." In the course of its development, a firm acquires a repertoire of routines that derives from its activities over the years. Note that *routines* refer to what an organization actually does, while *capabilities* also include what it may do if its resources are reallocated. Thus a firm's routines are a subset of its capabilities that influence but do not fully determine what the firm is competent to achieve. In a metaphorical sense, and often in a real one, the capabilities of the organization, and especially its routines, are superadditive in that they can accomplish more than the sum of the skills of the individuals in the organization. In addition to the "skill" of the firm's physical capital, there is also the matter of organization. How the firm is organized – how the routines of the humans and machines are linked together – is also part of a firm's capabilities. Indeed, "skills, organization, and technology are intimately intertwined in a functioning routine, and it is difficult to say exactly where one aspect ends and another begins" (Nelson and Winter 1982, p. 104). In effect, capabilities and routines are forms of knowledge about how to carry out productive tasks. Some of this knowledge may be tacit (Polanyi, 1958) and not easily articulated or transferred to others, but other capabilities may be generally available to those willing to make the investment necessary to acquire them.

Those routines and capabilities of a firm that are idiosyncratic – and the people who embody them – constitute the essence of that firm in the short and medium terms.[21] If the routines were to be quickly changed or the firm's activities were directed to areas requiring a heavy reliance on other capabilities, the firm would no longer have the knowledge required to undertake its activities with as much efficiency. Similarly, widespread and rapid changes in personnel would undermine a firm's ability to deploy its customary routines and capabilities. Finally, idiosyncratic routines and capabilities can be valuable because they are distinctive and it is unlikely that any other firm would possess exactly the same traits, competences, and behavior patterns.

Before moving on, we need to mention briefly two further considerations that we will deal with in considerable detail in the next chapter. First, the intrinsic core of a firm, as reflected in its capabilities and routines, does not necessarily define the borders of that firm. For various reasons of a transaction-cost nature, firms often find it desirable to internalize non-core, or *ancillary*, activities. Secondly, the nature of the core itself and of the non-core activities may change over time. Learning changes behavior and alters the nature and relative value of capabilities both within the firm and in the larger environment. It is therefore reasonable to expect that the activities of the firm and its relationship to potential suppliers and customers may also alter over the long run, with the result that the boundaries of the firm may contract or expand.

STRATEGY AND THE BOUNDARIES OF THE FIRM

One of the most important variables that affects the boundaries between firm and market is corporate strategy. Although there are many definitions of strategy, most agree that strategic decisions conform to several characteristics: they affect an entire firm or a significant portion of it ("a strategic business unit"); they are made by top level firm or divisional managers; they are long-term in nature; and they are based on perceptions about the future rather than on hard knowledge.

Neoclassical IO theory and its modern game-theoretic extensions are singularly incapable of shedding light on strategic activities because they disregard most aspects of strategy and regard many of the intended outcomes of strategic behavior with disfavor or even distaste (Mahoney and Pandian 1992; Foss, Knudsen, and Montgomery 1995). There is no scope for such behavior in a modeled world of unchanging technology, perfect knowledge, instantaneous adjustment, and identical access to resources for all firms. Real world strategies, however, must try to cope with the inherent uncertainty of the future: with markets that do not yet exist and products that potential buyers are unfamiliar with; with untried production processes; and with the use of specific skills and knowledge that may be in short supply and difficult or impossible to communicate to others. Moreover, while neoclassical economists have an inordinate fondness for market equilibrium, firm strategies often disrupt equilibria, sometimes intentionally.

Strategy formulation and implementation involve finding a match

17

between what a firm can do, or can induce others to do for it, and the technical requirements that a potential strategy imposes. This, in turn, requires a command over resources. These resources fit into several categories. Some, as we have seen, are peculiar to the firm, either because of idiosyncratic synergy or because other firms have not felt a need to develop the same combination of talents. Although idiosyncratic capabilities, including routines, cannot be imitated quickly, if at all, other capabilities can be reproduced more easily and promptly, especially by firms with similar existing talents, or they may be purchasable. Finally, there is the whole range of resources including capital equipment, raw materials, and standardized labor services that are generally, but not always,[22] available in the market. From this it follows that, since different firms have different bundles of capabilities, they vary in their ability to implement any given strategy (Penrose 1959; Nelson 1991).

But idiosyncratic capabilities, no matter how efficient, are not the only source of competitive advantage. Because of uncertainty, markets, where they exist, may function imperfectly, and those firms that cope best with uncertain conditions will be in the best position to implement their strategies. In this context, however, uncertainty has two separate meanings that need to be distinguished. The first, which we can call *structural uncertainty*, arises when a firm needs to base its decisions on judgments about future outcomes that are as yet unknowable. The second type of uncertainty, which we term *parametric uncertainty*, arises from the possibility of a range of market imperfections including bounded rationality and opportunism.[23] Whereas it is possible to adopt strategies to insure against parametric uncertainty, or at least to mitigate its effects, structural uncertainty cannot be eliminated strategically.

There are a number of ways in which firms may deal with parametric uncertainty. As we have discussed, writers in the capabilities tradition suggest that it is often best for firms to build on their existing capabilities and routines. This would be helpful in coping with problems associated with knowledge, for example, but can be extended to any area in which a firm has surplus resources that may form the basis of a new line of activity (Robertson 1990). But it is not always possible, of course, to build exclusively on resources that the firm already possesses. A second category of parametric uncertainty enters when a firm has to rely on a resource that it does not hold in adequate supply and that may be subject to opportunistic behavior on the part of suppliers or the bounded rationality of the firm itself. Strategies that involve the possibility of hold-up on the part of suppliers would, therefore, compel close attention by management in order to guarantee, as far as possible, that necessary resources are available as needed.

Questions of firm strategy and firm boundaries are thus closely related. Strategy implementation requires that firms compare their existing resources to their future needs and then determine how to make up any shortfall by either generating new resources internally or arranging to purchase them through the market. Alfred D. Chandler, Jr. investigates one aspect of this in *The Visible Hand* (1977) and *Scale and Scope* (1990), where he argues that the success of the corporate form was linked to investments in high-throughput production and mass distribution. In many if not most cases, this certainly implied integration of manufacturing functions and the elimination of middlemen. But it did not really imply massive vertical integration. The corporation often took purchasing out of the hands of brokers and middlemen – but it still purchased components and inputs. For the most part, Chandler seems to think, vertical integration was (and ought to be) merely "defensive," that is, designed to ensure secure flows of components, materials, and sales. Integration beyond this, he feels, has no economic function, and, as in the case of Ford in the 1920s, can be positively dysfunctional.

The historical firms that Chandler discusses were already operating in mature industries, however, in which product and process technologies had been largely decided and firms needed to protect existing large investments in plant and equipment. In an innovative situation, control over resources, as through vertical integration, can also be used offensively (Lazonick 1991a). Firms that can use resources to create new capabilities, especially idiosyncratic ones, can gain substantial competitive advantage that may last for extended periods if potential competitors are unable to replicate them quickly. Therefore, in theory at least, a firm may enhance its strategic maneuverability if it can gain preemptive control over valuable combinations of resources.

A strategy of offensive vertical integration is only useful, however, when the resources that are internalized really do lead to idiosyncratic synergy. If they do not, and defensive benefits are also missing, then it may be cheaper for a firm to remain specialized and buy its resources through the market. Furthermore, even idiosyncratic synergy does not guarantee permanent rents to a firm since, over a longer period of time, outsiders can often duplicate a firm's knowledge. If these outsiders turn out to be more efficient than the originating firm, in the sense that they can sell resources to the firm more cheaply than it can produce them itself, then offensive (like defensive) vertical integration will give way eventually to increased specialization.

The dynamics of these changes in the division of labor between firms, or differentiation, are rooted in changes in transaction costs. It is to these that we now turn.

3

A DYNAMIC THEORY OF THE BOUNDARIES OF THE FIRM

THE DIVISION OF LABOR

The dynamics of organization is a concern that goes back over 200 years in economics. One might even say that, in one form, it was the starting point for Adam Smith in the *Wealth of Nations*. Smith's theme was the division of labor. And his observation that the division of labor is limited by the extent of the market suggests a possible link between vertical integration and economic change in the form of market growth.

For example, Allyn Young (1928) assumed that the firms in an industry are initially vertically integrated and that increasing output leads to differentiation as various stages of the production process are spun off into specialized concerns. Small firms in industries with limited output might need to undertake the production of intermediate goods, since outside suppliers would not find it profitable to manufacture on such a limited scale. But an expansion of output of final products could permit the industry to take advantage of economies of scale as new specialized firms emerged to take over the production of intermediate goods. This differentiation is especially important where there are different levels of economies of scale for the various production stages – where, for example, the most efficient level of output of an intermediate product is greater than the amount needed by any single manufacturer of the final good. As an example of this kind of differentiation, Young cites the early printing industry, which over time evolved into not only the modern printing industry but also into firms turning out wood pulp and paper, inks, type and other inputs into printing.

Another economist who approached the boundaries of the firm through the division of labor was George Stigler. In a well-known 1951 article, he attempts to unpack the implications of Smith's observation by considering the various activities – he called them "functions" – in terms of their individual (Marshallian) cost curves. Why do firms with increasing-returns technologies not grow indefinitely large? he asks. His answer is that the increasing-returns activities are held back by other activities within the firm

20

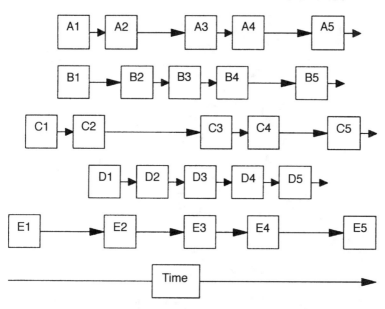

Figure 3.1 Crafts production
Source: Leijonhufvud (1986)

that exhibit decreasing returns. As the market for the final product expands, however, it becomes profitable for the increasing-returns activities to be spun off so that their economies of scale may be exploited by aggregating the demands for their services across the industry.

Stigler drew from this analysis his much-discussed hypothesis about vertical integration.[24] Since a larger market means more of this "spinning off," he concluded, "Smith's theorem suggests that vertical disintegration is the typical development in growing industries, vertical integration in declining industries" (Stigler 1951, p. 189). We will argue presently that this conclusion is unwarranted and, if taken narrowly, is probably exactly backwards. Before making that case, however, let us recast Stigler's analysis somewhat. Following Axel Leijonhufvud (1986), we can open up the black box of the Marshallian cost curve and look in a more Smithian fashion at the structure of production and the sources of economies of scale.

Consider first the paradigm of wholly undivided labor: crafts production. Here a single individual undertakes many of the relevant activities of production. Figure 3.1 shows this pictorially. Each of the artisans (**A** through **E**) performs sequentially all of the tasks (1 through 5). Consider now the reorganization of production in the manner of Smith's pin factory. In Figure 3.2, each artisan now performs only one task: **A** performs only task 1, **B** performs only task 2, etc. This allows for specialization and comparative advantage, permitting production to partake of all the

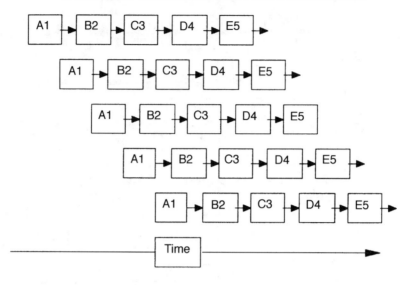

Figure 3.2 Factory production
Source: Leijonhufvud (1986)

economies with which Smith was impressed:[25] the increase in individual dexterity; the saving of time otherwise lost in "sauntering" between tasks; and the concentration of attention, which would lead workers to perceive opportunities for mechanization and (autonomous) innovation.[26]

There are several differences of note between crafts and factory production. In crafts production, each artisan requires relatively broad capabilities. The artisan must be adequately skilled in all the tasks necessary to complete the product. This implies a certain degree of flexibility. Innovation of a stage-specific, efficiency-enhancing sort is, as Smith argued, less characteristic of crafts production. But innovation of a more systemic sort is likely: for the artisan, systemic innovation – innovation across the stages of production under his or her command – is in fact autonomous because it affects only the activities of this one person. This accounts for the distinctiveness of, and the lack of standardization in, a crafts product (Gustafsson 1991, p. 84). It also suggests, once again, that an artisanal product is easier to change than one made in a factory, and that more-or-less radical product modification is cheap in this mode of production. Notice also that each artisan is the rival of all others, a factor that further encourages differentiated and nonstandard products.[27]

In factory production, by contrast, the worker's[28] on-the-job capabilities are relatively narrower in scope. Moreover, the use of these capabilities is hedged in by routines that provide some, and at times most, of the coordination between workers. The narrower scope of activity by the

individual worker and the smooth functioning of routines increase the
efficiency of production, and may even increase innovation – but it is
innovation of a stage-specific, efficiency-enhancing sort. For the artisan
in factory production, the opportunities for autonomous innovation are no
longer more-or-less coextensive with those for systemic innovation.
Increased production efficiency comes at the price of reduced flexibility,
including product flexibility, implying standardization, interchangeable
parts, etc. At the same time, the machinery used in production also
becomes more idiosyncratic and specialized (Leijonhufvud 1986, p. 215).

Notice also that the factory operatives are now *complementary* to one
another rather than rivals. Their interdependence may be controlled in
various ways, including direct supervision or the use of formal rules. But,
as we have seen, organization will frequently be effected by the use of tacit
procedures such as routines. Because these forms of coordination have
been designed, or have evolved, for specific and narrow purposes, they also
add to the element of inflexibility present in the factory system because
they may be inapplicable if the stages of production are altered significantly
in either a systemic or an autonomous fashion. When a major change
occurs in an organization with strong routines, either the introduction of
the innovation will be impeded by the persistence of routines developed for
other purposes, or there will be an "interregnum" in which old routines
have been abandoned but new routines have yet to be developed. Either
way, change may lead to transitionary inefficiency.[29]

Reorganization in the manner of Smith's pinshop is what most people
have in mind when they speak of the division of labor. But it is by no means
the entire story. Another possibility is the "division of industries" that also
occurs as markets expand.[30] In a pioneer society, members of a family
might have to engage simultaneously in food production, spinning and
weaving, soap making, construction, and various other occupations. As
settlement becomes more dense and transport linkages develop, however,
industrial specialization becomes feasible as some families concentrate on
farming, others go fulltime into cloth production or construction, soap is
imported into the community from distant manufacturers, and so on. One
important difference between occupational division of labor of the pinshop
variety and industrial division of labor, at least in its early stages, is that the
establishment of industrially specialized units does not necessarily carry the
implication of narrowed capabilities (or lowered human-capital requirements) on the part of workers; it may in fact mean an *increase* in human
capital per worker as Jacks-of-all-trades are converted into masters-of-one
(Leijonhufvud 1986, p. 212).

Leijonhufvud also distinguishes "parallel-series scale economies." Factory
production requires that the stages of production be closely coordinated in
time. Since the various stages are unlikely to be uniformly efficient,
however, some stages may be bottlenecks.[31] More interestingly, some

23

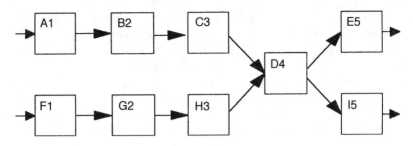

Figure 3.3 Parallel-series scale economies
Source: Leijonhufvud

stages may be anti-bottlenecks, that is, they may have excess capacity. Suppose one stage of production – stage 4, for example – is running at half capacity. If the firm were to double its sale of final product, it could run two assembly lines, both feeding into the same stage 4 (See Figure 3.3). The doubled output comes at the expense of less than twice the inputs. These economies of scale arise from organizational change rather than from technology, although mechanical innovation can renew the potential for generating economies by increasing the capacity of the stages.

If the demand for the output of stage 4 from diverse sources reaches minimum economic scale, then stage 4 can be "spun off" as in Stigler's story. Notice, however, that this spinning-off process is a manifestation of the division of labor quite different from what is implied in the pinshop reorganization. In Smith's terms, stage 4 has become a "peculiar trade" of its own. As in other cases of industrial division of labor, spinning off resulting from parallel-series economies of scale may lead to an *increase* in human capital per worker. Eventually, of course, whenever there is industrial division of labor, the newly independent stages may themselves undergo further occupational specialization as the market for their products grows.

The important point to notice about the division of labor story so far is that it is incomplete in a crucial way. The division of labor is at base a matter of *production* costs alone. But one cannot say much about the extent of internal organization without an overlying consideration of transaction costs. The industrial division of labor can take place within a firm, as when a separate division is set up to specialize in the production of a particular item that is then sold to outsiders as well as used as an input in some larger product manufactured by the firm itself. But, as we know, it is also possible for a subdivided stage to be spun off. Consider, as a historical example, the development of the American machine-tool industry (Rosenberg 1963). Before 1840, textile firms made their own machine tools as needed: in effect, the manufacture of such tools was a stage in the production of cloth into which the textile firms were integrated vertically. As the demand for

24

final products grew, the demand for machine tools – from the textile industry and elsewhere – increased to such an extent that the textile machine shops could spin off and become independent machine-tool firms.

There is, however, nothing in this story to tell us under what conditions such spinning off will occur or the division of labor will proceed under the umbrella of a single firm. We can just as easily point to industries in which the pattern has been quite different. Indeed, as we will suggest in Chapter 4, the automobile industry is a potential counterexample: firms were quite differentiated at an early stage in the industry's life but became much more integrated as output expanded. Production efficiencies by themselves say nothing about the choice of organizational form. This is precisely the difficulty with Stigler's analysis: he has made a case that there should be more (horizontal) division of labor when the market is growing (or, more correctly, when the extent of the market is large) and less division when the market is contracting (when the extent of the market is less). He assumes that this translates directly into statements about vertical integration; but without additional arguments, it really does not. Since Coase (1937), economists have begun to explain observed patterns of ownership and contract by their ability to minimize the sum of production costs *and* transaction costs.[32] And Stigler's argument is incomplete precisely because it ignores transaction costs.

One of the crucial ways in which classical value theory differed from neoclassical was in its preoccupation with costs of production. The classicals were interested in the long run. And in the long run, all factors are variable, implying production at constant returns to scale. In such a world, supply-side factors – and not demand – do indeed determine value. One way to understand our argument here is that the introduction of transaction costs into a Stigler-like explanation of organization is in some ways analogous to the change from classical to neoclassical value theory. To the extent that an explanation like Stigler's – or Smith's – focuses exclusively on production costs and largely ignores transaction costs, it implictly takes a long-run perspective. Production costs alone matter only when enough time has elapsed that transient "frictions" do not matter. As a result, a theory from production costs alone tells us much about the organization of the economy. But it also tells us less than we want to know about the boundaries of the firm, that is, about the ownership of the various stages of production and the nature of the contractual relationships among them.

The flip side to this analogy, of course, is that the Coasean theory of the boundaries of the firm is necessarily a short-run theory. Transaction costs are essentially short-run phenomena. This does not by any means make such costs unimportant. One cannot explain ownership and contracting structures without them. But the modern focus on transaction costs,

25

salutary as it has been, has nonetheless put into the background the richness of the classical cost-of-production theory.

A couple of points are worthy of note. First of all, the standard concept of the runs is, almost paradoxically, a timeless notion. That is, the time that passes between the short run and the long run is what Mark Blaug (1987, p. 371) calls "operational time" rather than real time.[33] The length of the run is defined entirely in terms of the variability of factors, not in terms of the external standard of a clock. The long run may come about in a week in some industries and a century in others.

Although this mechanical conception of the run is normally described as Marshallian, it was not in fact the way Marshall himself understood the concept (Currie and Steedman 1990, pp. 22–28). As he tells us in the preface to the eighth edition of the *Principles*, his use of static models is a matter of convenience rather than conviction, something appropriate to a textbook introduction. "The Mecca of the economist," he says, "lies in economic biology rather than in economic dynamics." As Brian Loasby (1989, 1990) has argued, Marshall's vision of economic progress was basically a Smithian one, overlain with this biological metaphor. The Smithian process of progressive specialization is not an economic process merely but a process characteristic of nature in its broadest. It is, Marshall says, a

> general rule, to which there are not very many exceptions, that the development of the organism, whether social or physical, involves an increasing subdivision of functions between its separate parts on the one hand, and on the other a more intimate connection between them. Each part gets to be less and less self-sufficient, to depend for its wellbeing more and more on other parts . . . This increased subdivision of functions, or "differentiation," as it is called, manifests itself with regard to industry in such forms as the division of labour, and the development of specialized skill, knowledge and machinery: while "integration," that is, a growing intimacy and firmness of the connections between the separate parts of the industrial organism, shows itself in such forms as the increase of security of commercial credit, and of the means and habits of communication by sea and road, by railway and telegraph, by post and printing press.
>
> (Marshall 1961, IV.viii.1, p. 241)

Economic progress is for Marshall a matter of improvements in knowledge and organization as much as a matter of scale economies in the neoclassical sense. We can see this clearly in his "law of increasing return," which is distinctly not a law of increasing returns to scale: "An increase of labour and capital leads generally to improved organization, which increases the efficiency of the work of labour and capital" (Marshall 1961, IV.xiii.2, p. 318). And, in arguing that long-run marginal cost is falling with

26

increases in output, he suggests that we "exclude from view any economies that may result from substantive new inventions; but we include those which may be expected to arise naturally out of adaptations of existing ideas" (Marshall 1961, V.xii.3, p. 460).

To say that a movement to the long run involves progressive changes in organization and knowledge is really to suggest an interpretation quite different from the standard neoclassical conception, in which substitution is supposed to take place with knowledge held constant. Adopting this learning-and-organization view, we argue, implies a shift to a real-time conception of the long run. In some sense, the long run is the period over which enough learning has taken place that adjustments are small and come only in response to foreseeable changes in exogenous conditions.[34]

TRANSACTION COSTS IN THE SHORT RUN

Our contention is that transaction costs lose their importance in *this* kind of long run. To the extent that transaction costs are "frictions" – a term one often hears applied – then such costs are bound to diminish over time with learning, all other things equal. In order to make this case, however, we need to examine the nature of transaction costs in more detail.

Alchian and Woodward (1988) have recently argued that there are two distinct traditions in transaction-cost analysis. "One emphasizes the administering, directing, negotiating, and monitoring of the joint productive teamwork in a firm. The other emphasizes assuring the quality or performance of contractual agreements" (Alchian and Woodward 1988, p. 66). The former is what we might call the measurement-cost view. The latter we may call the asset-specificity view. Looked at in the right way, however, these two traditions yield strikingly similar conclusions.

The basic notion of the measurement-cost approach is that it is often costly to measure the quality and sometimes even the quantity of the output of a stage of production (Barzel 1982; Cheung 1983). In the best-known example of this approach (Alchian and Demsetz 1972), indivisibilities in team production lead to shirking that is costly to detect, suggesting a rationale for a residual claimant to hire and monitor the team members. More recently, Barzel has provided a more general theory of how measurement costs affect organizational form. He suggests that "among factors contributing to the value of common effort, the greater the difficulty in measuring one factor's contribution vis-à-vis that of others, the more likely is the owner of that factor to assume the position of the residual claimant" (Barzel 1987, p. 105). Since the factor least easily measured is most tempted to moral hazard, output is maximized when that factor becomes the principal, leaving the factor(s) more easily measured to be agents.

The source of inefficiency in the asset-specificity approach is the tussle for rents after the fact of a contract (Klein, Crawford, and Alchian 1978;

Williamson 1985). Such distributive battles can arise only when there are assets that are synergistically related and cannot be redeployed costlessly if the contractual arrangement were to end. As a result, the costs to which the asset-specificity view looks are costs of post-contractual "hold up" rather than post-contractual moral hazard. As in the measurement-cost view, however, the possibility of these postcontractual costs leads to the selection (in some ill-defined sense) of institutional forms *ex ante* that mitigate the "opportunism" *ex post*.

The similarity becomes clearer when we look at one set of models that allies itself with the asset-specificity camp, namely the literature on incomplete contracts (Grossman and Hart 1986; Hart 1988, 1989; Moore 1992). Here contracts are incomplete in that, because the parties are "boundedly rational," the contract cannot provide in advance for all the contingencies that might occur, at least not in adequate detail. There are thus two types of rights a contract can allocate: specific rights and residual rights. Specific rights are those spelled out, while residual rights are the "left over" rights to control in any circumstances not specifically provided for. The possession of residual rights over an asset is what we mean by ownership of that asset. Thus a theory of the allocation of residual rights is a theory of the ownership of assets, which is a theory of the boundaries of the firm along the other of our two dimensions. What is interesting about this literature is the broad similarity of its conclusions to those of Barzel.[35] When contingencies can be adequately specified, or when the decisions of the cooperating parties don't affect one another, contracts are possible and integration is unnecessary. When the decisions are linked, however, that party should get the residual rights whose decisions are more important to the joint enterprise. As in Barzel, there is a kind of Coase-theorem result at work: the residual rights end up in the hands of the party whose possession of them maximizes the joint surplus.

There are also a couple of other ways in which these results are more similar to those of Barzel than initially appears. First of all, the concept of an agency cost – which is what really underlies Barzel's notion of measurement cost – includes not only the technological costs of monitoring but also any residual loss of value that comes from a misalignment of the agent's incentives with those of the principal (Jensen and Meckling 1976). Thus, to say that the owner of the residual right should be the party with the higher monitoring cost is in fact to say that that owner should be the party whose decisions are more important to the value of the enterprise. Second, the Grossman-and-Hart model relies on hold-up costs: the inefficiencies arise from non-optimal choices of specific investment *ex ante* in the face of a distributive game *ex post*. But the "property rights" approach, as Hart (1989) aptly calls this incomplete-contracts theory, is in fact more general than this. Indeed, one of the models in Hart (1988) relies on moral hazard *ex post* rather than hold-up.

28

TRANSACTION COSTS IN THE LONG RUN

F. A. Hayek (1945, p. 523) once wrote that "economic problems arise always and only in consequence of change." Our argument is the converse: as change diminishes, economic problems recede.[36] Specifically, as learning takes place within a stable environment, transaction costs diminish. As Carl Dahlman (1979) points out, all transaction costs are at base information costs. And, with time and learning, contracting parties gain information about one another's behavior. More importantly, the transacting parties will with time develop or hit upon institutional arrangements that mitigate the sources of transaction costs.

The incomplete-contracts framework makes this argument particularly clear. The reason contracts are incomplete is because of "bounded rationality," a somewhat misleading expression that better describes the limits to an agent's knowledge and decision-making skills than it does imperfections in the agent's rationality. In other words, then, contracts are incomplete because of limitations of knowledge. With time, however, agents engaged in similar transactions will learn the typical outcomes of those transactions and will include increasingly more specific provisions in their contracts. As a result, a progressively greater part of the transactions can be handled through specific rather than residual rights. More concretely, with repeated transactions in a stable environment one can expect (1) contracts to become "self-enforcing" because of reputation effects and (2) hold-up and moral-hazard problems to be attenuated by the evolution of norms of reciprocity and cooperation (Axelrod 1984; Sugden 1986). There is also another aspect to the argument. If the environment is genuinely one in which change is diminishing, then it is also one in which behavior must be becoming increasingly routine. And routine behavior is necessarily easier to monitor and measure than non-routine behavior. In an environment in which change is absent, the "plasticity"[37] necessary for moral hazard is also absent. For all these reasons, one would expect transaction costs to play a small role in the long run.

This is not immediately to say that the long run favors vertical disintegration, although there is obviously some reason to follow the likes of Stigler and Young in this direction. It may well turn out that one of the institutional responses to the moral-hazard or hold-up costs of the short run is in fact vertical integration, that is, common ownership and control of the ownable assets of adjacent stages of production. If this happens, subsequent organizational learning would take place (at least initially) within the framework of the firm, which may well affect the long-run pattern of integration. To put this another way, the result of a learning process of this sort depends in general not only on the present state of the system but also on the past states through which the system has traveled (Hayek 1967, p. 75). Such a system may display some of the properties of "lock-in" that Paul David (1985) and others have popularized. As a result, bursts of economic change may leave their mark in the long run (Langlois 1984, 1988).

We will return to these issues in later chapters. The point here is not that the effect of learning on transaction costs, let alone on the shape of organization, is obvious. Rather, the point is that one cannot have a complete theory of the boundaries of the firm without considering the process of learning in firms and markets. The reigning transaction-cost theories of vertical integration provide illuminating snapshots of possible institutional responses to a momentary situation. But they do not place those responses in the context of the passage of time. Most theories of the boundaries of the firm are static in an important sense. They take the circumstances of production as given and investigate comparatively the properties of market-contract arrangements, internal organization, and sometimes other modes of organization. What happens, however, when the technologies of production – and perhaps other environmental factors – are changing rapidly? In Williamson's view, the approach from asset specificity alone may then be less persuasive.

> The introduction of innovation, plainly complicates the earlier-described assignment of transactions to markets or hierarchies based entirely on an examination of their asset specificity qualities. Indeed, the study of economic organization in a regime of rapid innovation poses much more difficult issues than those addressed here.
>
> (Williamson 1985, p. 143)

To put it another way, the dominant transaction-cost theories of the boundaries of the firm are short-run theories that, unlike Marshallian price theory, have no long-run correlative. One important objective of this book is to attempt to sketch out a possible approach to connecting the long run and the short. In order to do this, we reassert the wisdom of the Smithian (long-run) view of organization and augment it by appending the capabilities theory of organizational learning discussed in Chapter 2.

CAPABILITIES AND GOVERNANCE COSTS

Like the theories of Smith and Marshall, the capabilities or resources view of the firm is a real-time account of production costs in which knowledge and organization have as important a role as technology. One implication of the boundedness of capabilities is that it is most unlikely that many firms – even the most integrated – have the ancillary capabilities necessary for all activities in the chain of production. The result is that firms must link up with other firms. This often takes place through the simplest of market contracts. One can, for example, buy off-the-shelf parts at spot prices and assemble a finished product out of them. But often, and especially when innovation is involved, the links among firms are of a more complex sort, involving everything from informal swaps of information (von Hippel 1987) to joint ventures and other formal collaborative arrangements (Mowery 1989). All firms must rely on the capabilities owned by others, especially to the extent that such ancillary capabilities are dissimilar to those the firm possesses. A firm could – and many do – acquire dissimilar capabilities complementary to the ones they already own. But there is no particular reason to do so unless there are specific transaction costs impeding contractual arrangements. And there are generally costs to owning dissimilar assets, especially when the acquiring firm cannot use or sell their full capacity.

In short, the capabilities view of the firm suggests that the boundaries of the firm are determined (at least in part) by the relative costs of developing ancillary capabilities internally or purchasing them externally through contracts with other firms. On the one hand, a firm may need to internalize a stage of production because the complementary capabilities that stage represents do not exist or are more expensive in the market. This would be a pure capabilities explanation for internalization. As Chapter 4 will suggest, the case of Henry Ford and the use of the moving assembly line and specialized cutting tools might fit this possibility. His process innovations gave him a cost advantage over outside suppliers, motivating a high degree of vertical integration. On the other hand, a firm may wish to internalize a stage of production even when the market possesses the requisite capabilities to at least the same degree as does the firm itself. If the firm does internalize, it must be because there are other costs to using the markets. An explanation along these lines would be a pure transaction-cost explanation.

Consider Figure 3.4.[38] On the X-axis we can array activities or stages of production in order of increasing cost of internal production. Specifically, ΔC graphs the normalized per-unit cost premium the firm must pay for the output of a particular activity if it integrates into that activity, measured relative to the per-unit cost it would incur by obtaining the output on contract from a distinct firm. Whenever this premium is negative, there is a cost advantage to internal organization. And the firm will acquire increasingly dissimilar activities until the premium is zero, in this case at B*. Activities in the range OB* are within the boundaries of the firm; the rest are left to the market.[39] One might well argue that, for some activities, the cost advantage to internal organization is effectively infinite in the sense that, at least in the short run, these activities are inimitable. In the terminology of the last chapter, these activities are idiosyncratic and non-contestable, and they constitute the intrinsic core activities of the firm. In Figure 3.4, the intrinsic core consists of those activities in the range OA*.

The cost premium, and therefore the location of B*, will depend on a number of factors. As transaction-cost economics suggests, it will depend on the bureaucratic costs of internal organization and the transaction costs

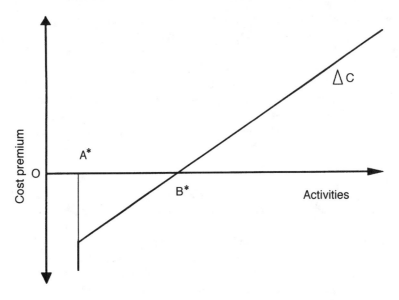

Figure 3.4 The activities of a firm and their cost premium
Source: Modified from Silver (1984)

of market relations. But in this story, the location of the ΔC curve also depends on the internal capabilities of the firm and the external capabilities available in the market. That is to say, the price premium includes both governance-cost and production-cost differences.

If we hold the value of these contestable capabilities constant, then we get the familiar account: whatever lowers bureaucratic costs on the margin will increase the extent of integration; whatever lowers transaction costs will reduce the extent of integration. If capabilities were unbounded, then governance costs alone would determine the boundaries of the firm. In such a case, the activities would be ordered according to the normalized per-unit governance-cost premium for internal over market procurement. By contrast, if governance costs were zero, the relative costs of contestable ancillary capabilities alone would determine the boundaries of the firm. In this case, the activities would be ordered according to decreasing similarity, measured from the activity in which the firm has the greatest cost advantage over the market. In both polar cases, "the firm" consists of all the activities in the range OB*; but those are not necessarily the same set of activities in each case.

TRANSACTION COSTS AND THE PASSAGE OF TIME

In the long run, we have argued, transaction costs might be expected to approach zero. One might also argue this for governance costs generally. In the long run, activities become increasingly routine. This reduces the cost of contracting, not in the sense that contracts become cheaper to write but in the sense that contracts are increasingly unnecessary: everything is done tomorrow the way it was done today. In this sense, then, the long run also arguably reduces the cost of internal management by reducing decision-making costs.[40] Thus, one might argue that, in the long run as we have defined it, the boundaries of the firm are determined entirely by the capabilities of the firm relative to the capabilities of the market.

If, however, we follow Marshall in seeing the long run as the asymptotic end-state of a process of learning, then we also have to consider the ways in which capabilities change over time. And here there are also two opposing effects. On the one hand, the firm is likely to become more "capable" over time. As more and more of the firm's activities take on the nature of routines, and as the firm's routines become more finely tuned, both the firm's total managerial capacity and its free managerial capacity will increase. Other things equal, this will shift ΔC down and increase the extent of OB*. On the other hand, however, the market will also become more "capable" as time passes. Other firms will also be increasing their capabilities. And techniques pioneered by one firm may diffuse to and be imitated by other firms. This would include the intrinsic core activities that, in the short run, were inimitable and non-contestable: with time and learning, everything is potentially contestable. All other things equal, the passage of time will have the effect of shifting ΔC up and lowering the extent of OB*.

The "classical" presumption – that is, the presupposition in Smith, Young, and Stigler – is that this latter effect predominates: in the longest of runs capability diffuses completely into the market, leading to full specialization and vertical disintegration (see Figure 3.5). In general, the relative strengths of these effects will depend on the relative learning abilities of the firm and the market. The firm's learning ability will depend on its internal organization. And the learning ability of the market will depend on technical and institutional factors, as well as on the learning abilities of the firms it comprises, considered both individually and as a system. This chapter is devoted to considering these two learning systems in somewhat more detail. It will set out some preliminary generalizations about how the level of capabilities in the firm and the market – and the nature of *change* in those capabilities – affects the boundaries of the firm.

First, however, we must raise a conceptual issue. We have so far tried to portray contestable capabilities as being in the nature of production costs, something distinct from transaction costs. But the line is actually far more blurred. Assume no transaction costs of the measurement or hold-up kind. And suppose that a firm chooses to undertake a particular activity internally rather than relying on the market. This must mean that the firm has a cost advantage over the market. But is that advantage in the nature of a

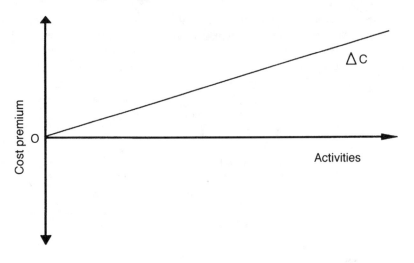

Figure 3.5 The "classical" presupposition

production cost or a transaction cost? In a recent critique of the transaction-cost approach to the multinational firm, Paul Hallwood (1994) argues that much foreign direct investment can be explained simply by production-cost advantages of the foreign firm over indigenous firms. For example, a foreign soft-drink company may choose to set up its own bottling plants in a particular country instead of licensing indigenous bottlers simply because its bottling capabilities are superior to – and thus its costs lower than – those of local plants. Viewed from another perspective, however, might we not say that the foreign licensor integrates into local production because the transaction costs of using the local market capabilities were prohibitive? This is not merely tautological if we specify that the transaction costs involved are those of somehow transmitting to local market participants the knowledge that would provide them with the necessary capabilities. As Hallwood suggests, this is not necessarily a helpful way to look at the issue, especially since, as we have argued, certain idiosyncratic capabilities involve tacit knowledge that can be gained only by a long process of apprenticeship.

At the same time, of course, "technology transfer" is in fact an option that presents itself. Instead of producing oneself, one may be able teach others how to produce and persuade them to do so. In principle, Henry Ford *could* have taught outside parts suppliers his innovative techniques and persuaded them to use them for high-volume production. The costs of doing so would have been prohibitive; but they would have been costs, in a straightforward foregone-opportunity sense. Similarly, a firm that opts to procure an input on the market *might* have chosen instead to acquire the necessary capabilities to produce internally if outside producers did not

34

possess inimitable advantages. The cost of acquiring those capabilities is the diminution in profit from not having taken advantage of the market's capabilities. We might not want to call these transaction costs, but they are certainly information or knowledge costs. And it is these costs that permit the notion of "capabilities" and "routines," unlike the classical or neoclassical notion of production costs, to help explain the boundaries of the firm.

Consider the following case. A firm's capabilities grow, allowing it to apply those capabilities to a new activity similar to the ones in which it is already active. If there are truly no transaction costs, and the issue were solely the firm's advantage over other firms in production costs, then there would be no reason for the firm in fact to own the new stage of production. It could costlessly license its knowledge to others and earn a specific contractual return. To say that the firm must extend its boundaries to encompass the new activity implies that it is costly to license its imitable capabilities, which means that there must be transaction costs of *some* kind.[41]

For want of a better term, we propose to call these *dynamic* transaction costs. They are a kind of cost that has been largely neglected in the explanation of the boundaries of the firm. As we will explain more fully below, we define dynamic transaction costs as the costs of persuading, negotiating, coordinating, and teaching outside suppliers. Another way to look at these transaction costs is as the costs of not having the capabilities you need when you need them. Indeed, if one follows Demsetz (1988) in using the term transaction cost to refer only to costs of using the market and never to costs of internal governance, then one ought to call these dynamic *governance* costs, since, as we shall see, it can also be a cost of internal organization not to have the capabilities one needs at the right time. When the market cannot provide the right ancillary capabilities at the right time, vertical integration may result; and when the firm lacks the right ancillary capabilities at the right time, vertical specialization may occur. This chapter examines the first possibility, and Chapter 5 examines the second.

THE SOURCES OF DYNAMIC TRANSACTION COSTS

We can begin to examine the sources of dynamic transaction costs by asking this question: Is rapid economic change likely to make market contracting more costly or less costly relative to internal organization? Almost without exception, writers who have asked this question (in one form or another) have concluded that, in such circumstances, internal organization is clearly superior to arm's-length contracting on transaction-cost grounds.[42]

What might the sources of these transactions costs be? Asset specificity is a possibility that is frequently cited. In a sense, this fits with the theme we have suggested: when there is a threat of hold-up, one might be afraid of not having the right capabilities available at the right time. For example, as we have shown, Alfred Chandler (1977) sees the backward integration of large manufacturing firms as largely if not entirely a defensive stratagem to avoid supply disruptions and ensure high-volume throughput. But as we have already hinted, the problem with the hold-up view is that it is neither sufficient nor necessary as an explanation for integration. It is not sufficient because, in the absence of uncertainty and a divergence of expectations about the future, long-term contracts, reputation effects, and other devices can remove the costs of arm's-length arrangements. It is not necessary because, in the presence of uncertainty and a divergence of expectations about the future, arm's-length arrangements can be costly even without highly specific assets.

One way to think about this is in terms of the flexibility of internal organization in comparison with that of a decentralized system of market contracts.[43] The firm, in one view, is a nexus of imperfectly specified contracts; this is in contrast with the more fully specified contracts of arm's-length transaction. In the face of rapid change, imperfect specification allows some maneuvering room to adapt adroitly. To put it another way, the decentralization of markets makes it difficult to coordinate a complex reorientation of production in the face of change; a more-centralized arrangement, by contrast, might permit lower costs of radical change, all else equal.[44]

COORDINATION AND APPROPRIABILITY

In an early work, Teece encapsulated the coordination problem nicely.

> If there is a high degree of interdependence among successive stages of production, and if occasions for adaptation are unpredictable yet common, coordinated responses may be difficult to secure if the separated stages are operated independently. Interdependence by itself does not cause difficulty if the pattern of interdependence is stable and fixed. Difficulties arise only if program execution rests on contingencies that cannot be predicted perfectly in advance. In this case, coordinated activity is required to secure agreement about the estimates that will be used as a basis for action. Vertical integration facilitates such coordination.
>
> This argument also reduces, at least in some respects, to a contractual-incompleteness argument. Were it feasible to stipulate exhaustively the appropriate conditional responses, coordination could proceed by long-term contract. However, long-term contracts are unsatisfactory when most of the relevant contingencies cannot be delineated. Given these limitations, short-term contracts are likely to be considered instead. . . . Even if short-term contracts are defective neither on account of

36

investment disincentives nor first-mover advantages, the costs of negotiations and the time required to bring the system into adjustment by exclusive reliance on market signals are apt to be greater than the costs of administrative processes under vertical integration.

(Teece 1976, p. 13)

Another way to say this is that unpredictable change makes it costly to specify contractual provisions, implying the need for expanded residual rights of control.[45]

Teece mentions this possibility as one of a string of possible explanations for vertical integration. Our contention is that this is in fact the general explanation, and that all other transaction-cost explanations are either derivative of this argument or apply only on an *ad hoc* basis to special situations. Ultimately, the costs that lead to vertical integration are the (dynamic) transaction costs of persuading, negotiating with, coordinating among, and teaching outside suppliers in the face of economic change or innovation.[46]

When would such costs be likely? That is to say, when would we expect vertical integration? As Teece suggests, the costs of coordinating among stages would be greatest when there is a high degree of interdependence among the relevant stages of production. But more than mere interdependence is necessary: the interdependence must be such that a change in one stage of production requires a corresponding change in one or more distinct stages. That is, it must be systemic.

It was autonomous innovation that Adam Smith had in mind when he argued that the division of labor enhanced innovation: each operative, by seeking ways to make his or her lot easier, would discover improved methods of performing the particular operation (Smith 1976, I.i.8, p. 20).[47] The innovations he had in mind were of a type that improved the efficiency of a particular stage without any implication for the operation of other stages. Autonomous innovation of this sort may even further the division of labor to the extent that it involves the cutting up of a task into two or more separate operations.

Instead of being *differentiating* in this way, however, an innovation may be *integrating*, in the sense that the new way of doing things – a new machine, say – performs in one step what had previously needed two or more steps (Robertson and Alston 1992). More generally, a systemic innovation may require small modifications of the way work is performed at each of a number of stages, and would thus require coordination among those stages. The possibility of systemic interconnectedness has long been the basis for an argument that vertical disintegration may retard innovation.[48] Innovation may mean replacing assets at more than one stage in the chain of production. If decision-making is decentralized, the costs of coordinating the innovation may be high, and the innovation may never take place.

Information impactedness (to use Williamson's term) can be reduced if the developer of an innovation and the user are in the same organization. Users – marketing or production teams – can make R&D experts (whether within their own organizations or elsewhere in the network) aware of specific commercial needs to which attention should be devoted. On the other hand, if researchers in such a network come up with an unanticipated development, they can easily alert others in the extended organization who might be able to use it. In the absence of coordination integration, potential benefits might be lost altogether or ceded to others.

In an unjustly neglected work, Morris Silver (1984) has articulated the outlines of a theory of vertical integration based on the costs of coordination. Citing Schumpeter (1934), Silver begins with the observation that innovation frequently involves the qualitatively new. The individual – the entrepreneur – who attempts to introduce something that is qualitatively new often meets with strong resistance. Such resistance may be cultural and psychological, as Schumpeter emphasized. But, more interestingly, it may also be informational. As we saw, the success of an innovation often requires the adaptation of complementary activities; if the innovation is indeed qualitatively new, many of the necessary activities will also be qualitatively new. The problem for the innovator is to call forth these specialized activities. To do this through arm's-length contracting, the innovator would have both to inform and to persuade those with the necessary capabilities. Since the innovator's vision is novel and idiosyncratic virtually by definition, this may not be an easy task. The innovator's potential contracting parties may have to invest in specialized assets, and it may take a high price to get them to bear the risk of an irreversible investment under such circumstances. This may make it less costly for the innovator to integrate into the cospecialized activities and to employ those parties with the relevant capabilities than to contract with them.

Silver sees the benefits to this largely in informational terms: Innovators can communicate the procedures and routines their employees are to follow more easily than they can put across to a contractor the detailed specifications of the end-product. There is also a cost to such internal organization: The innovator will probably be integrating into areas to which his or her own capabilities are relatively less adapted, that is, into relatively dissimilar activities.

Vertical integration can also redress adverse power relationships. As we saw, innovation may mean replacing assets at more than one stage in the chain of production. If ownership is decentralized, an innovation may never take place if some of the existing asset-holders, or the suppliers of factors complementary to the existing assets, have the power to block the innovation (through trade unionism, for example) to protect their rent streams. If innovation does occur, it may take place elsewhere in the economy (and perhaps elsewhere in the world) under the direction of a unified asset-holder and decision-maker who can ignore existing task boundaries. Under joint ownership, the owners or their immediate delegees can re-organize capabilities because they have ultimate (though not necessarily day-to-day) control. They can buy and sell and hire and fire. When the same organization is both the developer and the user of an innovation, then, the benefits are internalized and appropriability is no longer a problem.

Notice, however, that this argument applies to ownership integration, not coordination integration, since in principle the innovator need only take financial positions in the complementary assets – long positions in those likely to appreciate and short positions in those likely to depreciate.[49] How much coordination integration is necessary will depend on the pure information costs of informing and persuading those with *de facto* control over cooperating assets. Ownership integration itself does not guarantee enough coordination to solve the problem of information fragmentation, which could in principle be solved by a closely linked network that was not integrated in ownership.

Indeed, it is these problems of adverse power relationships – far more than the problems of coordination that Silver stresses – that have gained attention in the literature. For example, the more recent work of Teece (1986b) has stressed the importance of appropriability and asset specificity.[50] Appropriability is the capacity of one party (in this case the innovator) to appropriate the rents or quasirents of the innovation. The innovator's ability to appropriate these rents will determine the extent of internal organization. And that ability will depend both on the degree of complementarity and on the "regime of appropriability," the ability – both practical and legal – to create and enforce property rights in the innovation (Teece 1986a, p. 188). Again, the innovator need only take a position in – not control – all complementary assets in order to profit from his or her innovation. But when the assets involved are co-specialized, the transaction costs of highly specific assets – well-detailed in the literature – will make themselves felt. This implies the need for enough hands-on control by the innovator that his or her ownership can indeed overcome the transaction costs between cooperating stages.

The innovator may also have a motive to integrate into assets that are not co-specialized if imitators could otherwise quickly enter and bid away the quasirents of innovation. When, as is arguably the case in pharmaceuticals (Levin *et al.* 1987), the knowledge involved is of a sort easily protected by patent, licensing may obviate complete internal organization; but where this is not the case (as perhaps in some process technologies), internal organization may be the most effective way of protecting the quasirents.

Notice that much of the story here involves what we would ordinarily call "bottlenecks" in the innovation process.[51] In Teece's theory, bottlenecks cause transaction costs because they pose the threat of strategic expropriation of rents. "The owner of the bottleneck asset, realizing its strategic importance to the innovator, is in a position to threaten to withhold services, causing the price of its services to be raised" (Teece 1986a, p. 188).

This story is clearly quite akin to that of Silver; but it is also different in a crucial way. Silver has picked out the Richardsonian thread more clearly. He emphasizes the costs of coordination in a regime of economic change, that is, the costs of transmitting information that is novel and fundamentally qualitative in nature. Asset specificity, if it enters at all, does so in a secondary way. The threat to the specialized assets arises not from the opportunism of fully convinced asset-holders; rather it arises from the uncertainty in the innovation process, as perceived by asset-holders who may not fully grasp the innovator's vision. "In my scenario," says Silver (1984, p. 17),

> the entrepreneur does not "do it himself" in order to keep the profit-ability of good X a secret (Magee 1981). Just the opposite is the case! The innovator would prefer to concentrate his managerial resources narrowly on X. His problem is that he cannot, at reasonable cost, convey his implausible "secret" to those with the technical capabilities needed to produce the required operations at the lowest cost. Finding himself unable to secure the cooperation of the latter producers, the entrepreneur must direct his finite managerial resources into areas for which he does not have a comparative advantage. This in fact reduces the profitability of his innovation.

In order to distinguish these two variants of the theory, we will call Teece's the *appropriability* version and Silver's the *entrepreneurial* version. In both cases, of course, the innovator is motivated to integrate by a desire to "appropriate" the rents of innovation. But in Teece's case, he or she does so in order to prevent others from grabbing the rents, whereas in Silver's case, he or she integrates strategically in order to create rents that otherwise would not exist (or would not be as great).

CAPABILITIES IN THE LONG RUN

Access to capabilities, like transaction costs, alters as time passes. To the extent that capabilities are based on knowledge, they can be expected to become more widespread as others have an opportunity to acquire the necessary learning. Capabilities may spread very rapidly when the under-lying knowledge is well-known, but even tacit knowledge can be duplicated (and perhaps improved upon) with practice.

A further encouragement to dispersion occurs when capabilities gain multiple uses. For example, innovative techniques may spread from indus-try to industry as analogous uses are recognized. This process, which may take decades fully to work its way through the economy in the case of a truly systemic innovation such as electrification, eventually leads to a

40

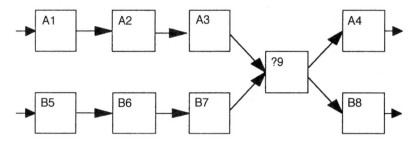

Figure 3.6 Two firms drawing on a single capability
Source: Inspired by Leijonhufvud (1986)

position like the one in Figure 3.6, with two firms, **A** and **B**, that are in different industries. Each firm has its own distinctive capabilities (**1**, **2**, **3**, and **4** and **5**, **6**, **7**, and **8**, respectively) but both draw on the common capability **9**. Initially, use of the common capability may have been confined to only one of the firms; but, as its use spreads, the possibility of vertical disintegration grows. In this case, the second firm may either purchase capability **9** from the initiator, or a common independent supplier or group of suppliers of the capability may develop to sell to both groups.[52]

One implication of this is that the process Silver describes could reverse as knowledge and appreciation of an innovation grow among outsiders, who then begin to produce inputs that they had originally refused to deal with. When this happens, if the transaction-cost position is suitable, vertical debundling may occur as the firm that reluctantly took on production initially now begins to delegate it to outsiders. Equally importantly, in this situation follower firms in an industry may be in a position different from that of innovators because their access to outside capabilities at the time of their founding may be greater. We might therefore expect some follower firms to be less vertically integrated than first movers in an industry.

Finally, the possibility that tacit knowledge might spread as time passes means that the core attributes of a firm might break down as inimitability of capabilities decreases. As this occurs, idiosyncratic synergy is converted into contestable synergy, transaction costs become relevant in areas where they previously had no importance, and the possibility of vertical disintegration grows.

THE SHORT- AND LONG-RUN BOUNDARIES OF THE FIRM

We are now in a position to bring together the capabilities and routines approach and the transaction cost approach to specify how the characteristics of a firm may change as time passes (Figure 3.7).

41

	Degree of idiosyncracy	Transaction costs	Availability of particular capabilities	Uses for particular capabilities	Relative cost of internalization	Degree of vertical integration
Short run	High	High	Thinly distributed	Few	Low	High
Long run	Low	Low	Widespread	Many	High	Low

Figure 3.7 The effects of spreading knowledge on the boundaries of the firm

In the *short run*, the core of a firm comprises those assets that are synergistic and idiosyncratically related to each other. When combined, these synergistic assets allow the creation of value that exceeds the value that the same assets would generate if deployed individually. Moreover, because the core assets are inimitable and not contestable, the rents that flow from their value creation are not simply transitory. As most physical assets are contestable in principle, the idiosyncratically synergistic core of a firm consists primarily in knowledge and patterns of behavior such as routines that are not readily communicated to outsiders and in the people that embody them.

When viewed from this perspective, the core characteristics of a firm reside in both coordination and ownership integration. In general, coordination of inputs is needed to achieve synergy, and the idiosyncratic nature of the core assets means that they are not contestable. Furthermore, even if the core assets were contestable in theory, they would tend to remain bound together by the bilateral (or, in the case of several inputs, multilateral) advantage that derives from coordination integration in that the inputs would not be as valuable (would not generate such high rents) if used individually or in other combinations (Williamson 1985).

The addition of further activities to the core depends on the relative transaction costs of internalizing the activities or purchasing them on the market. In many cases, as Chandler has noted, the decision to internalize an activity is defensive and designed to protect firms against hold-up or agency problems that cannot be adequately handled by contracts. In other cases, however, internalization can be a positive strategic decision if a firm wants to add new activities to its core in a way that will develop new forms of idiosyncratic synergy. In this way, a firm can hope to collect future rents by creating new combinations of inputs that, in the short run at least, are inimitable. Some of these rent-generating capabilities may be especially useful at the design phase in providing inspiration for new products and processes, but others, which we have termed routines, are part of the on-going activities of the firm.

In the *long run*, the spread of knowledge should lead to a *tendency* towards the generalized spread of capabilities that both breaks down idiosyncrasy and reduces transaction costs. As this happens, it is possible that the intrinsic core of the firm will erode because capabilities that were once based on tacit knowledge and therefore inimitable become more common as other organizations devote the time necessary to replicate knowledge that has not hitherto been contestable.

For ancillary capabilities that have always been contestable, the spread of knowledge over time should reduce transaction costs and make it more attractive in some cases for firms to buy inputs rather than produce them internally. Over the long run, we might therefore expect to find vertical disintegration as products mature, technologies spread by analogy to other industries, and capabilities become generally more contestable at reduced transaction costs. This, of course, is not inevitable, and the exact course of events necessarily varies from industry to industry, or even from firm to firm within an industry. Nevertheless, it represents a more plausible general tendency of development than Stigler's famous model.

One implication of this dynamic theory is that the desirability of vertical integration may depend on the existing array of capabilities already available in the economy. When the existing arrangement of decentralized capabilities is very different from that required by a major systemic innovation, vertical integration – which permits a quicker and cheaper creation of new capabilities – may prove superior. This may indeed help explain the prevalence of large vertically integrated companies in the historical periods that Chandler chronicles. The major rearrangements of capabilities enabled by rapid economic growth and the rapid decline of transportation and communications costs in the nineteenth century were refractory to the existing system of decentralized capabilities. Change came from large integrated firms who could sweep away ill-adapted structures in a wave of "creative destruction." But at other times and in other places, as we will discuss in later chapters, entrenched vertical integration can prove just as refractory to change.

THE DYNAMICS OF FIRM AND INDUSTRY EVOLUTION

When viewed from a broader perspective, there is continual flux in the relationship between firms and industries, as firms form and reform depending on changes in relative capabilities and transaction costs. As is shown in Figure 3.8, the pattern of change is not invariable, however, because the firm-specific nature of both production and transaction costs will render integration (or disintegration) desirable in some cases but not in others. Thus Firms 4 and 8 remain specialists throughout the period, but Firms 1, 2, and 3 first merge and subsequently spinoff some activities, a

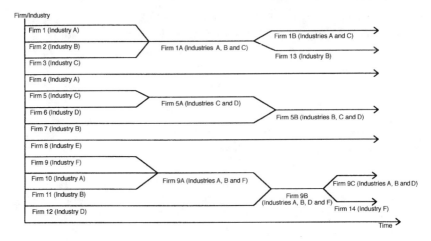

Figure 3.8 The convergence and divergence of industries

pattern that is also followed by Firms 10, 11, and 12. The merger of Firms 5, 6, and 7, on the other hand, leads to no spinoffs.

But this is by no means the end of the story, since we can expect technological change to upset existing relationships. In Figure 3.9, Firms 15, 16, and 17 produce innovative outputs that complement or replace the output of established firms. Whereas Firms 16 and 17 merge with older firms, Firm 15 remains independent. Moreover, as products become

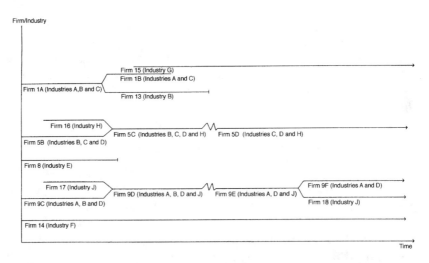

Figure 3.9 The effects of innovation and obsolescence on the convergence and divergence of firms and industries

44

obsolete, firms or whole industries may die. Thus, the outputs of Industries B and E are no longer needed and they go out of production.

The fact that our argument is couched in terms of *tendencies* and *varieties of experience*, however, does not imply randomness. On the contrary, the options for change at any given point are constrained by the nature of the environment at that point. Whether there is continuity, merger, or disintegration is a function of the cost structure at that time, which in turn depends on the existing distribution of capabilities and the degree of efficiency of markets. Hence change at the level of the economy as a whole is evolutionary, even when the effects of innovation on particular firms and industries may be revolutionary, because innovation has to fit within a functioning environment which can change only gradually as a response to stimuli.[53]

4

VERTICAL INTEGRATION IN THE EARLY AMERICAN AUTOMOBILE INDUSTRY

Chapter 3 presented a theoretical account of the interaction of innovation, the distribution of capabilities, and the level of transaction costs in helping to determine the boundaries of the firm. By examining the first four decades of the development of the American automotive industry, this chapter attempts to confront that theory with the historical record. It illustrates how changing patterns of internal and external capabilities and dynamic transaction costs altered firm boundaries in the *long run* as the industry progressed from its earliest stages to maturity. The auto industry is not, of course, a case that has never been studied before. It is, however, a case that has never been interrogated comprehensively and systematically on the question of vertical integration. Indeed, examples from the early auto industry appear in piecemeal fashion to support seemingly contradictory theoretical propositions about vertical integration.[54] What is lacking in the literature is a thorough treatment that sorts through both the facts of history and the claims of theory.

In the first phase of the industry, beginning at the very end of the nineteenth century, firms were generally assemblers that had few capabilities of their own and drew heavily on the skills of outside suppliers. Subsequently, as both the product and manufacturing processes became more sophisticated, the most innovative firms – in particular the Ford Motor Company – found that their inspiration and needs outstripped the talents of their suppliers. The automakers were therefore forced, in the manner suggested by Silver, to develop their own highly advanced capabilities in such diverse areas as components manufacture and tool making. By the late 1920s, however, these capabilities had become more widely dispersed and the degree of vertical integration receded as the auto firms could again draw on outside suppliers. Throughout this period down to 1940, there was a continual interplay between technology and capabilities that, as we have predicted in the theory of dynamic transaction costs, led to shifts in the balance between internal and external production.

INVENTION AND PRODUCT DEVELOPMENT

Robert Paul Thomas (1977, pp. 6–8) has divided the history of the American automobile industry into four periods: the era of invention, pre-1900; the era of product development, 1900–1908; the era of rapid expansion, 1908–1918; and the era of replacement demand, 1918–1929. Each period witnessed significant changes in the degree of vertical integration in the industry.

In the era of invention, the focus of all manufacturers – if they could be called that – was almost exclusively on product innovation. Here the industry came closest to the pattern suggested by Young and Stigler. Car makers like Winton, Olds, and Ford were craft shops, all highly integrated in the sense that they made – or, more accurately, improvised – most of their own parts (Epstein 1928, p. 28). One well-known example is Henry Ford making his first cylinder out of a piece of pipe (Nevins with Hill 1954, p. 142). What distinguishes the automobile industry from such earlier examples as printing or machine tools is that this early vertical integration and use of crafts techniques disappeared very quickly once genuine commercial production began in earnest. By the turn of the twentieth century, the capabilities to manufacture parts adaptable to the automobile of that period already existed in the American economy, and car makers quickly took advantage of them.

As is typical in the early stages of product innovation, the era of product development was initially characterized by a proliferation of automotive firms that put together a variety of models. By the end of this period, public taste had begun to coalesce to the point where demand for selected models allowed the prospect of mass production. As long as there was no consensus among consumers, however, the automobile remained a luxury product turned out in small numbers by a range of concerns that entered and exited from the market with relative freedom.

Although the degree of vertical integration varied from firm to firm, virtually all automobile companies began as assemblers rather than manufacturers. Early cars could be easily put together from components developed for other purposes, such as bicycle wheels, or from variations on known themes, such as wooden bodies. As Katz notes, "anyone organizing a motor car company in the early days could buy frames, axles, springs, wheels, motors, radiators, steering gears, and electrical systems – all set up and ready to install" (Katz 1977, pp. 14–15). Moreover, these components were available on credit terms of up to 90 days, which further reduced the capital requirements of new entrants to the industry as well as the skills that they needed.

Thus Silver's picture of vertical integration being forced upon an innovative industry does not strictly hold for the industry in this era because, from a technical standpoint, automobiles were not so much a new product

47

as a new way of deploying known components. Particularly in the United States, the term "horseless carriage" was an accurate description of the design concept that lay behind many cars. They were seen initially as improvements on existing forms of transport rather than as a new product that needed to be thought out *de novo*. It was only later that developments took place within a distinctive automotive paradigm. In addition, by the time that commercial production began at the turn of the century, the automobile had already received enough publicity to make customers and producers aware of its possible benefits, at least as an expensive toy. Early endurance tests and races generated potential orders that exceeded supply (Thomas 1977, pp. 44–47). Finding willing components manufacturers and dealers does not seem to have been a problem,[55] although raising capital was.

It is not surprising, therefore, that many of the early producers were already established in related industries. Pope, Winton, Thomas, Jeffery, and Pierce all manufactured bicycles, while the Duryea brothers and William S. Knudsen were bicycle mechanics and John N. Willys sold bicycles. Studebaker and the Fisher brothers made wagons or carriages. Ransom E. Olds manufactured gasoline engines with his father. And Henry M. Leland and the Dodge brothers operated machine shops. Some of these men introduced others to the industry by placing orders for components. When his factory burned down in 1901, Olds bought engines from Leland and Faulconer, transmissions from the Dodge brothers, and bodies from Briscoe. Two years later, the Dodges contracted to supply the first 650 chassis (engine, transmission, and axles) for the Ford Motor Company, of which they were charter investors. While Ford later became the strongest proponent of vertical integration, in the beginning he was an assembler like most of the pioneers in the industry (Katz 1977, pp. 18–22).

In many respects, the expansion of the industry in the first two decades of the century resembled a textbook example of the benefits of the external economies of a Marshallian Industrial District. Early in its development, the industry became concentrated in the East North Central states of Michigan, Ohio, and Indiana. In 1904, 53.3 per cent of total output by value came from those states, of which approximately one-half (26.6 per cent) originated in Michigan. A decade later, these three states accounted for 81.1 per cent of total output, with Michigan alone accounting for 62.9 per cent of total output. And, despite a reduction in later years, Michigan, Ohio, and Indiana still accounted for 67.6 per cent of output in 1925, with Michigan's share remaining as high as 51.7 per cent of total output (Seltzer 1928, p. 82).

Localization allowed assemblers to take advantage of external economies that flowed from concentrations of suppliers. But because of high transport costs for finished units, the structure of the industry has been compared to an hourglass, with parts from diverse suppliers funnelling into a small number of plants to make subassemblies that were then shipped to various plants around the nation for final assembly into automobiles (Hurley 1959, pp. 1–14). This was true, however, only of Ford and later General Motors, the largest manufacturers. Other firms concentrated their activities in the East North Central States or in New York.[56] Much as in the Lancashire textile industry or shipbuilding on the Clyde in nineteenth-century Britain, this made it possible for the auto firms not only to share parts suppliers but also to draw from a larger pool of skilled workers and to swap information more easily.

Recognition of the value of external economies resulted in two important agreements in 1910 and 1915. The first, sponsored by the Society of Automotive Engineers, led to the establishment of a set of standards for parts. In the early period of the industry, most independent suppliers built to specifications laid down by the assemblers. As a result, there were more than 1,600 types of steel tubing used and 800 standards of lock washers, with a similar proliferation of varieties for other components (Epstein 1928, pp. 41–43). Early attempts to set common standards had been unsuccessful, but the Panic of 1910 brought a crisis among assemblers. The failure of suppliers in the panic emphasized the vulnerability of small assemblers who were not readily able to switch to other firms because of peculiarities in specifications. Led at first by Howard E. Coffin of the Hudson Motor Car Company, over the next decade the S.A.E. set detailed standards for numerous parts, in the process increasing interchangeability across firms. After standardization, for example, the number of types of steel tubing was reduced to 210 and the number of types of lock washers to 16. Throughout the initial period of standardization, until the early 1920s, most interest was shown by the smaller firms, who had the most to gain. The larger firms such as Ford, Studebaker, Dodge, Willys-Overland, and General Motors tended to ignore the S.A.E. and relied instead on internally established standards (Epstein 1928; Thompson 1954, pp. 10–11).

A 1915 agreement to share patents also enhanced external economies. Because the increasing number of patent suits was costly and threatened to slow down the rate of adoption of improvements, approximately 100 members of the National Automobile Chamber of Commerce agreed to cross-license patents held by any of the signatories without royalty. With the exception of "revolutionary" improvements (which were few) and design features such as outside body shape, all patents were included in the agreement, which operated in its original form until 1925 (Epstein 1928, pp. 236–239; Seltzer 1928, pp. 44–45).

Nevertheless, even in the period before 1908 there were also pressures that promoted increased vertical integration. One was the Selden patent. Until it was declared uninfringed at the instigation of Henry Ford in 1911, the patent had been deemed to cover virtually all vehicles powered by gasoline-fueled internal-combustion engines. Allegedly in order to protect the public by eliminating fly-by-night organizations, the Association of

Licensed Automobile Manufacturers (ALAM), which administered the patent, tried to discourage assemblers in favor of firms that manufactured their own components. (The Association probably also realized that it would be easier to protect its rights if it could raise entry costs and therefore limit the number of possible offenders.) Because of its ability to deny licenses to firms that it did not find worthy of using the patent, the ALAM was in a position to encourage integration even if it could not closely monitor its decisions (Greenleaf 1961, pp. 84–85).

Before 1906–1908, the public also perceived some advantage in parts supplied internally. Epstein reports that in 1904 Maxwell-Briscoe advertised that "the Maxwell plant . . . is not an assembly plant, but one where every part of the Maxwell is actually made under the direct supervision of the designer, Mr. J. D. Maxwell." A few months earlier, Rambler had advertised that "excepting only the body, tires, and spark coil, every part of the Rambler touring car is made in our own factory" (Epstein 1928, p. 51). As late as 1920, however, a vehicle called the Cole was being advertised as a fully assembled car, one thus able to take complete advantage of the skills of its specialized suppliers (Rae 1984, p. 61).

Last, even at this early stage a number of automobile producers were beginning to integrate vertically for other reasons. For example, Henry Ford moved as soon as he could to eliminate much of the business he had been contracting to Dodge Brothers. By moving into the manufacture of chassis, Ford hoped to internalize the profits earned by the Dodges, a justification that on its own is unreasonable. However, the way in which Ford proceeded, by setting up a Ford Manufacturing Company that was distinct from the Ford Motor Company, also allowed him to force out minority stockholders who had challenged his control of the latter firm. In this way he began a pattern that was to lead eventually to the most heavily integrated firm in the industry (Nevins with Hill 1954, pp. 279–283, 324).

PRODUCT STANDARDIZATION AND MASS PRODUCTION

The last years of Thomas's era of product development also saw the standardization of automobile design that was to make mass production feasible. The ensuing innovations in both product and process soon eclipsed the capabilities of many outside suppliers and forced firms that, until then, had been largely assemblers to develop their own internal capabilities in order to undertake activities that were unknown elsewhere in the economy.

The first major question to be resolved was that of the power source. Electric motors had a very limited range of operation despite their heavy and expensive batteries. Steam cars, which initially seemed more promising, had similarly been discredited by 1904 by several well-publicized explosions.

This left the field to gasoline engines, which came to be perceived as "normal," while the alternatives became curiosities (Thomas 1977, pp. 47–48; Nevins with Hill 1954, pp. 203–204). The second move toward standardization came with the replacement of basic American designs with more advanced and complex French ideas. Although Americans originally conceived of cars as buggies without horses (like the curved-dash Oldsmobile runabout), the French thought in terms of a road locomotive. French autos had heavier, multi-cylinder engines mounted at the front, multi-gear transmissions, and differentials, all attached to a steel frame. The preference of wealthy customers for French imports induced American firms to begin manufacturing cars on the French pattern in 1901. The following year Rambler and Winton produced models with tonneau bodies and steering wheels rather than a tiller (Thomas 1977, pp. 52–54).

After 1905, the preference for cars on the French model was reflected in a shift of demand patterns toward more expensive cars. Before then, although the French type of design had become standard for American cars selling for over $2,000, there had been considerable elasticity of demand at the lower end of the price range: Horseless carriages like the Oldsmobile, which sold for $650, were produced in large quantities despite their obvious inferiority. But between 1904 and 1907, the average wholesale price of American-built cars actually increased from $1,056 to $2,150, as customers forsook motorized buggies for the dearer French designs (Thomas 1977, pp. 60–61). This left an enormous unfilled demand for a model that delivered the benefits of the French concept at a price comparable to the Oldsmobile. Ford's Model N of 1906–7 incorporated many of the features of the French design in a car selling for only $850. It still had the appearance of a buggy, however, and was therefore merely a stage en route to the development of a truly low-priced standard vehicle. Ford's subsequent success with the Model T was based on precisely that combination of modern features and low price.

In part, then, the success of the Model T is a story of product innovation. Although the French type of design was known and accepted, it still took considerable ingenuity to transform this into a cheap, reliable vehicle suited to mass use. This involved a high degree of standardization in manufacture, but Ford could and did make changes from year to year to improve the Model T slowly but significantly between 1908 and 1926 (Hounshell 1984, pp. 273–275). All these improvements remained, however, within a single design paradigm. The radical change in product characteristic of the era of product development had given way to incremental product change, and the focus began to shift to process innovation.

Process innovation – the development of mass automobile production – was the ultimate key to the success of the Model T. Ford pursued aggressively what would nowadays be called a strategy of overall cost leadership (Porter 1980, pp. 35–37). He also engaged in "learning curve pricing," reducing price in lock-step with reductions in cost and plowing back retained earnings into capital improvements aimed at lowering costs even further. Indeed, the Dodge Brothers sued Ford in the late 1910s for failing to issue adequate stock dividends and for proposing thereby to "continue the corporation henceforth as a semi-eleemosynary institution and not as a business institution."[57] The Dodges were simultaneously major stockholders in and major competitors to Ford Motors, and it is well known that Ford viewed his own success as therefore subsidizing the competition. But this pricing and investment strategy was almost certainly not motivated principally by a desire to squeeze the Dodges. Rather, it reflected Ford's appreciation of the standard-product, low-cost approach. Indeed, Ford thought it essential to sell the Model T solely on the basis of price as an undifferentiated product – even to the extent of trying to disguise or play down improvements in the car (Hounshell 1984, pp. 275–276). The low-priced car of Ford's imagination initially sold as an $850 touring car in 1908. By August 1916, the Model T had become a much improved $360 touring car or a $345 runabout. At the end of 1924, following the postwar inflation and deflation, the touring car was offered for $290 and the runabout for $260 – and, again, both models were greatly improved in comparison with earlier years (Chandler 1964, p. 33).

Ford's ability to reduce prices was based on two factors – savings in assembly costs and reductions in the costs of components. Although the former, which is associated with the development of the moving assembly line, is the more famous,[58] by far the greater savings were achieved by internalizing the production of components to take advantage of the firm's superior capabilities, particularly in cutting metals. It has recently been shown (Williams *et al.* 1993, pp. 73–78) that 55 per cent of the reduction in the price of the Model T between 1909 and 1916 can be attributed to cuts in component costs as the firm relied less and less on outside suppliers. The direct labor component of Ford's operations was always so small, however, that the savings from improved assembly methods were slight by comparison.

Mass production involved Ford in the large-scale design of machine tools, at least some of which also seem to have been manufactured by the firm. Although Thomas contends that the automobile industry was well served by outside machine tool firms in its early days, the greater extent to which Ford took the division of labor when he developed mass production and the assembly line called for a far wider use of special-purpose machinery than had been necessary for other firms. As Hounshell notes, Henry Ford's insistence on concentrating on a single model gave his engineers an unprecedented chance to install single-purpose machine tools (Thomas 1977, p. 269; Hounshell 1984, p. 233). Moreover, interchangeability of parts on the mass scale undertaken by Ford required extraordinary accuracy. Nevins and Hill list a selection of tools designed at Ford for the

Highland Park plant. These include an improved transmission-testing device, a double-ended tool for pressing tubes in radiator fins, and many others (Nevins with Hill 1954, pp. 458–461; Faurote 1915, pp. 184–201).

To meet their new needs, Ford and his engineers were forced to develop many of these devices themselves, which entailed generating the necessary internal capabilities. This was not because the technical advances in the tools were beyond the understanding of independent tool makers; rather, as Silver hypothesizes, it was because only the men at Ford understood the uses to which the new machines were to be put. It would have cost more for the Ford Motor Company to explain the process of automobile manufacture to the tool makers (a process that was in any case still evolving in the minds of Ford and his assistants) than it did to diversify into tool design on an *ad hoc* basis. A story told by Charles Sorensen, although discounted by Hounshell, illustrates the process.[59] Sorensen

> recalled that when Charles Morgana sent out specifications for a Ford-designed machine tool to machine tool manufacturers, the latter often came back to Morgana saying that there must have been an error because the machine could not do what it was supposed to do. Morgana would then show the tool builders that no mistake had been made because the Ford-designed and Ford-built prototype could indeed turn out the specified number of units within the specified limits of precision. "So it went with the thousand pieces of machinery that we bought," concluded Sorensen.
>
> (Hounshell 1984, p. 231)

But there is more to the story than the radical newness of the Ford machines. What is central to the innovation of mass production is, of course, its systemic character: its organization and timing of production activities. This systemic aspect had the effect of making vertical integration self-reinforcing in certain ways. Because much of the assembly activity was collected in one place, Ford engineers were able to perceive opportunities for grasping economies of scale that would not have been apparent to decentralized parts suppliers. Thus as an organization, Ford was able to collate in an idiosyncratic way knowledge encompassing diverse areas in order to bring about wide-ranging changes in product and manufacturing technologies. Although the required capabilities may have been present individually in various organizations spread throughout the economy, it is doubtful that they would have been combined so successfully if they had not been under the centralized control that Ford provided.

An example that perhaps illustrates this phenomenon is Ford's development of metal stamping techniques. Pressed-steel frames, which were much stronger than their structural-steel predecessors, were generally adopted in the industry by 1909. A couple of years before, however, the managers of the John R. Keim Mills, a producer of pressed steel in Buffalo, had approached Ford with a proposal to supply axle housings. Ford agreed, and by 1908 Keim was supplying a variety of parts. Ford and Keim engineers cooperated in perfecting the pressing process, and Ford invested heavily in machinery for the Buffalo plant. Finally, after the settlement of the Selden patent suit, Ford purchased Keim in 1911. When the workers at the Keim plant struck the following year, Ford ordered all of the machinery removed from Buffalo and shipped to Highland Park, where it was soon adapted to new ways of producing crankcases, axles, housings, and even bodies, moving Ford one step closer to the integrated mass production that was to come (Nevins with Hill 1954, pp. 458–461). Thus integration initially motivated by a desire to avoid hold-up problems and supply disruption led to further integration because of the possibilities for innovation it opened up in the Ford environment.

It is important to emphasize that integration at Ford in this period was a phenomenon of *dynamic* transaction costs arising from novelty and innovation. As we have defined them, dynamic transaction costs are the costs of persuading, negotiating, coordinating, and teaching outside suppliers, that is, the costs of not having the capabilities you need when you need them. But, because of the ability of outsiders to learn, dynamic transaction costs apply only in the short run. As soon as the outlines of the assembly-line innovation were clear, it diffused rapidly to independent parts suppliers, a process aided by Ford's openness to trade journalists (Hounshell 1984, pp. 260–261). Moreover, Ford engineers themselves soon learned that the production process could be efficiently decentralized. Ford's own account is worth quoting.

> We started assembling a motor car in a single factory. Then as we began to make parts, we began to departmentalize so that each department would do only one thing. As the factory is now organized each department makes only a single part or assembles a part. A department is a little factory in itself. The part comes into it as raw material or as a casting, goes through the sequence of machines and heat treatments, or whatever may be required, and leaves the department finished. It was only because of transport ease that the departments were grouped together when we started to manufacture. I did not know that such minute divisions would be possible; but as our production grew and departments multiplied, we actually changed from making automobiles to making parts. Then we found that we had made another new discovery, which was that by no means all of the parts had to be made in one factory. It was not really a discovery – it was something in the nature of going around in a circle to my first manufacturing when I bought the motors and probably ninety per cent. of the parts. When we began to make our own parts we practically took for granted that they all had to be made in the one factory – that there was some special

virtue in having a single roof over the manufacture of the entire car. We have now developed away from this. . . . So now we are on our way back to where we started from – excepting that, instead of buying our parts on the outside, we are beginning to make them in our own factories on the outside.

(Ford with Crowther 1923, pp. 83–84)

Once the innovation of mass production of parts became assimilated and disseminated – and as the extent of the market grew – centralization became more costly and less beneficial. At Ford, the ensuing decentralization took place within a vertically integrated structure for what are largely historical reasons.

It is also important to notice the importance of rapid growth and high demand in explaining the extent of vertical integration at Ford. The systemically innovative character of mass production is what called for a high degree of vertical integration; but "a high volume of orders furnished the necessity that was the mother of the invention." And, in the end, "mass production of automobiles was almost entirely Ford's response to orders too numerous to be filled any other way" (Rosenberg and Birdzell 1986, p. 222).

One way in which rapid growth affected vertical integration was in the changing capital position of the car companies. Early on, most if not all car makers were capital starved, financed largely by a bootstrap process of pressing dealers for immediate payment while taking credit from suppliers (Seltzer 1928, pp. 19–21). It was initially difficult to obtain outside financing, and most growth was on the basis of retained earnings. Ford was no exception; and with the success of the Model T, those earnings became large. Thus, whereas Ford relied on contractual arrangements early on – even when transaction costs were arguably high – he soon had much more capital with which to pursue integration. An example might be the development of vanadium steel, an innovation Ford considered a key to the success of the Model T. After extensive metallurgical experiments at the Ford Motor Company, Ford incorporated vanadium steel into the crankshaft, axles, gears, and springs of the first Model Ts. But production of the alloy was initially entrusted to outside steel manufacturers under guarantee (Nevins with Hill 1954, pp. 348–349, 389). Only later did Ford integrate into steel making.

This availability of retained earnings in a privately held corporation like Ford raises the possibility that some of the extensive integration, particularly in the latter part of this period, was in fact "mistaken":[60] that is, vertical integration had no particular efficiency rationale and existed only because Ford wanted it and the quasirents of the Model T could support it. By the mid-1920s, Ford had created a diversified empire on 2,000 acres bordering the Rouge River. There he manufactured steel and glass;

fabricated various intermediate inputs; and assembled vehicles. Beyond the Rouge, he became involved in iron and coal mining; lumbering; limestone; silica sand; Brazilian rubber; and railroad and shipping companies to bring these inputs to the plant. How much of this had an efficiency rationale? In the case of activities intimately related to automobile manufacture, Ford arguably could produce as cheaply as any outside supplier in the Model T era. The company kept detailed cost records, was aware of the costs of outside suppliers, and used those data as a benchmark (Hounshell 1984, p. 272). The cost-effectiveness of integration into dissimilar activities like glass, rubber, or railroads is less clear.[61] But these activities were probably not any great disadvantage in the era when demand for the T was strong. Only when the environment changed significantly – as it did in the fourth of Thomas's eras – would the extensive vertical integration at Ford appear a clear mistake.[62] But, as we have hinted, this perception of error is largely based on *ex post* reasoning. The fact that external capabilities spread and the transaction cost balance subsequently shifted away from internalization does not undermine the rationality of Ford's decision to integrate vertically in another period when conditions were different.

Significantly, the one other firm to attempt a high level of integration before 1920 was also run by a strong-minded visionary. In his two forays into General Motors, William Crapo Durant brought together not only a large number of automobile assemblers but also a collection of components suppliers. Under Durant, there was no systematic policy behind the expansion of General Motors, however, and no attempt to integrate the various divisions into a coordinated manufacturing group on the Ford model. As we will see, it was only after a decade of wrestling with their legacy that Durant's successors were able to rationalize the firm and then move toward genuine integration.

Like Ford, Durant believed strongly in the latent demand for automobiles, especially at the lower end of the price range. Unlike Ford, however, Durant's innovations lay not in production of the vehicles but in the creation of a marketing and distribution network. From the point of view of process technology, General Motors was very much a follower. For both of these reasons, integration at General Motors was of a very different sort than that at Ford, and it arose from motives that were also quite different.

Durant's entry into the automobile business came in 1904, when he took over control of the failed Buick Company. Here Durant applied principles he had developed as a successful carriage maker. He concentrated on marketing, leaving production to others as much as possible. Durant very quickly extended his reach backward into assembly and parts manufacture, of course. But, unlike Ford, he did so not by manufacturing his own parts in a way coordinated with assembly. Rather, he persuaded parts suppliers to move to Flint, where Buick was located, in what was in effect an attempt to create external economies by converting Flint into an industrial district. Weston-Mott, an axle-maker, moved to Flint in 1905, and Champion, the sparkplug maker, arrived in 1908 (Chandler 1962, p. 117; Sloan 1941, pp. 44–45). He persuaded other suppliers to shift to automobile parts from carriage making and other businesses. Durant also set up worker housing for similar reasons. As part of this effort to create production capacity, Durant often took financial positions in suppliers.

In 1908, Durant set up General Motors Corporation after a failed attempt to merge with Ford, Reo, and Briscoe. The new enterprise was a holding company, owning stock in a number of assemblers, notably Olds, Cadillac, and Oakland in addition to Buick. GM also bought a number of smaller companies, many of them with little real productive capability. More importantly, the company held stock in makers of parts, including bodies (F. W. Stewart Company), engines, gears, transmissions, lamps, rims, and steering mechanisms (Chandler 1962, p. 119). Chandler and others have cited as a principal motive for vertical integration Durant's desire to ensure adequate and timely supplies (Chandler, *loc. cit.*; Pound 1934, pp. 87–89). This is no doubt part of the story. But an arguably more important motive was Durant's desire, in the fashion suggested by Teece (1986b), to appropriate the benefits of his vision and his marketing innovations by taking positions in as many assets complementary to auto manufacture as possible. Durant was by no means a passive stockholder in these enterprises, of course. But capital markets for automotive securities were not yet developed enough to allow appropriation by passive investment: The first appearance of automotive stock on the New York exchange was the sale of General Motors voting trust certificates in 1911 (Pound 1934, p. 113).

It is certainly likely that some of Durant's vertical integration was also motivated by the desire to assure supplies, especially in view of the rapid growth of output, which suggests a disequilibrium in the market for parts. But it is also true that much of what Durant bought in the early heyday of GM turned out to be unnecessary or unprofitable. It is reasonable to conclude that this was largely because General Motors, unlike Ford, had no superior capabilities to bring to component manufacturing. After Durant was forced out in the financial crisis of 1910, the bankers who took over, headed by James J. Storrow, sold off both horizontal and vertical holdings (Pound 1934, p. 132).

In 1916, Durant returned to control of GM with some brilliant financial maneuvering. He immediately sold off a few more losing properties, but then began another buying spree. This time the investment was mostly vertical rather than horizontal, suggesting that assurance-of-supply motives were becoming more important as Durant sought to complete the General Motors package (Chandler 1962, p. 123). In May of 1916, GM added to its roster the United Motors Corporation, an agglomeration of parts and accessories makers that included Hyatt Roller Bearing, New Departure

Manufacturing, Remy, Delco, and Perlman Rim (Pound 1934, p. 162; Chandler 1962, p. 123).

By the end of the era of rapid growth, then, Ford and General Motors emerged as dominant firms in the automotive industry with structures that were, at one level, quite similar: They both engaged in large-scale production of low and moderately priced cars within a vertically integrated structure. At another level, however, the two organizations were quite different, and they had followed different routes to reach their positions. Whereas Ford had followed a Silverian *entrepreneurial* strategy, Durant had been more concerned with Teece's *appropriability* version of strategy. But, because Ford was able to back its strategy with superior capabilities whereas the firms that GM absorbed often had few capabilities whose quasirents could be appropriated, Ford's strategy was initially far more successful. As we will see, this legacy of history left the two firms with different sets of capabilities for dealing with the years after 1918. And while the value of Ford's capabilites had eroded by the mid-1920s, GM's capabilities proved to be more durable over the long run.

REPLACEMENT DEMAND AND MODEL CHANGES

In Thomas's last period, the era of replacement demand (1918–1929), patterns of vertical integration fluctuated as the industry matured. As both product and process innovation became less important and external capabilities dispersed, cost relationships between automobile manufacturers and potential suppliers became increasingly prominent. By the end of the period, a modest reduction in the degree of vertical integration had begun, based on a new appreciation of the flexibility that could be derived from outside suppliers.

The growth of the industry had been rapid after the introduction of the Model T. Registrations of new passenger cars increased from 63,500 units in 1908 to 1,165,792 units in 1917. Growth was more cyclical as the market came closer to saturation in the 1920s, but annual new registrations were routinely over three million units in the latter part of the decade and reached 4,455,178 passenger cars in 1929. Despite the dominance of the Model T until the mid-1920s, demand for many other makes had grown to the point at which it was feasible to take advantage of the production innovations pioneered by Ford. Although other firms did not attempt vertical integration on the scale undertaken by Ford, they did internalize the production of many components and adopt assembly line techniques. Independent suppliers had also learned many of the lessons of Highland Park.

As noted, General Motors had achieved a high level of integration by the 1920s, manufacturing a high proportion of its parts and accessory needs. After the departure of Durant for the second and final time, however, the firm consciously decided to limit its scope. As outlined in the annual report for 1920, the policy of the new du Pont regime was to restrict the firm to the production of items that were used principally in the construction of new vehicles. Therefore, tires, for which there was a large replacement demand, or steel, which was used primarily for other purposes, were not seen as proper activities for General Motors (Sloan 1965, p. 193). General Motors was thus clearly limiting itself to activities requiring similar capabilities and wished to avoid entering into fields in which external capabilities were well developed and transaction costs low.

The smaller companies also typically stuck to the basics of car building and drew on efficient external sources of capabilities. Studebaker's policy was to "buy all raw materials and half manufactured products which come from other industries – that is to say, iron, steel, aluminum and other metals, leather, textiles, lumber, glass, and tires – with the exceptions of these purchases they manufacture in a complete chain, do all of their own forging, stamping, and machining, and build their own parts units." Nash, however, adopted the Ford/GM strategy of internalization by producing many of its own inputs, although probably nowhere near the 93 per cent that was claimed at the end of 1934 (Katz 1977, pp. 254–255).

Estimates of the degree of internal value-added vary greatly. Ford stated in the mid-1920s that his firm purchased two-thirds of its inputs (Ford with Crowther 1926, p. 2). In 1933, after Ford had begun to use a higher proportion of components from the outside, *Fortune* nevertheless estimated that four-sevenths of a Ford car was produced by independent suppliers and the remainder by the Ford Motor Company. But in 1955, when the degree of vertical integration had almost certainly not been reduced further, Arjay Miller of Ford estimated that General Motors was 40 per cent integrated; Ford, 35 per cent; and Chrysler, 30 per cent (Katz 1977, pp. 252, 254). Crandall puts the figures for that year (the first year for which he has data for all three firms) at 51 per cent for GM, 44 per cent for Ford, and 40 per cent for Chrysler (Crandall 1968, p. 78).[63]

As late as 1937, the Federal Trade Commission found that Ford was still more highly integrated than General Motors and that Chrysler, which by then had surpassed Ford in sales, lagged far behind. But although Chrysler has been characterized as "a giant assembler which buys a maximum of the auto components it needs" (Katz 1977, p. 253), it also significantly increased its internal inputs in the late 1920s. The only major success among firms started after the First World War, Chrysler initially lacked forge, foundry, and other major manufacturing facilities. In part in order to gain control of these capabilities when it entered the low-priced field with Plymouth in 1928, Chrysler purchased Dodge Brothers from Dillon, Read, the Wall Street firm that had taken the firm over from the Dodge heirs. One of the few concerns that had patterned itself after Ford by limiting its models, Dodge Brothers had of course begun as a parts supplier and had

Table 4.1 Wholesale value of American motor-vehicle output compared with wholesale value of manufactured components and equipment purchased from others, 1922–1926

Year	Value of finished vehicles, $	Value of purchased components, $	Percentage
1922	1,787,122,708	982,952,384	55
1923	2,582,398,876	1,270,000,000	49
1924	2,318,249,632	900,321,000	39
1925	2,957,386,637	1,128,648,000	38
1926	3,163,756,676	823,394,000	26

Source: Lawrence H. Seltzer (1928), Table 4, p. 59

the plant to serve many of Chrysler's needs as it expanded (Seltzer 1928, pp. 240–247; Kennedy 1972, pp. 207–209). Nevertheless, Chrysler was able to take advantage of better developed external networks of capabilities than had been open to Ford or General Motors when they began mass production and, as Silver's theory predicts, Chrysler never reached the degree of vertical integration of the earlier firms.

Innovations and changing market conditions led to a reversal of the trend towards vertical integration in the later years of the decade. Between 1922 and 1926, the importance of components purchased from outside suppliers had declined from 55 per cent to 26 per cent of the wholesale value of American motor vehicles (Table 4.1). Even in dollar terms, the value of components had declined despite a near doubling in the total value of finished vehicles. By 1927, however, purchases of some components were already beginning to increase (Table 4.2), and vertical integration became progressively less important in the early years of the Depression, as dynamic transaction costs lost their earlier significance.

Katz has calculated an "index" of vertical integration for the years 1923–1934 (Table 4.3). A value of zero indicates a firm that only assembles parts supplied by others, while a value of 10 indicates that the firm supplies as high a proportion of its own inputs as is feasible (although less than 100 per

Table 4.2 Outside purchases of components by American automobile manufacturers, 1926–1927

Component	January 1926 (percentage)	July 1927 (percentage)
Engines	21.4	28.8
Clutches	47.8	70.4
Transmissions	31.0	31.5
Rear axles	30.2	33.4
Steering gears	63.5	69.9

Source: Shidle (1927), p. 146

Table 4.3 Index of vertical integration, 1923–1934

Company	Index[e]											
	1923	1924	1925	1926	1927	1928	1929	1930	1931	1932	1933	1934
Auburn	0	0	0	0	0	0	0	0	0	0	1	1
Chrysler[a]	3	5	5	4	3	4	3	2	2	2	5	4
Durant	1	1	5	3	5	5	5	3	3	1		
Ford	10	10	10	10	9	10	9	9	9	6	8	8
Franklin	6	5	6	5	5	4	5	2	3	2	3	3
GM[b]	6	6	7	6	6	6	6	6	6	6	7	7
Graham-Paige[c]	0	0	0	1	1	1	1	1	1	2	2	2
Hudson[d]	2	4	3	5	5	5	5	4	4	3	5	5
Hupp	5	3	2	2	2	2	2	3	2	3	3	2
Jordan	1	0	0	0	0	0	0	0	0			
Nash	5	4	4	4	5	4	4	4	5	5	5	5
Packard	8	5	6	6	7	5	4	4	5	5	5	4
Peerless	3	2	2	2	2	1	1	1	1	1		
Reo	7	7	7	7	3	4	2	3	3	2	4	4
Studebaker	6	5	6	5	5	4	3	2	3	3	4	2
Willys	6	5	7	7	6	5	5	5	5	2	4	5
Industry average	4.3	3.9	4.4	4.2	3.7	3.5	3.3	3.1	3.1	2.7	4.3	4.0

Notes: a Maxwell, 1923–25; Chrysler, 1926–28. b Chevrolet, 1929–1934. c Paige, 1922–1927. d Terraplane, 1933–1934. e See text for definition

cent). As one would expect, the two most integrated firms throughout the period were Ford and General Motors. The values of the smaller firms varied greatly, with some like Packard and Franklin scoring higher than might be predicted from their low level of sales. Chrysler's figure, on the other hand, is very low in view of the company's size. Almost all firms, however, show a marked decline in vertical integration from 1927 onwards, with a trough at the bottom of the Depression.

This may seem surprising in view of earlier trends. It is especially interesting for the early years of the Depression, when one would expect a capital-intensive firm to protect its own output of components at the expense of independent firms. The explanation for this pattern involves a number of factors that we will examine in more detail. Principal among these are: (a) the growth of the market for spare parts; (b) organizational innovation; and (c) the introduction of the annual model change.

Despite the increasing degree of vertical integration in the early 1920s, the aging of the national fleet of automobiles led to a proliferation of parts firms to supply the replacement market. While employment in automobile plants proper decreased by 43,628 over the period 1923–1925, employment in parts firms grew by 64,628 (Seltzer 1928, p. 50). Because of the low investment required to produce a limited range of items, most of the new parts firms were small or medium sized. Competition among them reduced costs to levels that frequently could not be reached by the automobile firms themselves, particularly as the need for flexibility grew near the end of the decade (Flugge 1929, p. 166). As novelty became an important selling factor, firms were forced to change models more frequently. Moreover, the number of models produced by each firm multiplied. This reduced the economies of scale open to automobile manufacturers, giving further advantage to the small parts firms that had gained capabilities that were earlier largely the preserve of the manufacturers.

Organizational innovation also helped shape the pattern of vertical integration in this era. In the 'twenties, the principal innovation had the effect of shifting the margin between firm and market in the direction of the market. Following the scares of the early 1920s, firms sought to keep their inventories small by purchasing only amounts that were immediately necessary. This led to the adoption of "hand-to-mouth" purchasing, a more colorfully named predecessor of the now-fashionable "just-in-time" practices[64] (Flugge 1929, p. 163). And, if modern proponents of this technique are correct, the adoption of hand-to-mouth purchasing had efficiency advantages over and above its ability to economize on inventories.[65]

But the most important factor influencing the pattern of vertical integration in the 'twenties and 'thirties was the annual model change and the product innovation that accompanied it.

The crisis of 1920 came as a shock to the automobile industry. Ford survived by cutting overhead and by shifting much of the burden of emergency financing to his dealers, who were shipped the company's entire inventory of cars "with draft bills of lading attached" (Seltzer 1928, p. 116). At GM, the crisis led to a more fundamental restructuring, including the ouster of Durant, financial intervention from the du Ponts, and the eventual ascendancy of Alfred P. Sloan, Jr. to the chairmanship. But the recession of 1920–1921 was only the first of four in a decade in which total car sales actually declined from past-year levels (Thomas 1973, p. 120). Automobile manufacture had ceased to enjoy predictable growth in sales and had become a cyclical industry. The market for new cars was becoming saturated, especially at the low end, where a growing fleet of used cars provided impecunious buyers with an alternative they had lacked in the industry's earlier days.

Cars like the Model T suffered most from this competition, since used versions of higher-priced models compared favorably with a new Model T. The manufacturers who did best during these cyclical downturns were the ones whose new cars offered significant advances in features over past models. These, it turns out, were the smaller, more innovative, and less integrated firms, including Hudson, Chrysler, and Dodge. These firms offered new models with styling and features that distanced them both from competing new-car makers and from used cars. In particular, these firms were pioneers in one particular innovation: the inexpensive closed steel body (Thomas 1973, pp. 128–130).

The decade of the 'twenties amounted, in effect, to what we might think of as a discontinuity in the automobile's product cycle. Instead of a continued evolutionary pace in product and process innovation, relatively radical product innovation had again become the order of the day. But here, in contrast to the changes surrounding the Model T, innovative capabilities were largely external to the manufacturers, and it was those firms able to draw on the product-improving innovations of decentralized suppliers that gained at least a temporary advantage.[66] Innovations like annealing, normalizing, and loose-rolling processes came from the steel industry, and independent body-maker Budd Manufacturing was responsible for automatic welding machines, improvements in sound-deadening materials, and the monopiece body (Abernathy 1978, p. 183).

The inexpensive closed body itself was developed in a joint venture between Fisher Brothers and Hudson before GM bought a share in the former in 1919, and it appeared first on the Hudson Essex in 1921 (Thomas 1973, p. 129). Dodge introduced the first all-steel closed body in 1922 (Abernathy 1978, p. 184). It was thus the small, less-integrated firms who were best able initially to succeed in the era of replacement demand. Abernathy believes, for example, that Chrysler's "strategy of design flexibility and shallow vertical integration proved very successful in the prewar period, when the rate of technological change in the product was rapid." Because Chrysler concentrated its energies in fewer areas, it was able to make good use of its resources. The firm pioneered in increased-compression engines in 1925 and aerodynamic body designs with a low center of gravity in the 1930s (Abernathy 1978, p. 37).

By contrast, Ford's high degree of vertical integration contributed to the firm's great difficulty in adapting to the changed conditions. Despite notable evolutionary changes in the Model T in the mid-1920s, Ford proved incapable of making a smooth transition to a new model. The firm was obliged to suspend production for nine months and faced severe teething problems thereafter (Hounshell 1984, chapter 7). Ford was later charged with callously abandoning its own highly paid workers in order to purchase more cheaply from independent suppliers, but the reality was more complex. For one thing, the Model A contained a number of important components that either were not manufactured by Ford or were so different from those of the Model T that existing plant and machinery could not be converted. New items included oil pumps, windshield wipers, distributors, water pumps, oil filters, air cleaners, and a variety of gauges[67] (Nevins and Hill 1957, p. 533). Among existing components, Ford could not produce large enough quantities of the more-complex bodies of the Model A and was obliged to buy more than half of its supplies from Briggs, Budd, and Murray Body (Abernathy 1978, p. 142; Katz 1977, p. 252).

The new regime thus had the effect not only of promoting the fortunes of firms employing relatively less vertical integration but also of prodding the highly integrated firms to become less so. "Major product innovations," as Abernathy argues, "destroy old paths of backward vertical integration and create opportunities for new ones. Product innovations thus generally reduce the degree of backward integration" (Abernathy, 1978, p. 64). And this certainly seems to have been the case at Ford. Moreover, despite the legend that Ford did not keep records, the firm knew as early as the mid-1920s that some components could be purchased more cheaply than Ford manufactured them. This message was reinforced by the transition problems that the firm experienced. By the early 1930s, these had convinced Ford executives that a smooth introduction of a new model was more likely if the burden of change were spread over a larger number of firms.

Of all the firms in the industry, however, General Motors was in the best position to take advantage of the new economics of replacement demand. Unlike Ford, GM had not optimized its production process for the single-minded manufacture of one unchanging model. Under Ford defector William Knudsen, GM installed a system of "flexible" mass production that allowed for model changes without trauma (Hounshell 1984, pp. 265–266). GM was also less integrated than Ford, and it was integrated in 1920 in a much looser way. This made it easier for GM to take advantage of the ideas and other capabilities of outside suppliers. Moreover, the company had always had something of a strategy of product innovation and model change. Dating back to Durant's early days at Buick, GM – unlike Ford – chose not to compete by reducing price on a standardized model but by improving the performance and amenity characteristics of a car with a more-or-less constant price (Thomas 1973, p. 122). At the same time, General Motors was also better placed than its smaller rivals to appropriate the benefits of product innovation and model change. GM possessed a richer package of complementary assets, notably its large distribution, dealer, and consumer-finance network. This gave the firm an ability to benefit, in a classic way, from both its own innovations and those developed by smaller competitors and independents.

And when GM lacked some of the relevant assets, it moved to acquire them. The most important example of this is GM's acquisition of Fisher Body. As we saw, Fisher pioneered in the development of the closed body. Although this was still a relatively unpopular option at the time, GM decided to tap into the technology by acquiring 60 per cent of Fisher in 1919. At the same time, GM signed a ten-year agreement to buy all of its closed bodies from Fisher. In return, GM insisted on stringent contract terms in order to avoid opportunistic behavior. As overall demand grew and preferences shifted toward closed bodies, however, General Motors became discontented with its arrangement with Fisher Body, which had become an extremely important supplier. Not only was the price charged now believed to be too high in view of the lower unit capital costs that Fisher Body incurred, but Fisher also declined to locate its body plants adjacent to GM assembly plants, a move that would have benefited General Motors but would also have limited Fisher's flexibility in dealing with other customers. Ultimately, General Motors was obliged to take over the remainder of Fisher Body in 1926 in order to protect its interests (Klein, Crawford, and Alchian 1978, pp. 308–310).

Klein, Crawford, and Alchian explain this episode narrowly in terms of the highly specific assets Fisher and GM had to commit to the venture and the attendant threats of hold-up and expropriation of rents. But it was not the specificity of the assets *per se* that made integration look better to GM than contractual alternatives. As we saw, the later years of the 1920s and the early 1930s saw a trend toward increased dependence on suppliers for parts, and many of these suppliers certainly employed assets highly specific to the task and produced components critical to the assemblers' flow of production. What led to high transaction costs in the case of Fisher was the very rapid shift in demand toward the closed body. In contrast to Ford's experience with the Model T, General Motors was not in the forefront of innovation in this instance.[68] Closed bodies had been available for years and had also been adopted by competitors.

In the long run, GM might well have been able to rely on outside body manufacturers as all other major auto firms, including Ford and Chrysler, were to do to some extent in the 1930s. In the mid-1920s, however, GM's larger volume and emphasis on flexibility made it especially vulnerable to hold-up problems. Because it was not an innovator, GM had to compete with other auto makers for scarce closed bodies as demand accelerated.[69] If it could not keep pace with rising consumer demand for closed bodies, GM stood to lose the benefits that its policy of up-to-date styling was supposed to provide. This might in fact have led to a permanent loss in market share if the public bought other brands by default. Rather than pay a premium to guarantee a reliable supply in a seller's market, GM decided to invest a relatively small sum to gain full control of a supplier in which it already held a majority interest.

Note that although sunk cost may be sunk, GM's prior investment made vertical integration into body building cheaper than for other firms that needed to begin from scratch. As the additional investments required to overcome the problem of hold-up were greater for other auto makers, those firms were more willing to incur whatever transaction costs derived from association with independent body manufacturers, especially since the carmakers could also offset these costs to a degree with the external economies of a competitive market.

Detailed estimates of vertical integration are not available for the years of the 1930s, but Katz believes that the use of outside suppliers was reduced as firms learned to cope with complexity and change (Katz 1977, p. 258). The effect of reduced – or institutionalized – innovation on the degree of vertical integration is an area in which theory is not well developed.[70] In the case of automobiles in this period, however, there were exogenous factors that tended to militate in favor of reintegration. One of these was the market for spare parts, an area over which car makers had an incentive to retain control in a period when replacement demand was growing. As original equipment and replacement parts were jointly produced – indeed, were identical – they could be turned out more cheaply where minimum efficient scale was large if producers had access to both markets (Robertson 1987, pp. 12–14). As we saw, the opposite may also be the case if there are low economies of scale, since the market for spare parts calls forth thick markets for components to which car makers could turn for cheap original equipment. Moreover, replacement parts have traditionally carried a higher profit margin than original equipment. Because automobile manufacturers forced their dealers to use only authorized replacement parts, they were in a position to pad their profits by producing parts internally.[71] In the 1930s, this appears to have paid off handsomely (FTC 1939, p. 1062).

Another factor favoring integration was organizational innovation. The corporate reorganization that Alfred Sloan put in place at GM in the 1920s is now hailed as a pioneering application of the multidivisional or M-Form structure (Chandler 1962, pp. 130–162). It was also a structure well-adapted to the institutionalized change of the annual-model strategy: It decentralized day-to-day decision-making to an extent that approached that of the market, while retaining a centralized strategic and coordination ability (Williamson 1985, pp. 279–285). The M-Form innovation thus arguably reduced the costs (increased the benefits) of internal organization, and helped move the firm–market margin in the direction of the firm.

Over its first four decades, the American automobile industry provides an excellent detailed example of the ways in which innovation can affect the boundaries of the firm depending on the distribution of internal and external capabilities and the extent of transaction costs. The history of the industry also shows why we term the transaction costs associated with innovation to be *dynamic* and how short-run internalization of functions, brought about by shortages in external capabilities, can lead in the long run to increased reliance on outside suppliers as capabilities become diffused and dynamic transaction costs erode.

5

EXTERNAL CAPABILITIES AND MODULAR SYSTEMS

The degree of vertical integration in an industry depends on both supply and demand conditions. In the 200 years since Adam Smith, the effects of such supply factors as the division of labor, economies of scale, and the presence or absence of external economies have taken center stage. And we shall not ignore supply factors, especially the relative abilities of alternative structures to encourage technological change. But demand factors have always received less attention in analyzing issues of industry structure.[72] In particular, the tendency of economists to assume product homogeneity has obscured the fact that the structure of an "industry" and the characteristics of the firms it comprises can vary greatly depending on how consumers define its "product." Over time, the nature of what consumers believe is the essence of a given product often changes. Consumers may add certain attributes[73] and drop others, or they may combine the product with another product that had been generally regarded as distinct. Alternatively, a product that consumers had treated as an entity may be divided into a group of subproducts that consumers can arrange into various combinations according to their individual preferences.

In this chapter, we explore the relationship between supply and demand conditions in shaping the nature of an industry and the scope of activities of specific firms. On the supply side, we consider the importance of technical and organizational factors in influencing the production cost, and therefore the price to consumers, of employing various degrees of vertical integration. We also recognize the vital role of suppliers as innovators who can bring new components and new arrangements of existing components to the notice of consumers. On the demand side, we look at how autonomous changes in consumer tastes and the reaction of consumers to changes introduced by suppliers help to shape the definition of a product.

Building on the theory developed in Chapter 3, we explore the role of Marshallian external economies – or what we might more appropriately call *external capabilities* – in economic growth. We have already suggested that, when a major entrepreneurial opportunity requires systemic change that an

68

existing decentralized network is ill-equipped to handle, the result may be large-scale vertical integration. Using both theoretical arguments and case studies, we now examine the opposite possibility. When markets offer a high level of capabilities relevant to an entrepreneurial opportunity, and especially when that opportunity permits innovation to proceed in autonomous rather than systemic fashion, the result may be economic growth within a vertically and horizontally specialized structure.

THE THEORY OF MODULAR SYSTEMS

In choosing what to purchase, consumers seek out a variety of attributes. Depending on the attributes they desire and their perceptions of which possibilities are – or will become – available, consumers may choose to combine components (or sources of attributes) in various ways consistent with their budget constraints. These range over a spectrum from an *appliance* – a product that brings together in a single standardized package components that provide all of the desired attributes – to a *modular system* that is acquired bit by bit, allowing consumers to construct for themselves the packages that meet their individual preferences for attributes. The nature of an industry and the extent of vertical integration therefore depend not only on which patterns of production minimize production and transaction costs, but also on which attributes consumers may wish. As a result of "bundling," "unbundling," and "rebundling" various attributes, the definition of a product and the structure of the industry that manufactures it may change dramatically.

For most kinds of products – toasters or automobiles, say – manufacturers offer preset packages. One can choose from a multiplicity of packages, but one can't choose the engine from one kind of car, the hood ornament from another, and the front suspension from a third. Not only are there transaction costs of such picking and choosing (Cheung 1983, pp. 6–7), there are also economies of scale in assembling the parts into a finished package. Indeed, it is these economies of scale more than transaction costs that explain the tendency of assemblers to offer preset packages. If there were only transaction costs of discovering which parts are available and what their prices are, we would expect to see not preset packages but a proliferation of middlemen who specialize in packaging components tailored to buyers' specific tastes. For most appliance-like products, however, the economies of scale of assembly lead to integration of the packaging and assembly functions.[74]

One way to think about this is in terms of the modern theory of product differentiation.[75] Instead of seeing a product as an ultimate entity, view it instead as an input (or set of inputs) to the production of utility through the consumer's "consumption technology" (Lancaster 1971). In technical terms, the consumer chooses among available bundles (or combinations

69

of bundles) to reach the highest indifference surface possible. Each bundle represents a location (technically speaking: a vector) in "product space," and each consumer has a preferred place in that space – a bundle with his or her favorite combination of attributes. If there are scale economies, some producers can gain advantage by choosing the locations in this space where they think the density of demand will be highest. An example of this is Ford's Model T. The undifferentiated, no-frills product may not have suited everyone's (or, indeed, anyone's) tastes exactly. But the progressive reductions in price that long production runs made possible brought the Model T within the budget constraints of a growing number of people who were willing to accept a relatively narrow provision of attributes rather than do without.[76] In the extreme case of no economies of scale, the entire space can be filled with products, and each consumer can have a product tailored exactly to his or her requirements. The type of product we have called a modular system approximates this extreme: both the transaction costs of knowing the available parts and the scale economies of assembling the package are low for a wide segment of the user population. By picking and choosing among an array of compatible components, the consumer can move freely around a large area of the product space.

In the case of sound reproduction, for example, the list of attributes can be extensive and the tradeoffs among them complex. The product technology the consumer chooses is a function of the attributes sought. As the range of the voice is limited, high fidelity can be achieved more easily for voice than for music: in contrast to lovers of piano sonatas, consumers who confine their listening to news broadcasts can get by easily with small radios and have no practical use for a sophisticated combination of components. When immediacy is needed, a radio or telephone will provide better service than a phonograph. The ability to store sound, on the other hand, can be accomplished using a record, tape, or compact disk, but not directly by a telephone or radio. For reciprocal communication, a telephone suits the purpose while a radio receiver does not.

When the bundle of overlapping attributes for different consumption technologies is small or they conflict in some way, consumers will use different appliances or systems. Although there are considerable technical similarities between the telephone and radio voice transmission, the differences have been more significant, ensuring that two distinct networks and sets of reception appliances have remained in use.[77] Where attributes do not conflict, however, the presence of a high degree of technological convergence will open the way for the development of multipurpose appliances or modular systems, as in the case of a stereo set featuring several sound media that share amplification and reproduction equipment. Again, compatibility is crucial. Producers may have an incentive to create proprietary products in an attempt to capture sales of most or all potential subcomponents. But, as we suggest below, such a strategy often backfires,

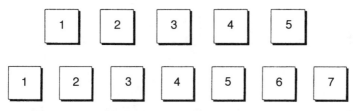

Figure 5.1 Components of the original and improved widget

and the high demand that unbundling allows can often force a compatible modularity on the industry.

Thus innovation can affect consumption technology in two major ways. First, new products can satisfy a desire for attributes that has not yet been met or, perhaps, even noticed. Second, through technological convergence, new ways of packaging or bundling consumption technology, and therefore providing attributes, become feasible. For example, there may be five components involved in the production of a particular good, the famous widget. Through a form of technological convergence,[78] two new components developed in other industries may turn out to be desirable adjuncts to the original good (Figure 5.1). The question is, will these new components be supplied by outside firms, perhaps their original manufacturers, or will they be internalized through vertical integration by the widget makers? The answer, as usual, will depend on the extent of economies of scale and the transaction costs involved. If the minimum efficient scale (MES) of production of the new components exceeds the needs of any individual widget maker, then the component manufacturers are likely to remain independent as long as the transaction costs of dealing with outside suppliers are smaller than the additional production costs the widget firms would incur by producing at less than MES (Williamson 1985, chapter 4).

Suppose, however, that the new components are not necessary – that they may, in fact, be superfluous or even repugnant to many widget users. In this case, the decision to purchase them could be delegated to the users rather than to the widget manufacturers. Users would buy the same type of widgets that they had traditionally purchased and then, if they wished, buy one or both of the additional components, perhaps from a different shop. The production of new widgets would then come to resemble Figure 5.2.

Alternatively, the rate of technological change of the various components that make up the widget may vary. Component 4, for example, might enter a new phase of rapid development while the remaining inputs do not vary. Furthermore, customers might have reason to believe that this component would continue to improve dramatically for some years. They would then wish to purchase a widget that embodies the traditional components 1, 2, 3, and 5, but that offers the opportunity to upgrade component 4 as improved variations come on the market.

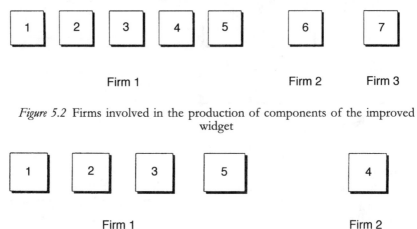

Figure 5.2 Firms involved in the production of components of the improved widget

Figure 5.3 Production of widgets with changing component 4

Again, whether component 4 would be manufactured by the widget maker or by someone else would depend on the relationship between production costs and transaction costs. If the widget firm decides that internalization is impractical, the situation in Figure 5.3 would arise. Customers would then purchase component 4 separately and the remainder as a package. In part this is a function of whether there are "economies of substitution." In the words of Garud and Kumaraswamy (1993, p. 362; italics in the original), "*[e]conomies of substitution exist when the cost of designing a higher performance system, through the partial retention of existing components, is lower than the cost of designing the system afresh.*" Production costs are also important, however, as are the costs faced by customers. If customers believe that they can save by updating components separately rather than by scrapping an entire system, they will opt for modular systems.

This assumes, of course, that the new variant is compatible with the other components. The established widget firms will have an interest in trying to avoid compatibility so that they can continue to sell the existing models that embody all five components. But the developers of the new variant of component 4 will want to achieve compatibility to allow consumers to adopt their product without fuss. In fact, if possible, the component developers will want to achieve compatibility with the products of all widget manufacturers. Component developers will also want to provide what Garud and Kumaraswamy (1993) term "upgradability," or compatibility across generations of a system. In the absence of upgradability, customers might still have to scrap their existing systems to obtain the benefits of an improved component, even though the new component was compatible with many types of systems of the latest generation.

In the situations portrayed in Figures 5.2 and 5.3, customers are no longer purchasing an appliance as they were in Figure 5.1. Instead, they have moved to a modular system in which they can take advantage of interchangeable components rather than having to accept an entire package that is prechosen by the manufacturer.

The vertical specialization that modular systems encourage leads also to the establishment of networks of producers. Two basic types of networks among firms are possible. The first (Figure 5.4) is a core one in which suppliers are tied to a "lead" firm, as in the Japanese automobile industry. *Decentralized networks*, however, of the type illustrated in Figure 5.5, are of more interest to the argument developed here (Best 1990).

W_1, W_2, and W_3 are the users of modular systems, which they assemble according to their individual requirements. A_1, A_2, A_3, C_1, C_2, and C_3 are the manufacturers of A and C, two of the components of systems of type W, and B_1, B_2, and B_3 are makers of subassemblies used in component C. Makers of components A and C must, therefore, ensure compatibility with each other's products and with other potential components if their output is to be suitable for modular systems of type W. But subassembly B needs

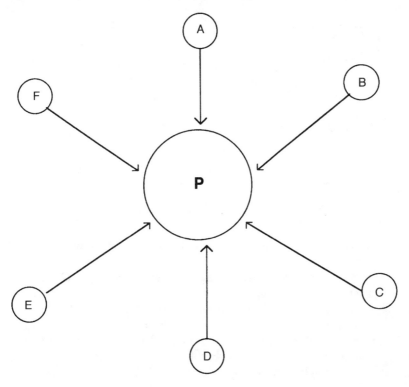

Figure 5.4 A core network

73

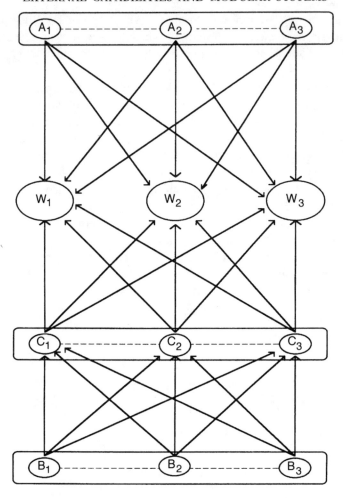

Figure 5.5 A decentralized network

to be compatible only with component C and not directly with other components

Taken together, all of the component manufacturers (A, C) and the ultimate users (W) make up a decentralized network. In contrast to centralized networks, in which the standards of compatibility are laid down by the lead manufacturers and may differ from one lead firm to another, in decentralized networks the standards are determined jointly by components producers and user/assemblers through market processes or negotiation. No single member of the network has control, and any firm that tries to dictate standards in a decentralized network risks being isolated if users and other producers do not follow. Even component variations that are demonstrably superior in a technical sense may be disregarded if users and other manufacturers are "locked in" to existing standards because the costs of change would be greater than the benefits permitted by the new variation (David and Bunn 1990).

A second type of network is important here. Even when there is no patent or other protection, horizontal networking of firms – for example, among A_1, A_2, and A_3 or C_1, C_2, and C_3 – can allow an innovator to earn higher profits than if it attempted to appropriate all of the benefits itself. As we suggest in the case studies, when a component maker (especially of software) is unable by itself to offer customers enough variety to justify the purchase of the associated components in a modular system, the most successful firms will be those that abandon a proprietary strategy in favor of membership in a *network of competitors* employing a common standard of compatibility.

The benefits of modularity appear on the producer's side as well as on the consumer's side. A modular system is open to innovation of certain kinds in a way that a closed system – an appliance – is not. Thus a decentralized network based on modularity can have advantages in innovation to the extent that it involves the trying out of many alternate approaches simultaneously, leading to rapid trial-and-error learning. This kind of innovation is especially important when technology is changing rapidly and there is a high degree of both technological and market uncertainty (Nelson and Winter 1977). In a decentralized network, there are many more entry points for new firms, and thus for new ideas, than in a vertically integrated industry producing functionally similar appliances. To this extent, then, a modular system may progress faster technologically, especially during periods of uncertainty and fluidity.

Another reason that modularity may spur innovation lies in the division of labor. A network with a standard of compatibility promotes autonomous innovation, that is, innovation requiring little coordination among stages. By allowing specialist producers (and sometimes specialist users) to concentrate their attention on particular components, a modular system thus enlists the division of labor in the service of innovation. We would expect innovation to proceed in the manner Rosenberg (1976, p. 125) and Hughes (1992) suggest: with bottleneck components – those standing most in the way of increased consumer satisfaction – as the focal points for change.

Systemic innovation would be more difficult in a modular system, and even undesirable to the extent that it destroyed compatibility across components. We would expect, however, to see systemic innovation *within* the externally compatible components. The internal "stages of production" within a modem or a tape deck can vary greatly from manufacturer to manufacturer so long as the component continues to connect easily to the network.[79] In other words, the components may be appliances. To the extent that the coordination this internal systemic innovation requires is costly across markets, we would expect to see greater vertical integration by makers of components than by purveyors of the larger systems.

PRODUCT DIFFERENTIATION AND THE PRODUCT LIFE CYCLE

When there is autonomous innovation within a system, manufacturers and consumers may give different answers to the question of whether the result is a variation on an existing product or an entirely new substitute product. From the standpoint of drivers, the successive changes from cotton to rayon and then to nylon and finally polyester tire cords between the 1940s and the 1970s were autonomous. They did not constitute a string of new products, but merely a change in the technology of an established one. To the tire manufacturers, however, the systemic nature of the changes was overwhelming, as each one involved the displacement of existing firms and the rise to leadership of, first, the American Viscose Company as a supplier of rayon cord, then Dupont for nylon cord, and ultimately Celanese for polyester (Foster 1986, pp. 215–216). The adoption of radial tires, on the other hand, was an even more significant (or systemic) product innovation from the perspective of the tire makers themselves, and they were soon overtaken by an innovator (Michelin) that had been unimportant until then in many markets. Again, however, the basic nature of the product has remained unchanged for the final users, who see tires as a generic good that is only one part of the system that they call a car, and who regard changes in tire design as autonomous within that larger system.

These differences in viewpoint mean, in turn, that one must exercise care in using the product life cycle, in its strict form, as a tool of analysis. Some products certainly conform to the traditional PLC S-curve that runs its course from introduction through a growth stage to maturity and, perhaps, decline. This cycle is more likely to pertain to components, however, than to entire systems. Manufacturers of individual inputs, therefore, will be more likely to perceive maturity and decline than consumers will. This is reinforced by the fact that, when there is a significant change in the technology of the product, but not in its use, it is relatively rare for leading firms to maintain their position (Cooper and Schendel 1976; Foster 1986).

From the perspective of consumers, the PLC might resemble more the overlapping wave pattern in Figure 5.6. In such cases, variations on a product succeed each other. Users substitute *within* categories, since there are only minor changes in the basic product attributes that they are seeking. Nevertheless, autonomous innovation encourages consumers to seek modular solutions. For technical or transaction cost reasons, of course, this may not always turn out to be feasible: Tires have remained entities despite changes in design and materials. When, however, modules can be purchased economically and fitted readily into a compatible network,

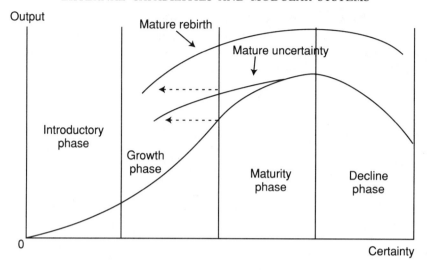

Figure 5.6 The consumer's view of the product life cycle

autonomous innovation will increase the attractiveness of systems at the expense of appliances.

THE DEVELOPMENT OF HIGH-FIDELITY AND STEREO SYSTEMS

The evolution of modular high-fidelity and stereo component systems in the post-Second World War period resulted from two separate but related developments, both of which originated before 1939. The first, the spread of an underground movement for greater fidelity in reproduction, involved better recording techniques and superior reproduction equipment. The second was the introduction of 33- and 45-rpm records and the associated use of vinyl, which greatly enhanced the usefulness of recordings, particularly for lovers of classical music. Thus the connection between changes in hardware (the components) and software (records and later tapes and compact disks) was established from the beginning.

Early developments

Before the 1930s, the phonograph[80] was an appliance. Even then, conservatism was strong in the industry and change was propelled largely by external forces, including the drastic decline that followed the spread of the radio in the 1920s. Record sales in the United States dropped from $52 million in 1920 to $21 million in 1925. At that time, records were still recorded and played back acoustically, using mechanical vibrations to cut

77

grooves into wax originals and to transmit sound from records to listeners via a horn. Although various instruments operate over a range of approximately 20 Hz to 20,000 Hz (20–20,000 cycles per second or cps), from the lowest note on the organ to the highest overtones of the oboe, acoustic records generally reproduced a range of 350 to 3,000 Hz (*Fortune*, September 1939, pp. 74–75, 92; Read and Welch 1976, p. 237; Inglis 1990, p. 29).

In the 1920s, the research department of Western Electric (which later became Bell Telephone Laboratories) developed electric recording techniques and later a superior phonograph. Victor, the largest record and record player manufacturer, turned down these improvements initially, arguing that the sounds produced would be unpleasant to listeners, who were used to the "true or miniature" sound of the acoustic Victrola. Nevertheless, falling sales soon motivated the adoption of electric recording methods. Sales of records rebounded quickly, reaching around 65 million units in 1929 (*Fortune*, September 1939, pp. 92, 94; Read and Welch 1976, chapter 17).

Early stages of modular systems

The origins of modularity in subsequent decades can be traced to the development of the Brunswick Panatrope. Although there had been earlier radio-phonograph combinations, they were essentially two appliances encased in a common cabinet, since radio signals could not be reproduced acoustically (Read and Welch 1976, pp. 268–269). The Panatrope, which had a vacuum-tube amplifier and a speaker, therefore permitted technological convergence, since both radio signals and signals transmitted from the phonograph pickup were now reproduced identically. This soon led to a degree of modularity. For example, as we will see, in 1933 RCA began to offer a record player for $9.95 that could be plugged into a radio (Wallerstein 1976, p. 58).

Although various enthusiasts attempted to achieve higher fidelity before 1939, significant improvements in both recordings and broadcasts did not come until the postwar period.[81] Hardware and software requirements went together, since high-fidelity components were of no particular value without high-quality recordings. At the end of World War II, most records cut off at 8,000 Hz because of distortion in the higher ranges. Even this limited span was further truncated by contemporary phonographs, which seldom reproduced sounds above 4,000 Hz. While this captured most of the fundamentals, the overtones were lost. In the early postwar period, English Decca[82] introduced Full Frequency Range Recordings (FFRR). At the same time, the company began to sell an inexpensive portable phonograph in Britain with a range from 50 to 14,000 Hz. However, for reasons that are obscure but that Read and Welch imply involve a conspiracy among

78

other manufacturers, the set was never introduced in the United States (*Fortune,* October 1946, p. 161; Read and Welch 1976, p. 338).

American record and phonograph manufacturers had long resisted attempts to improve the range of their products on the grounds that their customers preferred a diluted sound. One survey, conducted by the Columbia Broadcasting System, indicated that, by a margin of more than two to one, listeners liked standard broadcasts of up to 5,000 Hz better than wide-range programs that went up to 10,000. Owners of FM radios, who would have had greater exposure to wide-range reproduction, nevertheless preferred the narrow range by more than four to one. And, even more astonishingly, professional musicians voted by fifteen to one in favor of the standard range.[83] If, as it appeared, the most discerning of listeners were content with a cut-off of 5,000 Hz, there seemed to be no reason to improve recordings or equipment (*Fortune,* October 1946, p. 161; Read and Welch 1976, pp. 346–347).

Even before the war, however, there was a move for greater fidelity among some enthusiasts. The most famous of these was Avery Fisher, who had majored in English and Biology at New York University and later worked as an advertising manager and book designer for Dodd Mead. In 1937, he formed Philharmonic Radio to produce high-quality sets. He sold the company during the war, and in 1945 started Fisher Radio, the firm that would eventually make him a multi-millionaire (Eisenberg 1976, pp. 76–77).

The move towards systems in the postwar period

The high-fidelity movement gained impetus during the Second World War when U.S. Servicemen stationed in Europe became aware of the extent to which America lagged in both record and phonograph technology. In addition, many servicemen were trained in radio or electronic technologies that were transferable to high-fidelity uses, and some brought back equipment with them (Read and Welch 1976, pp. 333, 347–348; Mullin 1976, pp. 62–64). When their suggestions for improvement were rebuffed by the established firms, a number of them set up as components manufacturers.

While a few manufacturers like Fisher, Capehart, and Scott did produce high-quality phonographs and combinations in the immediate postwar years (*Fortune,* October 1946, pp. 190, 193, 195), there was a movement from integrated appliances to components that resulted from both supply and demand conditions. Many of the new firms were run by specialists who could not afford to manufacture across a broad scale even if they had had the expertise. On the demand side, interest in modularity was fueled by rapid but uneven rates of improvement across components that encouraged buyers to maintain the flexibility to update. The individualistic and subjective nature of "fidelity" also encouraged a proliferation of components as buyers sought to build systems to suit their idiosyncratic tastes.

One famous example was T. R. Kennedy, Jr., whom *Fortune* billed as a "'golden ear' of the richest sheen."[84] The magazine described the set that Kennedy, a radio engineer, put together for his own use.

> His receiver is well designed and, of course, has an FM circuit. His main amplifier was built at the Bell Telephone Laboratories. His speaker has three units. To forestall phonograph vibration, the motor is mounted separately, while a dental-machine belt carries the rotary motion to a turntable anchored in 600 pounds of sand. The pickup arm sports a feather-light sapphire needle, kept at an even temperature and humidity in an airtight container until just before it is used. Kennedy makes his own superior recordings of broadcast music. As a result, his parlor concerts are unsurpassed for fidelity. He has been accused of making a fetish of it, of listening to tone rather than to music. "Listen!" he says. "Compare music from my equipment with what the average combination gives. You'll throw rocks at your set."
>
> (*Fortune*, October 1946, p. 161)

Such an outfit did not come cheaply, especially in 1946. The total cost of around $1,400 comprised an FM–AM chassis costing $600; an amplifier, which had both bass and treble equalizers, for $150; a turntable for $175; a pickup for $180; and a custom-built speaker system for $250. (The cost of the sand was not given.)

As we have seen, components in the sense of add-on equipment had been available for many years. The Duo Jr. record player that RCA began to offer in 1933 was one example. In general, the "war of the speeds" between Columbia and RCA, who introduced 33- and 45-rpm records, respectively,[85] opened the field to component makers by disturbing consumer perceptions of the existing paradigm. This was soon reinforced in the early 1950s by even more options, such as tape recorders (Read and Welch 1976, p. 350). Listeners who took fidelity seriously now had a wide choice of equipment.

The importance of compatibility

Compatibility among the range of options was developed through the market as component manufacturers were forced to cooperate, at least up to a point, in order to be able to sell their products at all. In the words of Read and Welch (1976, p. 347):

> Another strong influence . . . was the competition for business on the part of the smaller manufacturers who specialized in such parts as pickups, amplifiers, and speakers; or even in such smaller components

as resistors, volume controls, etc. In their zeal, they were often forced to demonstrate the superiorities of equipment by assembling complete sound reproducing systems incorporating in them the requisite high-quality apparatus made by others. When the larger manufacturers refused to buy superior parts as a result of such demonstrations, which became frequent after the war, the answers were obvious. Consequently, many smaller manufacturers of improved components either went into the manufacture of more complete units, by acquiring licenses to manufacture other parts from other patent holders, or went into the business of selling directly to the public.

Packaged systems, of course, remained available. With the exception of Fisher and later Magnavox, which was originally a manufacturer of speakers, it was, however, rare before the 1970s for firms to produce both components and packages. Separate stores for high-fidelity and later stereo equipment developed in which customers could hear various combinations before deciding (Read and Welch 1976, pp. 351–352). Only components that were compatible could be demonstrated. Similarly, the growth of the kit industry relied on interchangeability. Indeed, as Britain and the Continent developed many of the best components, international standards became common.[86]

The origins of 33-rpm records

Although Decca's original FFRR recordings were on 78-rpm disks, a major impetus behind the development of high-fidelity reproduction was the introduction of long-playing 33-rpm records and 45-rpm singles. The history of the long-playing record well illustrates the distinction between autonomous and systemic change: because RCA tried to treat a systemic change as autonomous, the first introduction of 33-rpm records failed.

By the 1920s, the format of 10-inch and 12-inch 78-rpm records had been established. This was entirely adequate for the vast bulk of records sold, which were "singles," frequently popular tunes but also arias sung by well-known operatic soloists.[87] But, as the maximum playing time per side for a 12-inch 78 was barely five minutes, longer classical works required several disks and were frequently disrupted, sometimes in mid-movement. Moreover, as a result of the Depression and inept management in the industry itself, sales of records and phonographs slumped again in the early 1930s. Only 10 million records were sold in 1932, and total retail sales of both records and equipment in the United States fell from a peak of $250 million to around $5 million (*Fortune*, September 1939, p. 94). It was in this climate that RCA made the first attempt to market 33-rpm vinyl disks.

81

In 1932, RCA introduced 33-rpm records which, to reduce surface noise, were made from a vinyl compound rather than the shellac mixture used for the 78s. The RCA records featured grooves that were only a little narrower than standard 78 grooves, however, which limited 33-rpm playing times to only around twice that of 12-inch 78s. More importantly, the wide grooves required wide styli and heavy pickups, which cut through the soft vinyl after the records had been played a few times. RCA did not address these hardware problems. Because of the scarcity of suitable turntables and the fragility of the records, RCA terminated the experiment the following year (Wallerstein 1976, p. 57; Read and Welch 1976, pp. 339–340).

The early stages of LP records at Columbia

The man who made the decision to withdraw the 33-rpm records from the market in 1933 was Edward Wallerstein, the general manager of the Victor Division of RCA. He subsequently moved to Columbia, where, despite the Victor experience, he commissioned a team to develop the process further.[88] From the beginning, Columbia seems to have taken a systemic approach. As early as 1939, Wallerstein ordered that everything recorded at 78-rpm also be recorded on 16-inch 33-rpm blanks. These were then stored and available for reissue as LPs in the late 1940s (Wallerstein 1976, p. 57).

In order to increase playing time and (literally) reduce the wear and tear on vinyl, Columbia engineers concentrated on 1-mil microgrooves that could be used with a lighter stylus and pickup. Narrower grooves provided only part of the solution, however, as long as they were spaced as far apart as 78-rpm grooves on shellac-based records. As late as 1946, Columbia could provide only 11–12 minutes per side. To determine the desired length, Wallerstein surveyed the classical repertoire and found out that, with 17 minutes per side, 90 per cent of classical pieces would fit on a single two-sided disk. By approximately doubling the number of grooves to between 190 and 225 per inch, Columbia engineers were soon able to exceed the 17-minute standard, and the firm decided to market 33-rpm long-playing records from the fall of 1948 (Wallerstein 1976, pp. 57–58; Read and Welch 1976, p. 340).

Networks in hardware and software

Columbia recognized, of course, that simply offering the records would not be sufficient. Easy availability of 33-rpm record players would also be required. As Columbia, in contrast to RCA Victor, did not itself manufacture electrical equipment, the success of the LP (a Columbia trademark) depended on convincing one or more outside firms to manufacture players. Wallerstein recalled a promotional technique that he had used at RCA in

1933. In order to revive sales of records then, he established a record club that offered an inexpensive record player, the Duo Jr., that could be plugged into a radio set. RCA sold the player at cost, $9.95 (Wallerstein 1976, p. 58). Therefore, when Columbia discovered that it did not have the skills or time to develop its own record players, it approached several manufacturers. The company chose Philco as the initial supplier, with Columbia providing much (according to Wallerstein, all) of the basic technology. Wallerstein's recognition of the importance of networks was shown by his initial disappointment that only a single player manufacturer was chosen. "I was a little unhappy about this, because I felt that all of the manufacturers should be making a player of some sort – the more players that go on the market, the more records could be sold."

In any event, the price of the Philco "attachments" was soon reduced from $29.95 to $9.95, the cost at which Philco supplied them to Columbia. Columbia was able to leave the attachment business within a year as other manufacturers followed Philco's lead (Wallerstein 1976, p. 61).

Columbia also recognized the importance of networks of competitors. Recognizing that it would prosper if other recording companies adopted the 33-rpm microgroove standard, it offered to license the process, a proposition that was quickly taken up by other, smaller, companies. Buyers of classical records responded to the convenience of the LP, the alleged unbreakability of vinyl disks (which RCA had begun to market as 78s in 1946), and the sharp reduction in price. In 1939, for instance, Toscanini's recording of Beethoven's Fifth Symphony, a work of moderate length that could easily be accommodated on a single LP, required an album of four 78-rpm records that cost $2 apiece. As long as a work like Schönberg's Gurre-Lieder, which required 14 records at $2 each, could be expected to sell only 400–500 copies, few companies would be willing to take the risk of recording it (Wallerstein 1976, pp. 58, 60; Read and Welch 1976, pp. 339–430; *Fortune*, September 1939, p. 100). Given the high price elasticity of records, the lower price of LPs permitted an important broadening of the repertoire, which reinforced the density of the network and further encouraged consumers to switch to the new standard.

Thus, although there were no basic patents covering the LP process, Columbia was able to appropriate a large share of the profits by positioning itself as the leading firm in the network of competitors. Other firms that joined the network, such as English Decca, also prospered. But those that initially held out, including EMI and RCA, lost heavily and were eventually forced to conform. RCA, for example, lost $4.5 million on records between June, 1948 and January, 1950, when it began to issue its own LPs. Its classical sales were decimated, and a number of its most important artists, including Pinza, Rubinstein, and Heifitz, either deserted or threatened to do so. Over the same period, Columbia cleared $3 million (Wallerstein 1976, pp. 60–61).

RCA's response

RCA's first approach to the threat of the LP was to try to block the network by establishing its own incompatible system. Columbia had considered issuing six- or seven-inch 33-rpm records for the large singles market, but abandoned the idea. This left an opening for RCA, which introduced 45-rpm singles and produced its own record players and phonographs. In order to forestall competition, RCA chose to use a larger spindle that could not accommodate 33 (or 78) records (Wallerstein 1976, pp. 60–61; Read and Welch 1976, pp. 340–342). Although other companies followed RCA with large-hole 45s, however, the incompatibility turned out to be in one direction only, since 45-rpm records could easily be fitted in the center with a metal or plastic disk that permitted use with a standard spindle. Moreover, the 45-rpm microgrooves could be played with a stylus designed for 33-rpm records. In the end, RCA was unable to develop a proprietary hardware system fed by its own software variation. Even though the seven-inch 45-rpm format became the standard for singles, 12-inch 33-rpm LPs captured the market for longer works and collections.

RCA eventually joined independent manufacturers in producing phonographs and turntables that operated at all of the major speeds (including 78-rpm) and provided two styli (one for 78-rpm and one for 33- and 45-rpm microgrooves).

The development of FM broadcasting

The rapid spread of 33- and 45-rpm record formats contrasts sharply with the long delays required for FM receivers to become a vital part of high-fidelity systems.[89] In practice, FM broadcasts incorporate two important improvements: the use of wideband frequency modulation, in which the frequency rather than the amplitude of the radio signal varies with the audio signal being transmitted, and the use of very-high-frequency (VHF) waves for propagation, in contrast with the medium-wave frequencies used for AM broadcasts.[90] Together, these two characteristics result in greater reductions in man-made and atmospheric interference; relative immunity from other stations operating on the same frequency; and better fidelity of reproduction, especially in regard to dynamic volume range and frequency response.

Commercial FM broadcasts began in 1940, but on the range from 42 to 50 MHz. On this basis, the industry quickly grew in the United States. By the end of 1941, 58 stations had received construction permits and nearly 400,000 sets had been sold. When the U.S. entered the war, no further sets were built, although construction of stations did proceed. Nevertheless, the war accelerated technical developments in FM broadcasting as a result of government-sponsored research.

84

The real barrier to the spread of FM came at the end of the war, when the government decided on technical grounds to change the standard range of broadcast frequencies to 88 to 108 MHz. Although this led to improvements in reception and enlarged the number of channels theoretically available in any locality from 40 to 100, it had the disadvantage of immediately rendering obsolete all existing broadcasting equipment and receivers. In effect, the existing network simply disappeared.

The result was a decade-long decline in the popularity of FM. The number of on-air stations fell from 733 in 1951 to 530 in 1957. The fate of stations like WTMJ-FM in Milwaukee exemplifies the problems that FM broadcasters encountered. The station, which was owned by the *Milwaukee Journal,* was the fifth-oldest FM broadcaster in the United States. It began experimental transmission in February, 1940, concentrating on music in order to take advantage of the superior fidelity characteristics of FM. Through a systematic publicity campaign, the station was quickly able to build up a substantial audience, with 21,000 FM receivers in its listening area in early 1942. With the exception of occasional NBC war coverage, WTMJ-FM broadcast no programs in common with the *Milwaukee Journal's* AM station (Sterling 1968). At the end of 1945, however, the station was forced to change from 45.5 MHz to 92.3 MHz, in the process losing all listeners who had not purchased new receivers.

Because of the expense of building new transmitters to accommodate the frequency change, WTMJ-FM also abandoned its own broadcasts in mid-1946 and shifted entirely to simulcasts, presenting the same programs as its AM affiliate. Under the circumstances, it is not surprising that the FM audience dwindled, and in April 1950 the station left the air (Sterling 1968).

The resurgence of FM broadcasting

By the time that WTMJ-FM resumed broadcasts in 1959, a series of technical changes had begun to give FM new leverage with listeners. Initially, most popular recordings had a limited dynamic range and therefore did not require the increased fidelity that FM could provide.[91] Especially when most commercial stations concentrated on simulcasts, only the small proportion of classical-music listeners benefited from using an FM receiver, which meant that advertising revenues were also constrained. The increased dynamic range of popular music from the late 1950s, however, made FM reception valuable to a wider range of consumers. Secondly, FM stereo multiplex broadcasts began in 1961, which gave FM stations a distinct advantage that AM stations couldn't match. From that point, FM stations began to gain ground steadily. By 1975, the FM share of the total listening audience in the United States was slightly more than 30 per cent.

In 1979, AM and FM reached parity, and in 1988 the FM share was 75 per cent (Sterling 1968; Inglis 1990, pp. 141–145).

The importance of networks to the adoption of the LP and FM

The principal reason that purchasers of high-fidelity components were converted to LP turntables so quickly but resisted the charms of FM tuners for almost two decades was that LPs offered such important advantages when compared to 78-rpm records that a software network was created almost immediately, which consumers were then able to take advantage of through a series of individual purchases of relatively inexpensive record players and phonographs. The great majority of radio listeners, however, could see no immediate technical advantage in investing in FM equipment because the network of high-fidelity popular-music software did not exist. Moreover, radio listeners had less control because they were dependent on a network with two stages: the records and the stations that transmitted them. When, as a result of an exogenous change, the dynamic range of popular music was widened and then multiplex became available, the interests of popular- and classical-music listeners merged. Only at this point did the market become dense enough to justify greater investment by broadcasters in FM programming. The interests of FM consumers and producers therefore both evolved, but in a series of fits and starts, as each faced its own bottlenecks that had to be overcome before further progress was possible.

Products versus components

More recent developments, including cassette recorders and CD players, have strengthened the old principle of attaching new options to existing systems. Dedicated "audiophiles" continue to prefer separate components. In a recent discussion of integrated amplifiers and receivers,[92] *Stereo Review* recommended that listeners buy their preamplifiers, amplifiers, and tuners individually. As the product manager for one of the major component manufacturers explained, "The manufacturer of separate components is under fewer cost restraints. Higher-quality parts can be used. Construction is better, too, because components have more room to breathe on a circuit board. And separates offer greater control flexibility as you grow into a more complex system with video, surround sound, and subwoofers" (Gillett 1988, pp. 74, 77).

Because of the uneven pace of development among the various components since the 1940s, it is unlikely that consumers have regarded a high-fidelity or stereo-component system as a single "product." Instead, perceptions have approximated those in Figure 5.3, in which each set of attributes is treated separately. Thus, there has been a series of life cycles for a succession of types of software and their associated hardware requirements (78-rpm records, 33- and 45-rpm microgroove records, audio cassettes, and compact disks), amplifiers (monaural and stereophonic), and tuners (AM, FM, and AM/FM). Other components, principally speaker systems, provide similar development patterns. Modular systems in this case exist only insofar as they comprise components that supply the attributes users seek.

From modular systems to appliances?

After more than four decades of development, however, it is questionable if high sophistication is any longer of much value to the consumer. According to one estimate, 80 per cent of listeners are "rather deaf" at ranges above 10,000 Hz. Casual empiricism also suggests that many listeners prefer extra volume to better tone when playing music.

In contrast to microcomputers, stereo equipment serves only one basic use: the reproduction of sound. New components represent variations on a theme rather than departures into new realms. Except for the most golden of ears or snobs, the point has probably been reached at which high quality packaged systems[93] meet all reasonable technical specifications. At this mature stage of the product life cycle, the transaction costs of choice for most consumers may outweigh the benefits arising from picking and choosing. Preset packages cover almost the entire product space, not because consumers demand an undifferentiated no-frills product analogous to the Model T, but because with maturity a standardized product has become so well developed that it now meets the needs of almost all users. It remains to be seen when, or if, the microcomputer requirements of business and personal users will become similarly standardized.

THE MICROCOMPUTER INDUSTRY

Early developments

The first microcomputer is generally acknowledged to have been something called the MITS/Altair, which graced the cover of Popular Electronics magazine in January, 1975.[94] The machine was the creation of Ed Roberts, proprietor of a small Albuquerque firm that had made a variety of electronics kits for hobbyists. The Altair was also a kit, which Roberts offered through ads in hobbyist magazines for $379. Essentially a microprocessor in a box, the machine was built around the Intel 8080 chip. Its only input/output devices were lights and toggle switches on the front panel, and it came with a mere 256 bytes of memory.

But the Altair was, at least potentially, a genuine computer. Its potential came largely from a crucial design decision: the machine incorporated a number of open "slots" that allowed for additional memory and other devices to be added later. These slots were hooked into the microprocessor by a network of wires called a "bus." Roberts adopted this extremely modular approach partly in emulation of the design of minicomputers and partly because his small firm would have been incapable of producing a desirable (that is, more-capable) non-modular machine within any reasonable time. Indeed, the Altair sold beyond Roberts's wildest expectations, and his storefront operation had trouble meeting demand for the basic kit let alone developing its own add-ons.

Add-ons – especially memory boards – were definitely the first bottleneck of the Altair system. Very quickly, third-party suppliers sprang up, many of them literally garage-shop operations. But using a microcomputer, especially a primitive early model, required some less-tangible complementary activities as well: software and know-how. Third parties filled both of these gaps exclusively, the latter by grass-roots organizations called user groups. In effect, the hobbyist community captured the machine, and made it a truly open modular system. Like most manufacturers, Roberts wanted to keep the system as proprietary as possible. But when he tried to tie the sale of some desirable software to the purchase of inferior MITS memory boards, the main result was the dawn of software piracy. Moreover, the first clone of the Altair – the IMSAI 8080 – appeared within a matter of months. The Altair's architecture became an industry standard, eventually known as the S-100 bus because of its 100-line structure.

There were other microprocessors available, notably the Motorola 6800, which experts considered a superior chip. But the early success of MITS, IMSAI, and others anchored the popularity of the 8080/S-100 standard, especially among hobbyists, who were still the primary buying group. Lee Felsenstein, the influential leader of the Homebrew Computer Club in Northern California, argued that the standard had reached "critical mass," and, sounding like a present-day theorist of network externalities, forecast the demise of competing chips and buses (Moritz 1984, p. 123). The main reason was the impressive library of software that S-100 users had built up.

The Apple II

But the predicted dominance of the S-100 (and the CP/M operating system it used) never materialized. In 1977, three new machines entered the market, each with its own proprietary operating system, and two using the MOS Technology 6502 chip, an inexpensive clone of the Motorola 6800. The Apple II, the Commodore PET, and the Radio Shack TRS-80 Model I quickly outstripped the S-100 machines in sales and, by targeting users beyond the hobbyist community, moved the industry into a new era of growth.

The most important of the three machines was the Apple II. Apple Computer had been started a year earlier by Stephen Wozniak and Steven Jobs, two college dropouts and tinkerers. Of the two, Wozniak was the gifted engineer and the actual designer of the Apple II. A promoter and visionary, Jobs supplied the will to turn a hobbyist diversion into a serious company. In one area crucial to the present discussion, the two founders disagreed fundamentally. The hobbyist Wozniak, influenced, like Roberts, by the architecture of minicomputers, insisted that the Apple be an expandable system – with slots – and that technical details be freely available to users and third-party suppliers. Jobs saw the Apple as a single-purpose product, and he objected to the slots as unnecessary. Fortunately for Apple, Wozniak won the argument, and the Apple II contained eight expansion slots. Jobs exerted his influence – and aesthetic sensibility – in other ways, however, and the machine was something of a compromise. On the one hand, it was relatively open and expandable; but, unlike the hobbyist S-100 machines, it was compact, attractive, and professional, housed with its keyboard in a smart plastic case.

With early revenues coming almost entirely from sales of the Apple II, the company took in three quarters of a million dollars by the end of fiscal 1977; $8 million in 1978; $48 million in 1979; $117 million in 1980 (when the firm went public); $335 million in 1981; $583 million in 1982; and $983 million in 1983.[95] The machine's compromise between modularity and packaging was arguably one key to this startling success. By simplifying the microcomputer, Apple could target new areas of the product space. With the development of word processors like WordStar, database managers like dBase II, and spreadsheets like VisiCalc, the machine became a tool of writers, professionals, and small businesses. And, because of its slots, it could accommodate new add-ons – and therefore adapt to new uses – as they emerged.

Another key was timely innovation. In 1977, tape cassette decks were still the standard for data storage. Floppy drives were available, but they required expensive controller circuits. In what all regard as his most brilliant piece of engineering, Wozniak designed a wholly novel approach to encoding data on a disk and a vastly simplified controller circuit. This bottleneck-breaking innovation helped Apple beat Commodore and Tandy to market with a disk drive. "It absolutely changed the market," said Chuck Peddle, designer of the rival Commodore PET (Moritz 1984, p. 210).

The microcomputer as appliance: Osborne and Kaypro

By mid-1981, the uses of the microcomputer were becoming clearer than they had been only a few years earlier, even if the full extent of the product space lay largely unmapped. A microcomputer was a system comprising a number of more-or-less standard elements: a microprocessor unit with 64K bytes of RAM memory; a keyboard, usually built into the system unit; one or two disk drives; a monitor; and a printer. The machine ran operating-system software and applications programs like word-processors, spread-sheets, and database managers. CP/M, once the presumptive standard, was embattled, but no one operating system reigned supreme.

The emerging outline of a paradigmatic microcomputer gave Adam Osborne an idea: a cheap prepackaged computer. Rather than pushing the technological frontier, he would create a package that was technologic-ally adequate but also inexpensive. In this way he could carve out, as it were, a local maximum in the product space: "The philosophy was that if 90 percent of users' needs were adequately covered, the remaining ten percent of the market could be sacrificed." Osborne wanted a machine integrated into one package that users could simply plug into the wall, "as they might a toaster" (Osborne and Dvorak 1984, p. 11). The resulting Osborne I was an S-100 machine with a five-inch screen, two low-density drives, 64 kilobytes of memory, and bundled software that included a word processor, database manager, and spreadsheet. It came in a transportable package that could fit under an airline seat. Osborne's philosophy was echoed by Andrew Kay, whose Kaypro II, an improved clone of the Osborne, appeared in 1982. "We don't sell half a computer and call it a computer and then ask a person to come back and buy the rest of it later," he is quoted as saying. "It's like selling an automobile without wheels or seats and saying, 'Those are options.' IBM, Apple, and Tandy play that kind of game. But we don't" (Levering, *et al.* 1984, p. 68). The bundled transportables sold briskly. Osborne achieved sales of $93 million in 1983 before an abrupt collapse and bankruptcy; Kaypro became the fourth-largest seller of intermediate-price computers in 1984, reaching sales of $150–$175 million that year.

Modularity again: the IBM PC

But the signal event of 1981 was not the advent of the cheap bundled portable. On August 12, 1981, IBM introduced the computer that would become the paradigm for most of the 1980s. Like the Osborne and Kaypro, it was not technologically sophisticated, and it incorporated most of the basic features users expected. But, unlike the bundled portables, the IBM PC was a system not an appliance: it was an incomplete package, an open box ready for expansion, reconfiguration, and continual upgrading.

In July 1980, William Lowe met with IBM's Corporate Management Committee. John Opel, soon to become IBM's president, had charged Lowe with getting IBM into the market for desktop computers. Lowe's conclusion was a challenge to IBM's top management. "The only way we can get into the personal computer business," he told the CMC, "is to go out and buy part of a computer company, or buy both the CPU and software from people like Apple or Atari – because we can't do this within the culture of IBM" (Chposky and Leonsis 1988, p. 9). The CMC knew that Lowe was right, but they were unwilling to put the IBM name on someone else's computer. So they gave Lowe an unprecedented mandate: go out and build an IBM personal computer with complete autonomy and no interference from the IBM bureaucracy. Philip Donald Estridge, who quickly succeeded Lowe as director of the project, later put it this way. "We were allowed to develop like a startup company. IBM acted as a venture capitalist. It gave us management guidance, money, and allowed us to operate on our own" (*Business Week*, October 3, 1983, p. 86).

Estridge knew that, to meet the deadline, he would have to design a machine that was not at the cutting edge of technology. Moreover, IBM would have to make heavy use of outside vendors for parts and software. The owner of an Apple II, Estridge was also impressed by the importance of expandability and an open architecture. He insisted that his designers use a modular bus system that would allow expandability, and he resisted all suggestions that the IBM team design any of its own add-ons.

The IBM PC was an instant success, exceeding sales forecasts by some 500 per cent. By 1983, the PC had captured 26 per cent of the market, and an estimated 750,000 machines were installed by the end of that year. Yet PCs were still being snatched up as fast as they could be produced.

The emergence of a network of competitors

Because the machine used the Intel 8088 instead of the 8080,[96] IBM needed a new operating system. The company contracted with Microsoft to produce MS-DOS. IBM, which had long employed a proprietary strategy in its mainframe markets, wanted MS-DOS to become the industry standard. But the company chose to do this by allowing Microsoft to license MS-DOS to other manufacturers. One result was a legion of clones that offered IBM compatibility at, usually, a price lower than IBM's. But the other result was that MS-DOS – and the IBM PC's bus structure – did indeed become the new industry standard. Makers of IBM-incompatible machines went out of business, converted to the new standard (like Tandy and Kaypro), or retreated to niche markets (like Commodore and Apple, even if the latter's niche has been quite roomy).

IBM did have one trick up its sleeve to try to ward off cloners, but it turned out not to be a very powerful trick. The operating system that Microsoft designed for the IBM PC – called PC-DOS in its proprietary version – differs slightly in its memory architecture from the generic MS-DOS IBM allowed Microsoft to license to others. IBM chose to write some of the BIOS (or basic input-output system, a part of DOS) into a chip and to leave some of it in software. They then published the design of the chip in a technical report, which, under copyright laws, copyrighted part of the PC-DOS BIOS. To make matters more difficult for cloners, many software developers, especially those using graphics, chose to bypass DOS completely and access the PC's hardware directly. IBM sued Corona, Eagle, and a Taiwanese firm for infringing the BIOS copyright in their earliest models. These companies, and all later cloners, responded, however, with an end run. They contracted with outfits like Phoenix and AMI to create a software emulation (or sometimes a combination hardware and software emulation) that does what the IBM BIOS does, but does it in a different way. The emulation is also able to intercept the hardware calls and process them through the BIOS. This removed the principal proprietary hurdle to copying the original PC.

The era of the clones falls into two distinct periods. The early makers of clones fed on the excess demand for PCs. With one brilliant exception – namely, Compaq – these manufacturers disappeared when IBM began catching up with demand and lowered prices in 1983 and 1984. The second wave of clones began a couple of years later when IBM abandoned 8088 technology in favor of the PC AT, which was built around the faster Intel 80286 chip. By 1986, more than half of the IBM-compatible computers sold did not have IBM logos on them. By 1988, IBM's worldwide market share of IBM-compatible computers was only 24.5 per cent. IBM's choice of an open modular system was a two-edged sword that gave the company a majority stake in a standard that had grown well beyond its control.

What is especially interesting is the diversity of sources of these compatible machines. Many come from American manufacturers like Compaq, Zenith,[97] and Tandy, who sell under their own brand names. Another group would be foreign manufacturers selling under their own brand names. The largest sellers are Epson and NEC of Japan and Hyundai of Korea. But there is also a large OEM (original-equipment manufacturer) market, in which firms – typically Taiwanese or Korean, but sometimes American or European – manufacture PCs for resale under another brand name. The popular Leading Edge computer, for example, is made by Daewoo of Korea. Until recently, the AT&T PC was manufactured by Olivetti in Italy; the contract has now gone to Intel's Systems Division, which maintains a lively OEM business.

But perhaps the most interesting phenomenon is the no-name clone – the PC assembled from an international cornucopia of standard parts and sold, typically, through mail orders. Because of the openness and modularity of the IBM PC and the dominance of its bus and software standards, a huge industry has emerged to manufacture parts compatible with the PC. The resulting competition has driven down prices in almost all areas. Most manufacturers, even the large branded ones, are really assemblers, and they draw heavily on the wealth of available vendors. But the parts are also available directly, and it is in fact quite easy to put together one's own PC from parts ordered from the back of a computer magazine. By one 1986 estimate, the stage of final assembly added only $10 to the cost of the finished machine – two hours work for one person earning about $5 per hour. As the final product could be assembled this way for far less than the going price of name brands – especially IBM – a wealth of backroom operations sprang up. The parts list is truly international. Most boards come from Taiwan, stuffed with chips made in the U.S. (especially microprocessors and ROM BIOS) or Japan (especially memory chips). Hard-disk drives come from the United States, but floppy drives come increasingly from Japan. A power supply might come from Taiwan or Hong Kong. The monitor might be Japanese, Taiwanese, or Korean. Keyboards might come from the U.S., Taiwan, Japan, or even Thailand.

Today, the victory of the clones is essentially complete. Clone makers quickly followed IBM upscale to copy – and then lead with – machines using Intel's 80286, 80386, 80486, and now Pentium chips. IBM's early response, after a record with more failures than successes,[98] was to begin taking the PC proprietary again. In April, 1987, IBM announced its PS/2 line of computers built around a new proprietary bus called the Micro Channel Architecture (MCA). The original IBM PC had established an 8-bit industry bus standard, and the PC AT had established a new standard 16-bit bus called the Industry Standard Architecture (ISA). Though still serviceable for most uses, the AT standard was no longer optimal for high-speed 386 and 486 machines. In announcing the Micro Channel, IBM was attempting not only to set the standard but to prevent others from taking advantage of it. Nine of the major clone makers, with some nudges from Intel and Microsoft, quickly banded together to announce development of a competing 32-bit bus called the Extended Industry Standard Architecture (EISA) bus.

This development led many to expect a protracted, and perhaps fierce, battle of the standards. Essentially, however, no such battle emerged – or, rather, the battle ended quickly and decisively, with even IBM forced to abandon the MCA standard. IBM's attempt to take the PC proprietary was a failure.[99] The company was able to trade on its name and reputation to take rents for a while, selling high-priced machines to corporate customers and others seeking reliability over price and performance. But the passage of time, along with an increasing price-performance gap between IBM and its competitors, soon persuaded more and more corporate customers to buy clones. Newcomers like Dell, AST, Packard Bell, CompuAdd, Gateway 2000, and Zeos have gained sales through aggressive pricing – increasingly including sales to corporate buyers. The thickness and competitiveness of the market for components not only drove down PC prices but also increased reliability. A mail-order clone house could credibly offer better service than a big-name manufacturer simply by shipping overnight replacement parts to be swapped by the PC owner. This reduced the rents to a name brand. Moreover, experience with clones diffused through the user population, further reducing the advantages of a brand. IBM's ultimate response has been to cut prices and otherwise imitate the design and marketing techniques of its competitors. In essence, IBM has become one of the clones. Indeed, IBM has undergone a massive restructuring in response to problems that go well beyond its PC business (Ferguson and Morris 1993; Carroll 1993). The company sold off divisions and turned others into autonomous units. In effect, IBM has attempted to respond to a changing market with large-scale vertical disintegration.

The importance of the network

It is tempting to interpret the success of the original IBM PC as merely the result of the power of IBM's name. While the name was no doubt of some help, especially in forcing MS-DOS as a standard operating system, there are enough counterexamples to suggest that it was the machine itself – and IBM's approach to developing it – that must take the credit. Almost all other large firms, many with nearly IBM's prestige, failed miserably in the PC business. The company that Apple and the other early computer makers feared most was not IBM but Texas Instruments, a power in integrated circuits and systems (notably electronic calculators). But TI flopped by entering at the low end, seeing the PC as akin to a calculator rather than as a multipurpose professional machine. When TI did enter the business market in the wake of the IBM PC, its TI Professional also failed because the company refused to make the machine fully IBM compatible. Xerox entered the market with a CP/M machine that – in 1981 – was too little too late. Hewlett-Packard was also slow out of the blocks, offering an expensive closed-system machine with 32-column display and cassette drive – in 1980.

Consider, in particular, the case of Digital Equipment Corporation (Rifkin and Harrar 1988). DEC is the second-largest computer maker in the world, and the largest maker of minicomputers. In 1980, the company decided to enter the personal computer business. The Professional series was to be the company's principal entry into the fray. It would have a proprietary operating system based on that of the PDP-11 minicomputer; bit-mapped graphics; and multitasking capabilities. But, despite winning design awards, the computer was a commercial flop. Although DEC targeted the Professional to bring in 90 per cent of the profit, most of the 300,000 PCs DEC sold were Rainbow 100s, and many of those were sold at fire-sale prices. All told, the company lost about $900 million on its development of desktop machines. DEC's principal mistake was its unwillingness to take advantage of external economies. The strategy of proprietary systems and inhouse development had worked in minicomputers: put together a machine that would solve a particular problem for a particular application. The PC is not, however, a machine for a particular application; it is a machine adaptable to many applications – including some its users hadn't imagined when they bought their machines. Moreover, DEC underrated the value of software. And, unlike IBM, DEC chose to ignore existing third-party capabilities. Except for the hard disk and the line cord, DEC designed and built every piece of the Professional. The company tooled the sheet metal and plastics, manufactured the floppy drive, and even developed the microprocessor.

There is a similar story to be told about another spectacular failure, the Apple III. In 1979, Apple felt that, to capture the business market more securely, it needed to develop a new machine with capabilities greater than those of the Apple II. The new machine would be able to run most Apple II software, but only in an "emulation" mode. Afraid of cannibalizing its Apple II revenues, Apple actually added extra chips to make sure that, in this emulation mode, the Apple III could not take advantage of its advances over the Apple II. To use the new abilities would require new software. And Apple was trying to write the bulk of this software inhouse. The company was also angering the outside software firms by not releasing any technical specifications for or information on the machine. As head of research and development, Jobs pushed the project relentlessly and set unrealistic deadlines. Obsessed by technical elegance, he also insisted that the circuitry fit all on one board, even when that proved impossible. Because of this – and poor quality control – almost all of the first units shipped, in 1980, failed and had to be returned. The resulting bad reputation, coupled with the lack of software, effectively killed the product. Only 65,000 Apple IIIs were sold, less than the number of Apple IIs sold in 1980 alone. Total development costs were about $100 million for a product that ended up generating some 3 per cent of Apple revenues.

The importance of modularity

The Apple III – as well as the Lisa and even the Macintosh – also reflect the victory of Steve Jobs over Steve Wozniak. Wozniak grew increasingly annoyed as the company, in his view, turned its back on the Apple II and the philosophy behind it. In January 1985, he put it this way.

> The right way for one person is not the right way for another. We closed that machine [the Apple III] up to where somebody could have a very difficult time finding out how to add their own I/O drivers. We did not make it easy for the outside world. We thought we wanted all the markets for ourselves.

> You have to let the end users develop their own standards. You've got to give them the freedom to discover how they're going to use an

operating system, what sort of things they're going to buy. And if you're right and have provided a good solution, that's where they're going to settle. The thinking on the III was very much like a religion in that it could be done one way – our way. We made it very difficult for outside developers, instead of providing all the information as we did with the Apple II. . . . I think that when a new market evolves, like personal computers did, there's a period of time when you've got to let the world go in random directions, and eventually it will subside because it wants standardization. Then, once it's obvious what the standards are, they should be heavily supported by the manufacturer. You can't try to dictate the standard.

(Williams and Moore 1985, p. 178)

Wozniak described the proprietary attitude as "the most negative thing in our whole company, and it will be for years"[100] (Williams and Moore 1985, p. 178). Within a few months he had handed in his resignation.

But the essence of Jobs's view lay not so much in the proprietary character of the machine as in the basic nature of it. Jobs saw himself as designing not open-ended modular systems but "closed geographical systems" (Butcher 1988, p. 142). This was evident perhaps even more in the Lisa and early Macintosh computers, which bore Jobs's personal stamp. As Jef Raskin, the original Mac project director, put it, "Apple II is a system. Macintosh is an appliance" (Moritz 1984, p. 130). Upon the Mac's introduction in 1984, Apple decided it should be known as "the second desk appliance after the telephone" (Moritz 1984, p. 326). In large part, the non-systemic character of the later machines was simply a reflection of the fact that they were bounded in conception by a single mind: Jobs's. His approach was visionary, personal, and aesthetic. He wanted to design the ideal machine he would himself like to own. Alan Kay, a computer innovator who is now an Apple Fellow, describes Jobs and the Macintosh this way.

Take a look at the Mac. If you look at it from the front, it's fantastic. If you look at it from the back, it stinks. Steve doesn't think systems at all. Different kind of mentality. . . . Looking at the original Mac, you can see Steve. It's like Steve's head in a sense because it has the good parts of Steve and the bad parts. It has this super quality control and the parts where his brain didn't function.

(Sculley with Byrne 1987, p. 238)

Why were the most successful machines – the Apple II and the IBM PC – also the most modular? Microcomputer software is a popular example of the importance of network externalities. The value of owning a computer that runs a particular kind of software (IBM-compatible software under MS-DOS, for example) is dependent on the number of other people who

96

own similar machines, since the amount of software available is proportional to the total installed base of computers that can use that kind of software. But although this is certainly part of the story, its impact is less than might have been expected because the development of software networks has turned out to be a cheaper and more flexible process than was originally envisaged. By the summer of 1980, Microsoft had in place a system of software development in which code was first written in "neutral" language on a DEC minicomputer and then run through a translator program that would automatically convert the neutral software into the form needed by a specific machine. This made it possible to write machine-independent software. Now, smaller companies without this facility would still be tempted to write software specifically for one machine first, and the largest seller would offer the greatest temptation. But there are profits to be made writing or adapting software for even idiosyncratic machines, and a cottage industry like software development is particularly likely to seize such opportunities.

The explanation for modularity in microcomputers – modularity in hardware as well as software – is broader than, albeit related to, the phenomenon of network externalities. As we argued above, the benefits of modularity can appear on both the demand side and the supply side.

Demand-side benefits

In microcomputers, the economies of scale of assembling a finished machine are relatively slight. The machines are user-friendly in comparison with their larger cousins, and ample information is available through books, magazines, and user groups. There is also a lively middleman trade in the industry, revolving around so-called value-added resellers, who package hardware and software systems to the tastes of particular non-expert buyers. At the same time, the uses of the microcomputer are multifold, changing, and, at least in the early days, were highly uncertain. A modular system can blanket the product space with little loss in production or transaction costs.

Moreover, the microcomputer benefited from a kind of technological convergence, in that it turned out to be a technology capable of taking over tasks that had previously required numerous distinct – and more expensive – pieces of physical and human capital. By the early 1980s, a microcomputer costing $3,500 could do the work of a $10,000 stand-alone word-processor, while at the same time keeping track of the books like a $100,000 minicomputer and amusing the kids with space aliens like a 25-cents-a-game arcade machine.

Supply-side benefits

As we suggested earlier, innovation in a modular system typically proceeds in autonomous fashion, taking advantage of the division of labor. So long as it maintains its ability to connect to a standard bus, an add-on board can gain in capabilities over a range without any other parts of the system changing. Graphics boards can become more powerful, modems faster, software more user-friendly, and pointing devices more clever. The prime focal points of this innovation are often technological "bottlenecks," in this case bottlenecks to the usefulness of the microcomputer in meeting the many needs to which it has been put. The lack of reliable memory boards was a bottleneck to the usefulness of the early Altair. The 40-column display and the inability to run CP/M software were bottlenecks of the Apple II. The IBM PC's 8088 could address only a limited amount of internal memory. All of these – and many more – were the targets of innovation by third-party suppliers, from Cromemco and Processor Technology to Microsoft and Intel. In a wider sense, we can also include as bottleneck-breakers those innovations that extended the system's abilities in new directions – modems, machinery-controller boards, facsimile boards, graphics scanners, etc.[101] Sometimes a bottleneck is not strictly technological, as when IBM's copyrighted ROM BIOS became the focus of inventing-around by firms like Phoenix and AMI. Although "innovations" of this sort may not directly yield improvements in performance, they do help to keep the system open.

More importantly, a decentralized and fragmented system can have advantages in innovation to the extent that it involves the trying out of many alternate approaches simultaneously, leading to rapid trial-and-error learning. This kind of innovation is especially important when technology is changing rapidly and there is a high degree of both technological and market uncertainty. That the microcomputer industry partook of external economies of learning and innovation is in many ways a familiar story that needn't be retold. Popular accounts of Silicon Valley sound very much like Marshall's localized industry in which the "mysteries of the trade become no mysteries; but are as it were in the air, and children learn many of them unconsciously" (Marshall 1961, IV.x.3, p. 271). Compare, for example, Moritz's discussion of the effect of Silicon Valley culture on one particular child. "In Sunnyvale in the mid-sixties, electronics was like hay fever: It was in the air and the allergic caught it. In the Wozniak household the older son had a weak immune system" (Moritz 1984, p. 29). One could easily multiply citations. This learning effect went beyond the background culture, however. It included the proclivity of engineers to hop jobs and start spinoffs, creating a pollination effect and tendency to biological differentiation that Marshall would have appreciated. Moreover, the external economies of ideas were not in fact restricted to the physical realm of Silicon Valley –

or even Silicon Valley plus Route 128. As Austin Robinson anticipated long ago, external economies in a developed economy are increasingly intangible and therefore, in his phrase, mobile (Robinson 1935, p. 142).

Toward an open modular future?

We speculated above whether, for some market niches at least, high-quality packaged audio systems might not have achieved a practical superiority over modular systems. In computers, however, the opposite seems eminently clear: the future lies with open modular systems.[102] The PC world of today, as we have shown, is an open system within the architectural confines of the Microsoft DOS and Windows operating systems and the Intel family of microprocessors. As processors become more powerful, however, it seems inevitable that Intel's architecture will be challenged by the makers of higher-speed RISC chips.[103] There are several such challengers on the horizon,[104] including Sun Microsystems's SPARC family, DEC's Alpha chip, and the PowerPC chip produced by an IBM–Apple–Motorola consortium. The makers of these rival chips know that, to compete with Intel, they need not to assert a competing proprietary standard but rather to create an architecture that is even more open than the Intel-Microsoft standard. The PowerPC, for example, is being designed to run not only Microsoft operating systems but also such operating systems as Unix[105] and the new operating system under development by Taligent, the IBM–Apple joint venture. Sun is perhaps an even more dramatic example. Indeed, Sun's strategy in RISC workstations has paralleled closely the (unarticulated) open-systems strategy of IBM and the clone-makers in PCs (Garud and Kumaraswamy 1993). Sun has taken the non-proprietary alternative at every juncture,[106] tying its systems to the Unix standard and licensing its microprocessor technology to others. Moreover, the company has used a modular approach, building its machines from off-the-shelf parts and designing upgradeability into its systems. Sun may well be the leading contender to challenge Intel as the PC and workstation markets begin to merge.

OTHER EXAMPLES OF MODULAR SYSTEMS

So far the discussion has been couched in terms of user/assemblers. But the analysis also applies to intermediate products where consumers are often even more sophisticated and well-informed about product attributes than typical final consumers.

Chapter 4 discussed the role of the Society of Automotive Engineers in helping to set common standards for automobile components. Similar behavior has been common in other industries. Beginning in 1924, for example, radio manufacturers established a variety of standards committees to allow greater interchangeability and embed themselves in a decentralized network (Graham 1986, p. 40). A more recent case is the ongoing debate among semiconductor fabricators and equipment manufacturers over the Modular Equipment Standards Committee (MESC) architecture (Langlois 1992c), which is an open control and interface protocol that allows semiconductor fabricators to "mix and match" equipment from many different suppliers on a single assembly line. The MESC standards were instigated by a consortium of (typically small) equipment manufacturers, and it stands in opposition to the proprietary architecture of Applied Materials, Inc., the industry leader.

6

INERTIA AND INDUSTRIAL CHANGE

INTRODUCTION

One of the most persistent debates surrounding economic change is whether it is incremental or revolutionary in nature: whether, for instance, a period of change that lasted anywhere from seventy to one hundred years may be properly termed an industrial *revolution* (Cameron 1995; Landes 1991, p. 13). Regardless of the terminology used, however, it is clear that technological transitions in industrialized economies have frequently been prolonged and uneven. Despite the early adoption of the steam engine in the cotton textile industry, for example, the switch to steam power was for many decades confined to a few sectors in Britain and only became general after 1870 (Musson 1976). But the failure to adopt new technologies does not necessarily indicate stagnation. Although other sectors of the British economy retained traditional technologies and forms of organization well into the nineteenth century,[107] in many cases they underwent significant changes involving the *adaptation* of their existing technologies and organizational arrangements that, over time, led to significant growth in productivity in the period of early industrialization (McCloskey 1981, pp. 115–117; Berg and Hudson 1992, pp. 34–37; Hudson 1992, ch. 4).

Similarly, the "climacteric" after 1870, when Britain's relative economic lead was eroded, was a period of unevenness in change. Although dominance in newer sectors such as organic chemicals, electrical products, and steel was secured by American or German producers, the British retained their lead in most of the older areas including textiles and the manufacture of textile machinery; shipbuilding; and electrical-cable production. Again, as in the period of early industrialization, the older sectors – those in which Britain preserved its supremacy after 1870 – did not stagnate, because technological change grounded primarily in adaptations of existing technologies remained capable for many years of delivering improvements in technology.[108]

A further example of uneven and extended adjustment is the growing

101

economic leadership of the United States in the 1920s, which reflected an earlier adoption of capital-intensive technologies and greater efficiencies stemming from superior organization of production than occurred in Western Europe. Only after the Second World War did European firms begin on a large scale to adopt these innovations, and as late as 1960 Western European firms had, on average, not totally achieved the levels of output per worker that prevailed in the United States in 1925 (Nelson and Wright 1992; Denison 1967, pp. 334–335). More recently, the poor performance of some established industries such as automobiles in the United States since the 1960s has derived in part from the retention of older technologies and organizational forms in America after they had been superseded in Japan.[109]

In the world of neoclassical economics, older, and apparently less-productive, technologies or organizational forms should not coexist for extended periods with newer technologies or ways of organization. Perfect knowledge and instantaneous adjustment should induce producers to adopt improvements immediately as they become available. But in practice, adjustment is frequently prolonged, perhaps for several decades. The spread of electrification took nearly a century, for instance, and today, more than 45 years after the invention of the transistor, new uses for microelectronic devices are being found at a rapid (and perhaps still accelerating) pace (David 1991a).

In this chapter, we consider the reasons for prolonged adjustment and propose a model to indicate circumstances under which the retention of seemingly outdated capital equipment or practices (which we term inertia) *may* be economically rational. We then consider four hypotheses about inertia in the light of a variety of historical examples.

INSTITUTIONS AND INERTIA

There is a range of explanations of inertia. One set is the "real" or, in the narrow sense, "economic" explanations that look to abstract variables like demand levels, factor endowments, and relative prices to justify the failure of some organizations to change. A second reason for inertia is simple incompetence, when managers are either too stupid or too idle to adopt desirable new methods. This is a popular explanation of Britain's relative economic decline after 1870 (Aldcroft and Richardson 1969), and is also consistent with recent comments on American businessmen attributed to Japanese leaders. Alternatively, there may be cognitive or informational problems. Managers may not have access to new knowledge or they may not recognize improvements that do not fit their preconceptions (Gersick 1991, p. 18). Another set of explanations for inertia relies on cultural incompatibilities. For example, Wiener (1981) claims that the structure of

British society since the end of the nineteenth century has discouraged entrepreneurship and innovation.

Here, we concentrate on the influence of institutional variables on inertia.[110] Institutions may either retard or encourage innovation. If the institutional structure is rigid and unsuited to a new technology, change will be difficult to implement. When existing institutions are flexible or well-adapted to the requirements of an innovation, however, change will be accomplished relatively easily. As innovating firms may be affected by different sets of institutions, it is possible that one group may be impeded in its attempts to innovate while another group has a "head start" because it has already gained access to some of the necessary institutions for other reasons.

Both exogenous and endogenous institutions can affect the rate of innovation, as can a wide variety of institutional arrangements that are (depending on the level of analysis) either semi-endogenous or semi-exogenous. Exogenous institutions are those that are features of the economy or society at large, such as tariffs or the tax system in a given nation. Endogenous institutions comprise those that are specific to a particular firm or industry, including research and development departments, codified and uncodified corporate rules and procedures, and trade associations and lobbying groups.

In one kind of institutional explanation, the impeding or encouraging structures are only partly endogenous. That is, the institutions that retard or enhance adoption of new organizational and technological practices have been created by the self-interested behavior of individuals, but, once created, stand somehow outside or independent of that behavior. For example, the profit-maximizing behavior of a set of firms may lead to a particular kind of labor-relations policy, which in turn leads to the creation of a particular sort of labor union. Once created, this union may then affect, exogenously as it were, the subsequent behavior of the firms.

A second type of semi-endogenous institution comprises those that are generated by wider societal action and may not be especially targeted at specific firms or industries but that nevertheless create conditions that vitally affect the ability of firms to innovate. Most nations, for example, have systems of schooling that turn out potential workers with an assortment of skills of various grades. Employers must then provide further training and education to meet firm-specific needs. When the system of public education is appropriate to the technological and other needs of employers, little further training is needed. If, however, there is no public education or it is directed to other ends or is otherwise inadequate, a far greater burden falls on the employers. Moreover, what is highly efficient in one context may be entirely inappropriate to meet the challenges posed by significant innovations. As a result, some firms may find that a hitherto excellent system of education has become a source of inertia, while other firms, which were not well-served with educational facilities to cope with the old technology, discover that types of education that they had thought to be impractical or useless do, in fact, mesh well with the needs created by innovation.[111]

There is also a sense in which the institutions retarding change can be more straightforwardly "endogenous." The behavior patterns of the individual actors – their routines[112] – are themselves "institutions." Like institutions more broadly, routines (and their organizational and technological correlatives) can become obsolete. Moreover, institutional change can often take place through the more-or-less slow dying out of obsolete institutions in a population and their replacement by better adapted institutions – rather than by the conscious adaptation of existing institutions in the face of change.

The nature of markets themselves may also provide an institutional explanation for inertia because of the low level of price elasticity in many mature industries. There is little incentive for established firms to sponsor innovations if lower prices (or *de facto* lower prices, as when extra longevity more than compensates for higher sticker prices) will lead to decreased total revenue as a result of inelastic demand. Innovation will be favored, however, by new entrants that stand to gain market share at the expense of existing concerns if they can exploit better product or process technologies. This helps to explain, for example, why it was Wilkinson Sword rather than Gillette that introduced stainless steel razor blades, and why American tire manufacturers were reluctant to produce the long-life steel-belted radial designs promoted by Michelin.[113]

THE ROLE OF ROUTINES AND CAPABILITIES

Overall, inertia exerts two principal influences on the ability of firms to cope with innovation. Inertia is often a product of successful adaptation to earlier innovations, as a firm develops ways of operating that appear to be so well suited to its internal and external environment that it sees no reason to change. In many instances, this adaptation may prove so effective that the firm can retain a total cost advantage for a prolonged period despite using an outdated technology because it can still capitalize on its mastery of compatible support and ancillary operations, while firms adopting a new, and technically more efficient, technology are still wrestling with the expensive process of acquiring the endogenous and exogenous institutional backup necessary to gain full value from the innovation (Hannan and Freeman 1989).

When inertia retards the learning process necessary to deal with a subsequent important innovation, however, firms that are otherwise in a position to make the eventual transition to a new technology may be so slow in coming to grips with change that dominance shifts to new entrants who are unencumbered by prior developments, learn new adaptive procedures more quickly, and are able therefore largely to appropriate the market by the time the established firms have learned to cope with the innovation. The obstacle in this case may be termed "lockout," as leaders using the old technology find that they cannot successfully make the transition when there is a significant innovation (Cohen and Levinthal 1990, p. 137).

Routines and capabilities are at the heart of both of these aspects of inertia.

From the standpoint of the internal operations of a firm, the adoption of an innovation may be conceived of as a form of diversification. The Wrigley (Scott 1973) and Rumelt (1974) classifications of the degree of diversity or relatedness of intrafirm operations are based on the extent to which technological or marketing activities are shared across operations. The adoption of a radically new product or process technology for an existing product would lead a firm into unfamiliar, albeit still related, territory, in the same way as would diversification into a new product that shared marketing or technological bases with other products of the firm. The ability of the firm to master such a change would then depend on whether it possessed the technical and organizational flexibility to cope with an extended range of activities.

Routines and capabilities, as we have shown, form the basis of a firm's activities because they comprise the inputs that the firm can bring to bear to achieve its goals. As Penrose (1959), Nelson and Winter (1982), and others have argued, by building on its routines and capabilities a firm can create a position of strength in the marketplace. Teece (1980) and others have generally neglected the negative side of Nelson and Winter's analysis, however, and fail to note that the inflexibility, or inertia, induced by routines and capabilities can raise to prohibitive levels the cost of adopting a new technology or entering new fields. Such inertia can develop to the extent that existing rules are both hard to discard and inconsistent with types of change that might otherwise be profitable. Therefore, in adopting a product or process innovation, firms must look for a total-cost solution by weighing up possible increases in transaction costs caused by a departure from their existing capabilities and routines against savings or profitable marketing opportunities brought about by the change in technology. Moreover, the ensuing transaction costs may have two components, those that derive from disruption of existing operations and those that result from the need to learn a new set of capabilities appropriate to the new product or process technology.

Technological change, as we have shown, comes in a variety of forms that affect the likelihood of it being assimilated into existing firms. First, it is necessary to distinguish between minor and radical changes. A technological change may be characterized as "a bit-by-bit cumulative process until it is punctuated by a major advance." In general, these frequent minor changes can be assimilated in passing, and characterize the equilibrium stage. This is not true, however, of major innovations, which are "advances so significant that no increase in scale, efficiency, or design can make older technologies competitive [in direct cost terms] with the new technology" (Tushman and Anderson 1986, p. 441). Assuming that the adoption of a major innovation is feasible, the speed of adjustment will depend on the compatibility between the capabilities required by the old and new technological regimes. Some innovations are "competence destroying" whereas others are "competence enhancing" for particular organizations. Whereas major competence-enhancing innovations may, in time, be assimilated, the creation of entirely new organizations may be needed to deal with innovations that undermine the capabilities or competences of existing firms. Alternatively, there may be existing firms in other fields that are better able to cope with the innovation because it demands capabilities that, perhaps fortuitously, are compatible with their existing routines (Tushman and Anderson 1986, pp. 439–465).

LEARNING AND INERTIA

Learning is the antidote to inertia because it allows organizations to switch paths by augmenting their routines and capabilities. Organizations that learn quickly, cheaply, and accurately therefore have a degree of flexibility that is denied to organizations that can only learn slowly or at great expense, or that cannot learn at all. Thus, while "[i]nertia is . . . a profoundly functional organizational characteristic in stable/predictable environments" (Tushman and Romanelli 1985, p. 195), it is ultimately destructive when it impedes learning at times of significant change.

Stiglitz (1987) distinguishes between learning by doing and learning by learning. Under the familiar concept of learning by doing (Sahal 1981, pp. 108–110), organizations improve their efficiency and effectiveness through experience. Stiglitz applies this notion to the learning process itself. "Just as experience in production increases one's productivity in producing," he explains, "so experience in learning may increase one's productivity in learning. One learns to learn, at least partly in the process of learning itself. . . . By specialization in learning, one may improve one's learning skills" (Stiglitz 1987, p. 130). But learning is not an all-embracing process. Rather, it is localized in that learning about one field of study may not yield significant increases in an organization's ability to learn about other fields (Stiglitz 1987, pp. 126–130). There may be some spillovers that result simply from the process of learning how to question, but specific knowledge about a technology in a given industry may be of little value in dealing with a particular innovation in the same industry but with unfamiliar characteristics.[114] Recently, Stiglitz's observations on learning by learning have received some support from Kelly and Amburgey (1991,

p. 606) who show that prior experience in dealing with a similar type of change increases the chances of an organization coping successfully with subsequent changes, but experience in dealing with dissimilar changes does not.

Some types of learning can also be picked up externally, by watching and benefiting from the experience of others. Learning by learning remains important, however, because some knowledge is tacit and cannot be verbalized and transferred to outsiders, while other knowledge is proprietary and not publicly available. The ability of an organization to overcome inertia by learning is therefore limited by the timing of the learning effort and the method of learning that is chosen. Both Spence (1981) and Silverberg, Dosi, and Orsenigo (1988) have shown through simulations that lack of learning presents substantial barriers to entry. In large part, this is because organizations can readily pick up knowledge in the public domain but will be less efficient than experienced competitors if they cannot tap their own sources of tacit and proprietary knowledge. As the only way that an organization can learn the latter[115] is through learning by doing, the later the organization enters a new field or adopts an innovation, the further behind it is likely to be in efficiency. In such cases, established firms faced with mastering an innovation may encounter barriers to entry in the same way as new entrants to the industry. They may therefore find it hard to make the transition from the old to the new technology if they delay for very long.

As we have seen, Cohen and Levinthal (1989, 1990) call the ability of a firm to pick up information from external sources its "absorptive capacity," which is a function of its existing knowledge. Absorptive capacity can increase a firm's potential to fend off inertia to a degree because organizations that already have some background in a given area may be quicker and find it cheaper to acquire new related knowledge than organizations with no prior experience in the area. Cohen and Levinthal point to basic, or generalized, R&D activities as an important way to improve a firm's chances of spreading its external nets widely in acquiring useful knowledge from its surrounding environment. But, as it is not feasible to have a basic background in all areas, the problem is still to determine which fields are likely to prove sufficiently fertile in the future to justify an investment in basic background knowledge now. Firms that do not make the correct decisions (that do not know how to learn what they specifically need to learn) may lose irrevocably.

A firm without a prior technological base in a particular field may not be able to acquire one readily if absorptive capacity is cumulative. In addition a firm may be blind to new developments in fields in which it is not investing if its updating capability is low. Accordingly . . . firms may not realize that they should be developing their absorptive capacity

107

due to an irony associated with its valuation: the firm needs to have some absorptive capacity already to value it appropriately.

(Cohen and Levinthal 1990, p. 138)

Furthermore, as Penrose (1959, p.150) has noted, some organizations have better initial learning capabilities than others. Each organization is unique, and its ability to acquire the knowledge necessary to adopt a significant innovation successfully differs from that of existing or potential competitors. If the innovation is competence destroying, the inertia generated by mastery of an older technology may preclude the rapid acquisition of knowledge that will permit the transition. Competence-enhancing innovations, on the other hand, can benefit either existing firms or new entrants depending on whether the competences that are strengthened are related to or distinct from those associated with the old technology.

THE POPULATION DYNAMICS OF MARKET DOMINANCE

As vital elements of internal learning are needed, first to determine which capabilities a change demands, and then to master them, inertia will be strong and the adoption of major competence- or capabilities-destroying innovations can be expected to be gradual. In the interim, the industry may be composed of two sets of firms, the representatives of the older technology who will gradually wither, and those of the new technology who, as will be shown, may or may not gain the momentum required to establish themselves permanently. The survival of the older technology rests on the mastery of appropriate capabilities by existing firms who have learned to make the most efficient use of their resources under existing conditions. If capabilities for the new technology have not yet been worked out, therefore, a prolonged period may follow in which the total cost of production of the representatives of the old technology is less than that of the newer because the transaction cost savings arising from the use of efficient routines more than offset the direct savings in production costs that can be attributed to the new technology (Hannan and Freeman 1989, ch. 4). In fact, under certain circumstances, it may pay firms to continue to invest in a dying technology even though they would incur an accounting loss as a result (Tang 1988).

But, within any given population of firms, the withering of the representatives of the old technology and their replacement by firms that have adopted the innovation are not symmetrical processes. This is because there may be competition between as well as within populations. It is conceivable that there may be different endowments of capabilities and other resources that make the firms in one population, for example the

108

producers in an industry in a particular country, better able to adopt the new technology than producers elsewhere. An obvious example would be an endowment of some vital mineral that is highly localized, expensive to transport, and unnecessary under the old technological regime. If an innovation rendered this mineral necessary, not only would firms using the old technology in locations distant from the mineral deposits be at a severe cost disadvantage if they innovated, but distant new entrants would also face a severe handicap.

Equally importantly, there may be artificial differences among populations that lead to differential rates of success in adopting the new technology. This could arise, for instance, if one nation had, for independent reasons, already invested in a set of capabilities needed for the efficient use of an innovation, say those associated with technical education, but other nations had not. If this nation's firms were thus enabled to achieve rapid control over the new technology, they could potentially appropriate the innovation and gain a lasting market dominance (Abramovitz 1986, p. 388).

A second, and more pervasive, artificial means of gaining market dominance is through the use of tariffs. Assume that, under an existing technology, production in an industry is controlled by firms in a single country who have gained an early lead. These firms have used their cost advantages, based in large part on the efficient use of learned capabilities, to blanket domestic and export markets to such an extent that there are few foreign competitors.[116] When a major new technology is developed that dramatically reduces direct costs of production, many of the existing firms are initially reluctant to adopt the innovation because their capabilities still give them an overall cost advantage. A few pioneers, however, venture into the new technology and slowly develop the capabilities necessary to use it at its most efficient level. After a period of time, the capabilities of the representatives of the old technology are no longer great enough to compensate for higher direct costs of production and these firms are obliged either to adopt the new technology belatedly (a risky and probably futile gesture[117]) or to quit the field.

In the meanwhile, a second country, which has not had a successful group of firms using the old technology, imposes a tariff (or equivalent trade barrier) to protect local firms that adopt the innovation. Because of the tariff, these firms do not have to compete against the foreign first movers whose mastery of capabilities associated with the old technology still gives them an advantage in the early stages of adoption. Furthermore, if the pioneering nation gives no tariff protection to its own producers, firms in the follower country are able to compete on equal, or nearly equal, terms with the representatives of both the old and new technologies in the pioneer's home market. If the market in the follower nation is large enough to accommodate available economies of scale, firms adopting the new technology there are able to move down their learning curves much faster than similar firms in the pioneering nation that face competition from imports as well as from the local firms that have retained the old technology. Under this scenario, it is entirely plausible that the adopters of the innovation in the follower nation are able to learn so much more quickly that they can appropriate the greater part of the market by the time the older firms in the pioneer nation finally succumb, and that the adopters of the innovation in the pioneer will have been relegated to a minor role or eliminated altogether.[118]

Nevertheless, the retention of the old technology by the pioneering firms may be rational. For example, a discounted cash flow analysis could show that the pay-off to "harvesting" the existing operation, by reducing investment and letting it run down to the point of extinction, is greater than that from shifting to a new technology because of the much higher profits to the old technology in the early years, when capabilities appropriate to the innovation are still under development. David (1991a) gives a good example of harvesting in the defense of DC electrical power that Edison mounted during the Battle of the Systems. According to David, Edison was not being quixotic when he took elaborate, and sometimes bizarre, steps to contain the spread of an AC power system that even he must have known was superior in many ways. Edison needed funds for experimentation in new areas and had neither the patents nor the financial resources to enter AC transmission himself. What he really wanted to accomplish was an orderly transition that would permit him to liquidate his substantial investments in the DC technology at a good price so that he could get on with his new work. By resisting until the rotary converter was perfected, which allowed AC power to be converted to DC and thus ensured the viability of the existing DC network,[119] Edison was able to sell out at a greater profit than if he had either sold during the earlier period when the continued viability of DC was uncertain or shifted to AC as a follower.

The diagram in Figure 6.1 illustrates graphically the possibility of harvesting and a consequent shift in leadership among firms. The solid lines are experience curves (Abell and Hammond 1979) for two different basic technologies for producing the same good. The downward slope of the curves derives not only from learning by doing but also from such factors as economies of scale and minor competence-enhancing innovations. Indeed, the curves are drawn on a double-log scale, which emphasizes that, in the early stages, relatively small increases in cumulative output lead to relatively large decreases in production costs, but after the product matures much larger increases in cumulative output are needed to generate the same absolute decreases in production costs.

Initially, there are four firms employing the old technology: an experienced and relatively low-cost producer at A_1, an inexperienced and relatively high-cost producer at B_1, and two intermediate firms at C_1 and D_1.

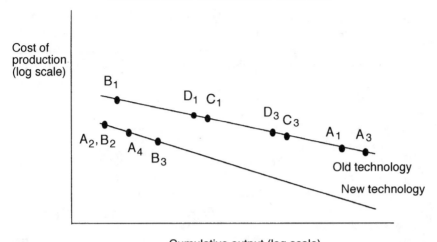

Figure 6.1 "Harvesting" and leadership-shift among firms

Firms A, C, and D are in one nation and firm B in another. Assume now that there is a major innovation that, if implemented, shifts a producer to a new and lower experience curve.[120] Both firm A and firm B have equal capabilities to adopt the innovation and would therefore be at the same point on the new experience curve (A_2, B_2). Firm B would find the innovation desirable and adopt it, but firm A would face inertia because it is already producing at far lower cost. Not only would firm A endure lower profits if it adopted the innovation, but it might even face extinction if other domestic producers using the established technology (firms C and D) declined to innovate and instead engaged in stiff price competition. Because of its higher initial cost structure, firm B, of course, would not be able to survive during this transition phase unless it were somehow insulated from competition. This, however, is perfectly feasible if B is in a different country and can be protected by a tariff.

After a period of time (years, or perhaps even decades) in which both firms have gained experience on their respective curves, A will have moved to A_3 and B to B_3, at which points their production costs are equal. But B's costs will be falling faster. If firm A wishes to change to the new technology now, however, the best it can hope for is to enter at A_4 because, although it will have access to publicly available knowledge concerning the innovation, A will not be able to tap the tacit and proprietary knowledge that firm B has gained. C and D will be at a similar disadvantage. Thus, the leading firms when the old technology was dominant will become the followers after the new technology takes hold because they will always have less knowledge and therefore relatively higher costs if they do not innovate initially at the same time as firm B. Under such circumstances, if the transition period is

111

long and the initial cost differential high, the rational course for firms A, C, and D is to harvest their investments by collecting higher profits over the period of transition even though the eventual result is to become followers or perhaps be driven from the industry when the innovative technology has become established.

The same basic mechanisms can operate either for entire national industries, as illustrated here, or for leading firms within a particular national economy that are less well equipped than some domestic competitors to cope with a significant innovation.[121]

The evolutionary explanation presented here should be distinguished from the now-familiar notion of technological lock-in (David 1985; Veblen 1915, pp. 126–127). In the broadest sense, we are, of course, arguing for a kind of lock-in. Because of the continuing possibility of learning along a particular technological or organizational path, there are, in effect, transaction costs impeding movement to a new path. This is very much a matter of path-dependency. But the cause of the lock-in is not (necessarily) increasing returns arising from the presence of network externalities or from fixed costs in complementary activities. Rather, the dependence on path arises simply from the persistence of routines. In a neoclassical world of fully informed actors, one needs a specific nonconvexity to achieve lock in. In a more believable world of ignorance and bounded rationality, the following of rules – as a necessary tool of cognition – is enough to do the trick.

FOUR HYPOTHESES

The analysis we present suggests a class of explanations that help to predict which firms will appropriate the benefits from an innovation. Here, we illustrate four hypotheses with a variety of historical and modern examples.

> Hypothesis 1   A firm that is adept at employing an existing technology will be less likely to adopt a new technology that is incompatible with its current capabilities than will a firm that is less adept at using the existing technology, even if the new technology offers the prospect of long-run increases in profits for both firms.

This is the hypothesis with which we are most concerned. It is illustrated in Britain after 1870 by electricity generation and electrical machinery and, perhaps most paradigmatically, by cotton textiles.

The relatively stunted development of the electrical products industry in Britain is a reflection of an older legacy, in this case in the use of gas for lighting and of steam, pneumatic, and hydraulic tools in industry. The electrical-machinery branch of the industry was especially weak in Britain, but British firms had trouble in competing even in simple items. Imports of electric lamps in 1908 were nearly as large as total domestic production in

1907, and imports of incandescent light bulbs were half again as large as domestic production. The older telegraphic equipment branch, and in particular cable manufacturing, was somewhat stronger, but in general the British produced less sophisticated varieties of equipment for home consumption and for export to the underdeveloped areas of the globe (Byatt 1968, 1979).

In large part, the failure of the British to attain greater success in electrical products manufacturing can be traced to the slow adoption of electricity for lighting, traction, and power purposes in the United Kingdom. Many of the reasons for this were political. By 1913, there were only a few large generating stations in both Chicago and Berlin, serving centralized power and light systems in each city. By contrast,

> Greater London had sixty-five electrical utilities, seventy generating stations averaging only 5,285 kw. in capacity, forty-nine different types of supply systems, ten different frequencies, thirty-two voltage levels for transmission and twenty-four for distribution, and about seventy different methods of charging and pricing.
>
> (Hughes 1983, p. 227)

This failure to consolidate was based on legislation that gave each municipality effective control over both public and private supply within its boundaries. Moreover, as late as 1912, the majority of electrical power used in Britain was actually generated by users rather than purchased from generating stations, further increasing the fragmentation of supply (Byatt 1979, ch. 6; Hughes 1983, pp. 227–38, 249–50).

In several important respects, however, the slow adoption of electrical power can be traced directly to the existing provision of other types of power in Britain which were not matched by developments in the U.S. or Germany. In contrast to the United States, inexpensive gas lighting was available in many British cities before electric lighting was feasible. Even in the early years of the twentieth century, electrical power was more expensive relative to gas in Britain than in the U.S. (Byatt 1979, p. 24). The use of electricity for industrial purposes in Britain was retarded in two ways by existing structures. Many firms were already using steam or other forms of power, and the slow rate of expansion of the economy left less scope than in Germany or the U.S. for the construction of entirely new plants that could be laid out to make the best use of electrical power rather than, as in the past, built around a central steam power plant that optimized the use of shafts and belting but did not take advantage of the flexibility that electricity could provide. In addition, the structure of the economy itself reduced the spread of electrification since cotton textiles and coal mining, which were of greater importance in Britain, were less susceptible to conversion to electrical power than many fast growing industries in America and Germany (Byatt 1979, chs. 3–5).

Nonetheless, it remains the case that the institutions retarding change

113

in the electrical industries were in large part quasi-exogenous governmental ones. For this reason, the cotton textile industry provides a purer example in which the principal "institutions" retarding change were the endogenously developed skills and capabilities of firms and workers. ·

Mass and Lazonick (1990) have recently provided a thorough summary of the debate on the British cotton industry in which they have been prominent participants. Their analysis of the sources of British dominance in the industry draws in most respects on a set of facts that are not broadly in dispute, even if these authors place their own interpretation on them. The facts are these. Combining their early capabilities in the premechanical textile trades with mechanical innovativeness, the British developed a set of productive capacities in mass-produced cotton textiles ahead of any other nation. These capabilities arose in an extremely decentralized manner that partook of Marshallian external economies. Among these capabilities was a highly developed market in cotton fiber. Technologically, these capabilities came to center around the self-acting mule and the power loom, which guided incremental innovation and conditioned the skills of the labor force. Although the exact productivity figures may be in dispute, it is clear that these competences in the British economy allowed the industry to follow an experience curve like those in Figure 6.1. And Britain was further along this curve than all others.

In the 1890s, however, a new technological paradigm emerged with the development of the automatic loom by Draper in the U.S. This device allowed for higher throughput and required less-skilled operatives. In order to benefit from its advantages, however, one needed yarn more resistant to breakage (for a given count) than that produced by the mule. The ring frame, which also required less labor skill and which, quite rationally, was little used in skill-rich Britain, thus became an important complement to the automatic loom, as it produced the needed stronger yarn. Coupled with new techniques for blending grades of cotton for ring spinning, the combination of the automatic loom and the ring offered a technological trajectory different from the one on which Britain had embarked. The U.S., Japan, and others speedily adopted these techniques behind tariff walls. In the Mass and Lazonick account,[122] Japan was particularly adept at honing the labor skills complementary to this new technology. And after the First World War, that country led a pack of low-wage countries – all of which depended on ring spinning and automatic looms – in a successful assault on British dominance. Britain attempted belatedly to adopt the new technologies, but found itself perennially behind on the experience curve.

Hypothesis 1 is also consistent with the experiences of a number of modern firms. In addition to the razor blade and tire industries, which are discussed above, the recent history of IBM is a classic example of a company that deliberately tried to forestall innovation in order to protect current product lines. IBM has maintained a prolific R&D program over many decades that has continuously generated important new products, but it has been reluctant to market many of its innovations because they would "cannibalize" highly profitable product lines in which the company had invested heavily in the past. IBM's insistence on maintaining compatibility with its 370 series mainframe computers and its AS400 minicomputers has been based on the enormous revenues that it has continued to generate from those machines and its realization that even immense success in the workstation and personal computer markets could not produce sales and flow-ons anywhere near the size of its past achievements. For example, IBM has produced an excellent RS6000 workstation that it is hesitant to market strongly because it is so powerful that it can replace earlier-generation IBM equipment costing far more. As Ferguson and Morris point out (1993, p. 87),

> a top-of-the-line AS400 [minicomputer] costs almost $1 million; and customers are beginning to catch on that RS6000 workstation-based networks can do the same job for a fraction of the cost. They get irritated when they ask about workstations and the IBM salesman starts pushing the AS400; so they call Sun or Hewlett-Packard instead.

This does not mean that IBM has been stupid in continuing to push its old lines, but simply that it is in a far different position from other workstation producers who have nothing to lose if their products replace larger machines. In recent years, around 70 per cent of IBM's revenues have been derived from the sale of products associated with mainframes and minicomputers. These include not only the hardware ($15 billion in 1991), but even greater sums from the sale of peripherals, software and services, and maintenance ($32.1 billion). Although sales in these latter categories would continue for a few years if IBM were not able to sell its larger computers, they too would disappear eventually and the company would "implode," to use a favorite term of Ferguson and Morris (1993, pp. 205–214). It is indeed conceivable that this may happen, bringing about IBM's demise, but the decision to resist the cannibalization of its major products by other lines in which the firm has fewer distinctive competences may nevertheless have prolonged the firm's existence and brought greater benefits to its shareholders and employees at all levels than would have eventuated if IBM had embraced the new technology at its inception.

The deterioration of the position of American automobile manufacturers is also a function of inertia, in this case in the face of important changes in process technologies by Japanese firms. These changes, which to a large extent involve organizational innovations, are based on a total rethinking of the nature of mass production in the light of improvements in quality monitoring mechanisms in recent decades. By linking low costs in mass production to high quality output – in contrast to the Taylor-Ford premise that there is a trade-off between cost and quality – Japanese automobile manufacturers have been able simultaneously to gain a significant advantage in costs of production and a marketing advantage sustained by a reputation for high quality. Despite eventual adjustments by U.S. and European automobile producers, it seems clear that a substantial share of the market has been permanently ceded to the Japanese (Womack, Jones, and Roos 1990; Smitka 1991).

> Hypothesis 2   If there is no major innovation in an industry, the incumbent leaders will probably retain leadership.

It is well established that firms that gain market dominance are likely to hold on to it unless there is a major technological change (Lieberman and Montgomery 1988). To reverse the examples cited under Hypothesis 1, the following firms all held market leadership under relatively stable conditions for several decades until challenged by major innovations: Gillette in razor blades; Goodyear, Firestone, and Uniroyal in tires; and General Motors, Ford, and Chrysler in automobiles. Similar examples of long-term dominance in mature markets apply in typewriters, electrical products, and many other industries.

  In the late nineteenth and early twentieth centuries, British industries were also able to retain their market dominance when there were no major innovations, even when firms in related industries were being supplanted by foreign competition. British cottons maintained their dominance of international markets until well into the twentieth century, particularly in piece goods. Imports failed to penetrate the home market and, despite increased foreign competition, there was seldom any absolute decrease in exports except in the case of yarns (Tyson 1968). In engineering the older sectors such as cotton-textile machinery also kept their international dominance. The ring frame may have been a competence-destroying innovation from the point of view of the British spinners, but it was competence-enhancing from the point of view of the machinery firms, who strengthened their position through its production (Saxonhouse and Wright 1984). The market for British locomotives and rolling stock held up as well, especially in the Empire and South America. In boilers and prime movers, Britain exported more than the United States or Germany in 1913, and in agricultural machinery, more than Germany (Saul 1968).

> Hypothesis 3   If there is a major innovation, but it is highly compatible with existing capabilities (is competence enhancing), the incumbents will probably retain leadership.

In their discussion of the automobile industry, Abernathy and Clark (1985) list a number of innovations that were highly significant but nevertheless competence enhancing. Moreover, they note that, since a firm can have important competences in several areas, an innovation that is destructive of one competence can bolster others. Thus the introduction of the

116

inexpensive V-8 engine and steel bodies eroded some of the technical competences of major firms but allowed them to enhance their existing marketing competences.

A further example in Britain is the advent of the steel hull for oceangoing merchant vessels in the 1870s. This innovation reduced hull weights by as much as 15 per cent in comparison to iron hulls and offered improved strength and flexibility. It was, however, a change that fitted in well with the capabilities of both existing shipbuilders and steel makers in Britain. By the 1890s, virtually all major ships were built of steel and Britain had retained its leadership (Pollard and Robertson 1979).

> Hypothesis 4   If the innovation is, for all practical purposes, entirely new (that is, there is no significant existing industry), then the benefits of the innovation will be appropriated by the population of firms that already has the best access to the most important relevant capabilities. These may be either entirely new firms or incumbent firms in related fields.

EMI's experience with the CT scanner illustrates the problems a technical pioneer can encounter if it does not possess complementary capabilities (Teece 1986b). Although EMI had the technical sophistication to develop the scanner, the device required a higher standard of training, servicing, and support than hospitals had needed until then. EMI was not in a position to provide these services, but GE and Technicare, two firms that were similarly sophisticated in electronics, were also established medical suppliers. Teece (1986b, pp. 298–99) reports the final result.

> By 1978 EMI had lost market share leadership to Technicare, which was in turn quickly overtaken by GE. In October 1979, Godfrey Houndsfield of EMI shared the Nobel prize for invention of the CT scanner. Despite this honor, and the public recognition of its role in bringing this medical breakthrough to the world, the collapse of its scanner business forced EMI in the same year into the arms of a rescuer, Thorn Electrical Industries, Ltd. GE subsequently acquired what was EMI's scanner business from Thorn for what amounted to a pittance. . . . Though royalties continued to flow to EMI, the company had failed to capture the lion's share of the profits generated by the innovation it had pioneered and successfully commercialized.

Mitchell (1989) has since shown that incumbent firms with related capabilities in other branches of medical diagnostic imaging are also more likely to enter new fields in imitation of pioneers than are incumbent firms without related capabilities.

Another example of Hypothesis 4 is the substitution of iron hulls and steam propulsion for wooden-hulled sailing vessels around 1850 (Pollard and Robertson 1979). These changes thoroughly undermined the distinctive competence of North American shipbuilders, which lay in their sources of cheap timber, and instead placed a premium on access to iron plates and steam boilers, both fields in which Britain had already established the basis for leadership. Similarly, Britain developed a strong bicycle industry at the end of the nineteenth century, based in large part on the country's strong external economies in the manufacture of mechanical parts (Harrison 1969).

In other cases, late Victorian and Edwardian Britain did not possess the right capabilities to capture the benefits of wholly new innovations. In some electrical and chemical industries, for example, countries with systems of technical education more developed than that in Britain were in a better position to appropriate the benefits of innovations that relied on the use of technically trained labor. As in the case of other types of education, it was difficult to align the costs and returns from technical training and, as the government and potential students were less willing to pay in Britain than in some other countries, technical education there was stunted (Robertson 1981). Firms in Britain, which could rely on their initial capabilities arising from a stock of skilled labor, were confirmed in their reliance on manual skills and became less able as technologies evolved to make the transition to more highly technical routines. This, in turn, determined not only the work practices of firms in older industries but helped to steer British entrepreneurs away from industries where technical knowledge was vital because they knew that suitable workers would be expensive to hire. In Germany, the U.S., and Switzerland, a readily expandable pool of technically educated workers was already available when the electrical and chemical industries began to take hold. As these foreign firms had many of the necessary capabilities for innovation on hand before the innovations were actually adopted, they were able to learn other routines much more quickly and to seize market share before British firms could become meaningful competitors.

CONCLUSIONS

The model presented here is intended as only one explanation among many for the coexistence of a variety of competing technologies and organizational forms even in nations at similar stages of development. Other factors such as deficiencies in real resources, limited markets, labor intransigence, or entrepreneurial failure may also have been important factors influencing technological choice. Furthermore, the model does not, at first glance, explain some of the more interesting cases of inertia. For example, one appealing working hypothesis is that the existence of strong pig and wrought iron industries in Britain before the advent of Bessemer steel would have retarded vertical integration and put British steel manufacturers at a disadvantage in comparison to integrated German and

American competitors who could convert hot pig iron directly, without reheating. Elbaum has pointed out, however, that Bessemer firms in Britain were as highly integrated as those elsewhere and that the problems can be traced to the subsequent early conversion of the British to open hearth technology at a time when economies of scale offered by the Siemens-Martin process were too small to justify vertical integration. On this reading, the origins of fragmentation were technical and cannot be easily traced to an early start and subsequent inertia (Elbaum 1986). Also, although (as our analysis would predict) German steelmakers seem to have benefited from having tariff protection at a time when their competitors did not (Webb 1980), the effects of cartels and control by the banks may have been more ambiguous. Because separate cartels were organized for each major stage of production, they created an artificial barrier between the pig iron and steel producers that, in at least one important case, inhibited vertical integration (Whale 1930, pp. 53, 62; Webb 1980, p. 312). Before a firmer conclusion can be reached, more detailed studies of the steel and iron industries in the three countries will be needed.

It is nevertheless clear that institutional factors, especially those embodied in capabilities and routines, can both improve the ability of a firm to exploit an existing technology and make it more difficult to innovate by generating an inertia that is hard to overcome. Not all organizations are equally well equipped to adapt to change, however, and firms that are adept at using an existing technology may have fewer of the capabilities required to cope with innovation than a new entrant or a firm that was less successful under the old regime. When this is true, a change in industrial leadership is probable, with the hitherto dominant firms becoming either followers or leaving the industry altogether because they are no longer competitive. From this perspective, the slow and uneven pace of technological change across sectors and among nations since the middle of the eighteenth century becomes a little easier to understand.

119

7

INNOVATION, NETWORKS AND VERTICAL INTEGRATION

This chapter concentrates for the most part on the short-run effects of capabilities and transaction costs in the context of innovation. We argue that the choice of an organizational form suitable for a particular context depends, among other things, on the nature of the innovation, the uses to which it will be put, and the existing distribution of available capabilities in the economy, including sources of information. Because of the variety of possible forms and the importance of on-the-spot knowledge, the choice among organizational forms should not be tightly constrained by government policy but should be left to firms to adopt the arrangements that best suit their individual circumstances.

INTRODUCTION

The debate over the institutional forms most conducive to economic growth has intensified in recent years. In the mid-1980s, Michael Piore, Charles Sabel, and Jonathan Zeitlin challenged the notion that the growth of large businesses in twentieth-century Britain and the United States had been either necessary or desirable. On the basis of developments in Continental Europe, they have contended that communities of skilled craftsmen are as capable of generating high standards of living as are giant, vertically integrated firms (Piore and Sabel 1984; Sabel and Zeitlin 1985; Sabel *et al.* 1987; Sabel 1989). Moreover, they claim, small firms are more flexible and thus better adapted to engendering and adopting innovations. To take advantage of these capabilities, they recommend reorienting the American economy towards small, craft-based firms that operate in a cooperative environment. This call has been reinforced by Michael Best, who questions the efficiency of both vertically integrated Western firms and Japanese networks, and calls instead for the growth of geographical concentrations of small firms organized along cooperative lines as in the "Third Italy" (Best 1990).[123]

Piore, Sabel, and Zeitlin support their analysis with historical examples.[124] To them, the adoption of the paradigm of mass production represents the triumph of an idea rather than an economic necessity. Because of the highly publicized triumphs of producers such as Henry Ford, large firms came to be regarded as the norm. Nevertheless, craft production retained advantages in flexibility and variety that were overlooked as Britain and the United States moved towards gargantuan factories in the twentieth century. As counter-examples, Sabel and Zeitlin cite industries in France and Italy that maintained their craft traditions and prospered as a result. Piore, Sabel, and Zeitlin maintain that large firms often fail to cope successfully with the accelerating rate of innovation that they perceive, or to take advantage of the flexibility permitted by new production technologies. They recommend instead that the American economy be reoriented towards smaller firms, clustered in industrial districts similar to those in the Third Italy, where they can develop symbiotically.

Other analysts believe that large, vertically integrated firms are in the best position to develop and exploit innovations. In contrast to Piore and Sabel and Best, William Lazonick contends that economies of scale will remain overwhelmingly important and that small firms will not be able to compete effectively in many areas. As a result, Lazonick believes, growth must be based on giant firms that are able to combine strategic flexibility with access to economies of scale. But to survive, such firms need to be vertically integrated into marketing and the supply of inputs in order to provide the security to justify investments in large production facilities (Lazonick 1990 and 1991a).

Like Piore, Sabel, and Zeitlin, Lazonick uses extensive historical evidence to support his policy recommendations. He draws heavily on the work of Alfred D. Chandler, Jr. to demonstrate that the growth of manufacturing since the late nineteenth century has been closely correlated to the degree of horizontal and vertical integration in technologically advanced industries. In *The Visible Hand* (1977), Chandler showed that the rapid growth of firms in a number of American industries between 1870 and 1940 was based on significant and continuing increases in economies of scale. In order to take advantage of these scale economies, small firms that had been restricted to local markets merged to serve regional or even national markets. Horizontal integration in itself was rarely if ever enough to guarantee viability, however, because such collections of small enterprises could not gain the benefit of scale economies unless they were rationalized into larger units under central control. Thus the "visible hand" of management was needed to initiate and direct the new giant firms. Moreover, because of the larger investments in fixed capital which were required, enormous size entailed greater risk. As a result, managers attempted to shield giant firms from market uncertainties by integrating forwards and backwards in the hope of ensuring supplies of inputs and, in particular, increasing the demand for finished products to keep pace with growing productive capabilities.

More recently, Chandler has extended his analysis to British and German history. He states, for example, that Britain's relative decline as a manufacturing power after 1870 occurred because "British entrepreneurs failed to make the essential three-pronged investment in manufacturing, marketing, and management in a number of the capital-intensive industries of the Second Industrial Revolution."[125] In other words, the British erred in not building large facilities or, when they did, in continuing to rely on market mechanisms and not providing adequate internal marketing and management skills to coordinate and protect their investments.

This, essentially, is the model that Lazonick projects into the future. He believes that to prosper nations must take advantage of substantial economies of scale in major industries, and that this requires centralized management and a high degree of vertical integration to overcome market deficiencies. To the extent that American firms are inhibited – either through government policy, market fragmentation, or managerial ineptitude – from matching the control that foreign competitors hold over resources, they will, he feels, lose out in a world of increasing returns.

Richard Florida and Martin Kenney also believe that a high degree of vertical integration is desirable, but stress the need to coordinate basic research and development activities with product development and manufacturing in order to gain maximum benefits from scientific and engineering breakthroughs (Florida and Kenney 1990a). Florida and Kenney and Lazonick are critical of Piore and Sabel and of current American developments in Silicon Valley and along Route 128 in Massachusetts because, they claim, small firms cannot fully realize the potential that seminal discoveries offer. As a result, well-articulated Japanese and Korean industrial conglomerates are appropriating the bulk of the benefits of American discoveries and, increasingly, themselves making the important breakthroughs on which future growth will be based (Florida and Kenney 1990a, ch. 6).[126]

An intermediate position has been staked out by Michael E. Porter. Porter believes that, in order to be successful in international markets, firms must first develop the knack of competing domestically. To achieve this, he advocates a high degree of rivalry among firms in their home markets. He also cites the importance of networks of suppliers to provide inexpensive and flexible access to inputs (Porter 1990). And, like Piore and Sabel, Porter believes that geographic concentrations of producers can increase productivity by enhancing access to knowledge and other factors of production. Although Lazonick (1991b) has criticized Porter's support for a high degree of domestic competition and networks of support firms, it is clear that, in contrast to Piore and Sabel, Porter is not advocating the establishment of ateliers when economies of scale are present.

There appear to be two basic differences between Porter and Lazonick. First, Porter believes that the American economy is large enough in most

122

industries to justify competition among several large firms, whereas Lazonick supports monopolies or very tight oligopolies in the domestic economy. To Lazonick, the most important rivalry is on the international stage and industries on the national level should conserve their strength for competition with firms from other countries. Second, Porter believes that an extensive web of outside suppliers and regional agglomerations of producers provide flexibility to cushion downturns and give broad access to technical improvements, whereas Lazonick emphasizes the security that arises from maintaining resources under centralized control.

Prescriptions for government industrial policy also vary among analysts. Lazonick (1990, 1991a, 1991b), for example, contends that governments should promote centralization and concentration to permit firms to meet competitive challenges from large foreign firms. Piore and Sabel (1984) and Best (1990), on the other hand, recommend that governments actively support the growth of small firms and industrial districts by generating policies that simultaneously promote competition and cooperation. Finally, Porter (1990) believes that governments should emphasize the creation of environments that encourage domestic and international competition by promoting technological change, but that governments are in general ill equipped to provide detailed economic direction.

All of these observers are correct in the sense that both large and small firms have thrived historically and continue to exist. But neither set of examples precludes the other because different industries are involved. In certain industries, such as iron and steel, automobile manufacturing, and some branches of chemicals, economies of scale proved so strong that small firms were virtually wiped out in the first half of the twentieth century.[127] Chandler, however, probably overestimates the importance of these industries (Supple 1991; Landes 1991). In many other cases, economies of scale were limited although increases in productivity may nevertheless have been great. In these latter industries – which include some branches of machinery manufacture, clothing, and retailing – small, highly competitive firms have been able to retain strong positions.

All of these authors are grappling with the same problem of locating the patterns of industrial and firm organization that are most efficient in permitting a firm to innovate and gain or maintain productive superiority. Their concern in terms of policies and outcomes is at the level of both the firm and the nation.[128]

What is needed is a way of predicting how economic institutions will behave within their particular environments to affect the behavior of firms. Because of the diversity of those environments, however, analysis requires the use of a selection of models appropriate to circumstances and the questions under consideration, rather than an overarching model that may be inadequate to deal with the needs of any particular institution.

NETWORKS AND NETWORKS

Vertically integrated firms and loose webs of small producers are only two of the types of networks operating in modern economies.[129] As we showed in Chapter 2, organizations can be classified according to their degrees of both coordination integration and ownership integration. In this chapter, we use this as a starting-point in examining various kinds of actually existing networks and how they respond to innovative conditions (Figure 7.1).

The loosest type of network is the Marshallian industrial district. Alfred Marshall (1961) based this concept on a pattern of organization that was common in late-nineteenth-century Britain in which firms concentrating on the manufacture of certain products were geographically clustered. In some cases, these clusters were highly specialized. While Lancashire as a whole was the center of cotton textile production, for example, individual towns within the county concentrated on spinning or weaving and on specific counts of yarn or styles of fabric. Similarly, different shipbuilding districts specialized in particular classes of vessels, and various Midlands cities such as Birmingham and Coventry became centers of different branches of the engineering industry. The characteristics of Marshallian industrial districts are similar to the "social structures of innovation" listed by Florida and Kenney: "integrative systems comprised of . . . technology-oriented enterprise, highly skilled labor, considerable . . . private R & D expenditures, extensive networks of suppliers, manufacturers and vendors, support firms such as law firms and consultants . . ., strong entrepreneurial networks, and

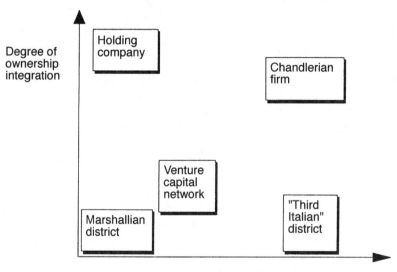

Figure 7.1 Integration, networks and the response to innovative conditions

124

informal mechanisms for information exchange and technology transfer" (1988, p. 130).

The two dominant characteristics of a Marshallian industrial district are that capabilities are widely distributed and transaction costs are minimal. In a Marshallian district, there are high degrees of vertical and horizontal specialization and a very heavy reliance on market mechanisms for exchange. Firms tend to be small and to focus on a single function in the production chain. Suppliers of intermediate goods commonly sell their stocks locally, within the district, although the final products may be marketed internationally. Firms located in industrial districts are also highly competitive in the neoclassical sense, and in many cases there is little product differentiation. The major advantages of Marshallian industrial districts therefore arise from simple propinquity of firms, which allows easier recruitment of skilled labor and rapid exchanges of commercial and technical information through informal channels. Tacit knowledge and idiosyncratic synergy are relatively insignificant. As Marshall described them, industrial districts illustrate competitive capitalism at its most efficient, with transaction costs reduced to a practical minimum; but they are feasible only when economies of scale are limited.

Recent commentators have revived the term "industrial district" to describe somewhat different types of organizational arrangements. As applied to the Third Italy, the term indicates a higher degree of cooperative coordination than would be present in a Marshallian industrial district. In this part of Italy, vertical and horizontal specialization are again high and firms are generally small. Competition is high and barriers to entry and exit are low. In contrast to Marshallian districts, however, product differentiation rather than price is the dominant competitive characteristic. Tacit, idiosyncratic knowledge is central to firm performance and competition is limited to certain spheres of activity in which firms might be expected to develop distinctive competences (Lazerson 1988, Malerba 1993).[130] In general, this means design, especially in industries such as ceramics and textiles. For those activities in which economies of scale extend beyond the range of individual small firms and the degree of standardization is high, firms in industrial districts in Italy tend to favor cooperative arrangements, which are normally government sanctioned. Cooperation is common in such activities as business services, including bookkeeping; sponsorship of trade fairs and other domestic and, in particular, international marketing ventures; and the provision of utilities and other infrastructure.[131] Cooperation also extends to the provision of capital, which the banks lend directly to official cooperatives, who guarantee the loans and determine the distribution of funds among member firms (Brusco and Righi 1987). As a result, small firms are able to sell their output in world markets and to gain some of the benefits of scale economies while continuing to compete strongly with each other.

Because of the legal advantages that pertain to small firms, many producers in the Third Italy are reluctant to employ directly more than fifteen or so workers. To avoid expanding too far, however, firms do take ownership positions in "satellite firms" that maintain legal independence. Interestingly, the satellite firms are not generally used to expand output and increase market control, but to protect the core competences of the original enterprise by providing intermediate goods at lower cost or with greater security. The acquisition of satellites is also used to gain control over complementary design capabilities. The networks of satellites therefore represent small islands of ownership and control integration within the larger horizontally integrated networks of the cooperatives (Lazerson 1988).

A second recent variation on the industrial district is the Innovative Network, as represented by Silicon Valley and Route 128. Because the pace of change is so rapid, firms in Innovative Networks rely for their competitiveness on knowledge that is tacit or closely held. As in Marshallian industrial districts, coordination integration is low in these districts,[132] but some coordination is supplied by the venture capitalists who put up the initial seed money. The venture capitalists are specialist investors who have close connections throughout the districts and are also able to provide new firms with entrepreneurial and managerial guidance and connections with potential suppliers and customers (Florida and Kenney 1988).[133] Under this arrangement, there are two networks, one of producers that approximates the market orientation of the Marshallian industrial district, and a second network of venture capitalists that is superimposed on the network of producers. In addition, the degree of local focus is frequently reduced to the extent that the venture capitalists come from other regions.

Although there is a stronger orientation towards cooperation in the Third Italy than in Marshallian industrial districts, both models are based on organic growth. Even the government sponsorship of collective action in Italy is a reinforcement of a socialist ethos that has been the dominant attitude among small producers in Emilia-Romagna and Tuscany for nearly a century. Where the appropriate institutions do not exist, formal cooperation and coordination are less likely to take hold. Jones (1993) has investigated the nature of cooperation in Australia, a country in which there has traditionally been little enthusiasm on the part of businessmen for government intervention. His study of the boat-building industry, which is clustered in New South Wales and southern Queensland, reveals that despite thick networks – in one instance, over twenty builders are sited within a distance of three kilometers just south of Brisbane – the builders were resistant to suggestions that they organize along the lines of business in the Third Italy. They showed little interest in sharing design roles with suppliers and were overwhelmingly opposed to any form of government-sponsored cooperation. In part, this stemmed from a desire to preserve their distinct competences in design, but it appears also to have been generated by poor experiences with the government in the past and the prevalence of a long-standing anti-government ideology. As a result, the boat-building districts are heavily Marshallian in their informality of organization.

In such Innovative Networks as Silicon Valley and along Route 128, there has been a similar organic growth: The development of nuclei of isolated firms into large clusters required more than two decades (Dorfman 1983; Miller and Côté 1985). The imposition of a network of venture capitalists, however, marks a significant step in the direction of centralization and outside control. As a consequence, the organic nature of competition in the local industries is reduced and industrial districts dominated by venture capitalism represent a movement along the dimensions of both coordination integration and ownership consolidation, even if such arrangements fall far short of vertical integration in the Chandlerian vein.

Modularity, which we discussed in detail in Chapter 5, is a form of organization that is related conceptually to industrial districts. When there are few economies of scale in assembly and consumers prefer the ability to choose components rather than pre-packaged sets, vertical specialization will occur, with firms concentrating on individual modules. But while firms retain significant independence in design, manufacturing, and marketing, they cannot be totally oblivious to the practices of either their competitors or of manufactures of other modules because assembly requires a high degree of standardization to permit compatibility. When there is modularity, therefore, both vertical and horizontal networks may arise, perhaps with government enforcement as in the case of radio frequencies (Robertson and Langlois 1992).

Writers like Piore and Sabel extol industrial districts for their "flexible specialization," which allows swift adaptation to market changes and permits the realization of a wide range of separate visions as manufacturers concentrate on product niches (Piore and Sabel 1984; Saxenian 1990). Industrial districts are less appropriate, however, when there are potentially large economies of scale or high transaction costs. Under these conditions, different types of organization are needed.

One possibility is the establishment of core networks. As the name implies, these are organized around a single firm, which is usually a large assembler (Figure 5.4). The satellite firms supply intermediate inputs to the core, which effectively coordinates the network as a whole. The relationships between U.S. and Japanese automobile manufacturers and their assemblers illustrate two types of core networks. U.S. auto firms have traditionally dealt with suppliers at "arm's length," using short-term contracts and exacting discipline by switching to other sources if they are dissatisfied with price, quality, or regularity of delivery. To the extent that there is any synergy, it is definitely contestable: Suppliers fill orders as

127

detailed by the core purchasers and are seldom given any discretion over design (Helper 1991).

American core networks often approximate monopsonistic market relationships. Although, in theory, suppliers may serve a variety of firms, in practice this may be precluded by asset specificity, as dies and other capital equipment cannot be readily transferred to other uses. As a result, large U.S. firms are able to use their bargaining power to exact low prices when dealing with small suppliers operating in competitive markets. The transaction costs of maintaining impersonal market relationships may be great, however, as the willingness of U.S. core firms to switch suppliers engenders little loyalty from the latter, who therefore tend to stick to the letter of contracts and are reluctant to offer help when they are able. In any case, given the centralized nature of decision-making, there is only a slim chance that suggestions emanating from suppliers – including internal captive suppliers – would attract any attention at the core.

By contrast, the networks of Japanese automobile firms (Figure 5.5) arguably serve to reduce transaction costs by establishing what Florida and Kenney (1991, p. 395) have termed "tightly networked production complexes." Fruin (1992) has identified three distinct but closely-related industrial forms in Japan (see Figure 7.2). At the lowest level of aggregation are what Fruin terms "focal factories," which concentrate on particular products. The activities of focal factories go well beyond manufacturing and more closely approximate those of strategic business units in Western corporations. R&D and market and product planning as well as

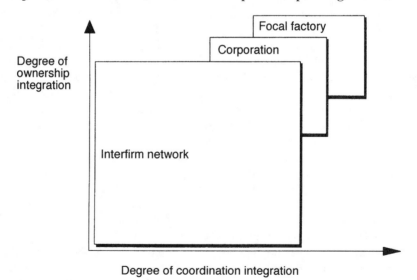

Figure 7.2 Japanese firm relationships

128

manufacturing are undertaken at focal factories, which thus serve as learning organizations that accumulate deep knowledge concerning narrow lines of output.[134] Integrative learning, on the other hand, is provided by corporations and interfirm networks. Complex corporations may have thousands of interfirm relationships. Toshiba, for example, has approximately 1,900 interorganizational connections that are distributed widely along both the coordination and ownership dimensions. Toshiba has ties to about 600 affiliated and subsidiary companies, but the strength of these relationships varies considerably. Thirty-three consolidated firms are more than half owned and Toshiba holds shares of between 20 and 50 per cent in sixty-five to seventy other firms. Toshiba owns little if any proportion, however, of 1,300 other suppliers of parts, components, and sub-assemblies (Fruin 1992, pp. 20, 220). Thus the organizational forms in Japan cover virtually the entire quadrant in the figure, but with differing degrees of density.

One aspect of this networking lies along the coordination dimension in the form of synergy that may shade from the contestable into the idiosyncratic. As Smitka (1991) and others have argued, the longer-term "relational" contracts among Japanese assemblers and suppliers, supported by rational, economically motivated structures of trust, reduce the transaction costs of bilateral monopoly. Moreover, such contracts, by encouraging the sharing of information, spur supplier-generated innovation in a way foreclosed to the American firms. Another, less-noticed, aspect of Japanese automotive networks is that they represent a more effective decentralization scheme. Rather than hoarding most technical and design knowledge inhouse, Japanese lead auto firms parcel out discrete modules to suppliers. "Typically," as Helper and Levine (1992, p. 563) write, "a Japanese automaker will not undertake the design of a part that it requires for a new model. Instead it will specify exterior dimensions and performance characteristics, and allow a specialist supplier to design the part to best match its process." For example, an American firm typically assembles a car seat from parts supplied by some 25 different subcontractors. By contrast, a Japanese firm will subcontract the entire seat to a "first-tier" subcontractor, who will then assume primary responsibility for design, quality, and compatibility (Womack, Jones, and Roos, 1990). This efficient modularization also serves to reduce transaction costs, allowing the network of outside suppliers to achieve a higher level of productive capabilities than in the American system. The suppliers respond in Japan by increasing product specialization to a high degree (Odaka, Ono, and Adachi 1988), giving the system some of the character of a Marshallian network.[135]

Another aspect of the Japanese supplier network in automobiles lies along the ownership dimension. Although Japanese core firms directly produce a smaller proportion of their components than do their American competitors and have a far smaller number of workers per unit produced, they often own a substantial stake in their suppliers, who are therefore not truly independent. Japanese suppliers are also provided with help in finding land close to the core factory to facilitate just-in-time deliveries. In part, the virtues of this ownership quasi-integration derive from the coordination integration it facilitates. Because of their close financial connections, Japanese core firms have an interest in the prosperity of their suppliers and an incentive to engage in reciprocal cooperation that is not present in America. But a dynamic perspective casts the ownership aspects of the network in a somewhat different light. Such ownership ties are part of efforts by the lead firms to create and cultivate the network of suppliers rather than efforts to manage the network once created. The approach of creating an external network rather than producing inhouse has long been a conscious strategy in the Japanese auto industry, albeit one forced on the industry in part in response to labor unrest in the early 1950s (Smitka 1991).

A substantial portion of part of the difference between American and Japanese core networks in the automotive industry centers on the way in which they manage the balance between internal and external capabilities. Most of the inputs that firms in both countries draw from outside suppliers are based on capabilities that are technologically simple and could be easily learned. In order to retain the bargaining advantages that stem from quasi-monopsonistic relationships, U.S. car firms deliberately discourage suppliers from acquiring a wide range of capabilities, especially in the area of design, by strenuously refusing to delegate any functions that would use those capabilities. At first glance, Japanese core firms follow a far different policy of actively delegating design functions. Because of the ownership stakes that Japanese firms hold in many of their leading suppliers, however, it is far from clear that they are actually encouraging a broad-based spread of capabilities. It appears that in both types of networks, the core firms still believe that the transaction cost situation favors internalizational of many capabilities that the market is technically competent to provide.

In fact, it is possible to exaggerate the degree of disparity in supplier relationships between Japanese and American firms. Richardson (1993) points out that, while Japanese automakers may maintain single sourcing for particular parts on specific models, they also protect themselves against opportunism by fostering contestability. This is done through "parallel sourcing," in which very similar parts for different models are provided by a range of firms. Even though any given item may be single-sourced, therefore, firms are able if necessary to switch orders to other suppliers with whom they have already established relations and which possess very similar capabilities. Overall, the suspicion remains that variations in performance between Japanese and Western firms do not result so much from formal organizational differences – for there are close parallels across nations – but rather from differences in the way in which

130

these organizational forms are implemented and in the behavior of the various actors.

Formal vertical integration is at the far end of our spectrum. Here, stages of production are under common ownership, and administrative coordination prevails over arm's-length coordination. Again, ownership integration does not by itself lead to centralized control, as firms may choose to have divisions deal with each other on an arm's-length basis to simulate market transactions. Alternatively, central management may through oversight or weakness lose control over internal divisions, which are then able to act independently. Indeed, it is important to remember that the innovation of the multi-divisional (M-form) structure was in one sense an innovation in decentralization. What made the large vertically integrated firms possible was an efficient parcelling out of knowledge and control to modular subunits, with the core retaining only higher-level strategic functions.[136] This system is thus rather closer to the Japanese core network than one might think, except that strategic control is arguably greater in the M-form firm and, as Williamson argues in theory and students of industry have confirmed in practice,[137] internal supply divisions lack the "high-powered incentives" of a financially independent (or at least quasi-independent) relationship. When vertical integration is chosen despite these drawbacks, it indicates either that the required capabilities are concentrated and potential outside suppliers are not competent to meet the needs of the producer, or that the transaction costs of purchasing the capabilities externally outweigh any savings that might ensue.

Thus, in practice, the degrees of vertical integration available to producers are finely graded and may be chosen according to needs. For example, as Chi has noted (1994, p. 283), "a firm may . . . be able to gain control over certain crucial decisions in an adjacent stage of production without acquiring full control over the whole operation." There is no single degree of integration, or form of firm or industry organization, that suits all purposes. In some cases, firms may even mix forms as in the case of taper integration, in which firms produce a proportion of their needs for a given input internally and purchase the remainder from outside suppliers (Harrigan, 1983).

The degree of horizontal integration is also important in determining how effectively an innovation is adopted. The ability to generate research funds, for example, and the variety of options that might be tried in an uncertain research environment may be affected by the size of firms and their ability to cooperate. Small firms are often lauded for their ability to focus their capabilities in response to the need for change. Moreover, many independent research efforts may generate more ideas than a few larger teams (Nelson and Winter 1977). When research is expensive, however, small firms may be unable to pay the price of admission while large firms and consortia can tap greater pools of resources.

Forms of horizontal integration also vary. In a Marshallian industrial district, firms are independent for most purposes.[138] Formal horizontal combinations characterize the industrial districts of the Third Italy, however, and *ad hoc* horizontal combinations promoted by venture capitalists operate in American industrial districts that feature Innovative Networks. In general, large U.S. firms are discouraged by antitrust laws and other regulations from horizontal cooperation, but this is less true in Japan and Europe. As in the case of vertical integration, the most efficient form of horizontal integration for promoting innovation depends on the circumstances of the particular case.

SPECIALIZATION AND APPROPRIABILITY

Specialization and the appropriability of benefits also exert conflicting influences on the choice of organizational form in an innovative environment. The advantages that flow from specialization and the division of labor should lead to a low degree of vertical and horizontal integration. The ability of an originator to appropriate the benefits arising from an innovation may be constrained, however, if the adoption and use of the innovation depend significantly on the capabilities of other firms, either at the same or different stages in the production process. When there are important appropriability problems (when the benefits flowing from an innovation are likely to elude the originator and fall into the pockets of others), increases in horizontal and vertical integration may therefore enhance the probability of both origination and adoption.

We have already canvassed the advantages of specialization for promoting innovation. Adam Smith believed that workers would become more alert to improvements as they concentrated on performing fewer activities. They would accordingly develop suitable capabilities to bring about change. By analogy, vertically specialized firms would also be expected to be more adept than integrated firms at isolating and solving problems through focused alertness and the development of specialized capabilities. Horizontal specialization could also foster innovation by increasing the number of competing units searching for solutions to a given problem. Whereas there would be only a few groups of problem solvers in an oligopolistic market and the number of firms in which innovations could be implemented and tested would be limited, competition among a large number of firms could generate significantly more ideas, increase the range of firms with appropriate capabilities, and provide more opportunities for trial and adoption. Furthermore, if firms were clustered and the mobility of personnel high, as in an industrial district, rapid exchanges of information would speed up the sorting process leading to the identification of the best solution.

However, this method of problem solving might be inappropriate for certain types of systemic innovation. When the innovation involves changes

132

that span stages of production or even industries, the same sort of concentration of activity that Smith praises could make it less likely that linkages would be discovered – that information would flow to where it is needed. As a result, specialization could retard recognition that an innovation produced for one purpose could serve other needs. Moreover, innovations adopted at one stage of a production chain could prove to be suboptimal for efficiency at other stages. Thus excessive specialization might hamper both the development and adoption of innovations. Development, for example, would appear less attractive if only a portion of a wide variety of potential uses were envisioned initially; and adoption would be less likely if potential users were unaware of innovations that were developed for other purposes but might be of use to them.

Such factors underlie the appropriability problems discussed by Teece (1986b) and Mitchell (1989, 1991). There are two essential sets of barriers that could keep the developer of an innovation from gaining a high enough share of the benefits to make development worthwhile. These barriers correspond to our two dimensions of coordination and ownership. The first, as we have just discussed, is imperfect information flows. When people are unaware either of the existence of suitable solutions for their problems or of problems that can be beneficially treated by particular solutions, then the payoff to, and incentive for, innovative activity will be reduced. The second set of barriers concern power relationships. Discoverers of a breakthrough who are not directly involved in the industry to which the innovation is to be applied may have very limited bargaining power because they cannot themselves bring about implementation. In order to gain any benefits, they may therefore be forced to sell or license the innovation at a small fraction of its ultimate value to the user if they are to gain any profits at all. Moreover, if imitation is easy – if patents or trade secrets do not effectively protect the innovator – an innovating firm may be at the mercy of competitor (or even supplier) firms who can enter quickly and take cheap advantage of the capabilities created at high cost by the innovator. To profit well from innovation in such circumstances, the innovator would have to own many of the assets complementary to the innovation.

Both of these kinds of obstacles point towards vertical integration as a means of speeding up the rate of innovation. Information impactedness can be reduced if the developer of an innovation and the user are in the same organization. Users – marketing or production teams – can make R&D experts (whether within their own organizations or elsewhere in the network) aware of specific commercial needs to which they should devote attention. Furthermore, if researchers in such a network come up with an unanticipated development, they can easily alert others in the extended organization who might be able to use it. This is related to what Cohen and Levinthal (1989; 1990) refer to as a firm's "absorptive capacity," and is in fact a reflection of a particular set of capabilities. When firms have a basic knowledge of a particular technology, they also have an enhanced ability to learn more about that technology in comparison to firms that are totally ignorant. Therefore, firms that develop a rudimentary set of capabilities concerning a technology also acquire a "capability to learn" still more. In the absence of coordination integration, potential benefits might be lost altogether or ceded to others. It is arguable, for instance, that the relative decline of many mature industries in Western economies in recent decades is in part the result of their stark separation from many industries, particularly in semiconductors, in which relevant innovations have been generated. In the more coordinated *keiretsu* system of Japan, however, the separation has been muted and manufacturers of mature products have had better access to the information and other capabilities needed for innovation.

Vertical integration can also redress adverse power relationships. Under joint ownership, the owners or their immediate delegees can reorganize capabilities because they have ultimate (though not necessarily day-to-day) control. When the same organization is both the developer and the user of an innovation, then, the benefits are internalized and appropriability is no longer a problem. Potential developers would not be deterred by the prospect of surrendering a high proportion of the payoff. But, as we noted earlier, this argument applies to ownership integration, not coordination integration, since in principle the innovator need only take financial positions in the complementary assets in order to benefit. How much coordination integration is necessary will depend on the pure information costs of informing and persuading those with *de facto* control over cooperating assets. Ownership integration itself does not guarantee enough coordination to solve the problem of information fragmentation, which could in principle be solved by a closely linked network that was not integrated in ownership.

Also of relevance here is Morris Silver's contention (1984) that innovating firms sometimes are forced to integrate forwards or backwards because they cannot find specialists who appreciate the full potential of the innovation and are willing to associate themselves with a new product. This may be either because suppliers literally cannot understand what the innovators need or because they do not believe that the innovation is commercially viable; in order to implement their ideas, innovators may have as a result to engage in tasks they would rather delegate to existing specialists through market mechanisms, as when Ford built prototypes of many of its machine tools.

Nevertheless, when there is integration forward from an intermediate stage of production, there are potential losses through restrictions in learning-by-using (von Hippel, 1976). Firms that are unable to tap the experience of diverse customers may be shut out from important information channels, thereby impeding their ability to innovate. For example, SKF,

134

the Swedish ball bearing producer, sold half of its shares in a captive steel producer in 1985 in order to make it possible for its one-time subsidiary to gain better access to important skills. Similarly, half a century earlier, in 1935, SKF sold Volvo in order, among other things, to gain the ability to interact with other car-producing customers, who could now dare to co-operate with SKF without fearing that confidential information would leak to Volvo (Lundgren 1990, p. 119).

NETWORKS AND ECONOMIC CHANGE

Bound up in the preceding discussion were two distinct characteristics of innovation that affect the appropriateness of organizational forms, namely, the systemic character of the innovation and its radicalness. These two factors often ride together, but in principle they are separable. Following Teece (1986), we can talk about an innovation as systemic if change in one part of the system (one stage of production, for example) necessitates corresponding change in other parts; by contrast, an innovation is auto-nomous if change in one part can proceed without materially affecting the rest of the system. The conventional view, which we have followed so far, is that decentralized networks of innovation do well under conditions of autonomous innovation but that systemic innovation calls for integration of both ownership and coordination in order to surmount adverse power relationships and avoid information impactedness. Moreover, one would typically think of systemic innovation as more "radical" than autonomous, since changing many parts of a system is clearly a relatively drastic procedure, whereas adjusting only a part seems to be necessarily an incremental business. But there is an often-forgotten sense in which autonomous innovation can be the most radical of all; or rather, in which the most radical of innovations is necessarily autonomous.

Consider an innovation that most would view as radical: the personal computer. This innovation required bringing together information from many diverse areas: semiconductors, programming, electronic assembly, etc. Yet this innovation was not the work of large vertically integrated firms whose capabilities spanned many disciplines. Rather, it was the work of small firms, whose early attempts to get the large organizations to take them seriously were persistently rebuffed. As we saw in Chapter 5, many large firms failed miserably in the business, and even the success of IBM came as the result of almost completely abandoning its internal capabilities in favor of those of the market.

Although the radicalness to which internal organization is adapted may be greater than that to which certain kinds of market-based networks are adapted, there is in the end a kind of radicalness (or newness or uncer-tainty) that large organizations do not handle well. For this type of uncertainty, a decentralized network does much better (Langlois and

135

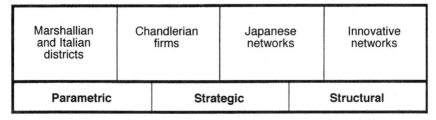

Marshallian and Italian districts	Chandlerian firms	Japanese networks	Innovative networks
Parametric		**Strategic**	**Structural**

Figure 7.3 Degree of radicalness of uncertainty

Everett 1992). But such a network may be very different from the kind of decentralized network adapted to slow or incremental change. Consider the following distinctions (see Figure 7.3). At one end of a spectrum we might think of parametric change, that is, change of certain known variables within a known framework.[139] For example, it may be highly uncertain which grade of cloth or which style of tile will be demanded this season, but it is well known to all what it means to produce a grade of cloth or a style of tile. For this kind of uncertainty, Marshallian and Third-Italian structures arguably work well. A more radical kind of uncertainty or change we might call strategic. This would typically involve rearranging capabilities in fairly drastic ways, but within known boundaries. Here a vertically integrated firm may have an advantage over a pure market network, for many of the reasons detailed above. Once the dynamic random-access memory chip became a known commodity, for instance, large Japanese (and, more recently, Korean) firms were able strategically to redirect capabilities into their mass production more decisively than less-integrated American firms. At the most radical extreme, however, is what we may call structural change. The personal computer may be an example. Here the ability of a decentralized Innovative Network to generate a wide diversity of information signals and to move rapidly may be an overwhelming advantage. Of course, as time passes, the same technology will change status, suggesting, as we develop more fully below, that the appropriateness of organizational structures varies over the product life cycle.[140]

INDUSTRY STRUCTURE AND THE SCOPE OF INNOVATION

If, as we have outlined, there is a tradeoff between the diversity of ideas that specialization and fragmentation may encourage, on the one hand, and the ease of implementation and internalization of returns permitted by vertical integration, on the other, then the choice of an appropriate industry structure will vary depending on the market forces operating within and upon the industry. These will be reflected primarily in the prevailing levels of transaction costs. When, for example, appropriability is not a problem, vertical specialization will be favored more strongly than when the originators are unlikely to capture the returns to an innovation themselves. The optimal degree of horizontal integration is also a function of specific influences surrounding an innovation, especially when development costs are beyond the resources of small firms.

Our discussion here concentrates on two factors that we consider to be particularly important. In this section, we investigate the ways in which the range of uses of an innovation – its scope – might influence the pattern of industrial structure that maximizes the benefits derived from the innovation. In the next section, we consider the effects of different product life-cycle patterns in the using industries on the adoption of an innovation.

Most innovations have a limited number of uses. This is true of much incremental change and also applies to significant innovations that are confined to one or a few industries. When the scope of an innovation is limited, the need for communication between developers and users is restricted to a narrow and easily definable group. In these circumstances, information exchange is especially easy when there are existing channels of communication, as in an industrial district in which suppliers and customers deal with each other regularly and have a good idea of their respective needs. Even without geographic clustering, established market mechanisms can work well when the scope of innovation is confined. For example, specialist machine manufacturers who supply a particular industry may have good national or international connections that allow them to provide information on new models to potential customers quickly and cheaply. Another channel for communication would be the trade press, which can pick up news on developments from diverse sources and supply it to other interested firms.

There are, however, limits to the ability of firms to use markets effectively. When there is product differentiation, the producing firms are relatively small, and the population of customers is diverse and geographically dispersed, as in the ceramic tile, clothing, or textile industries, information problems may be overwhelming because neither the firms nor their environment may have the capabilities needed to diffuse and interpret new knowledge. Under these circumstances, the costs of spreading and acquiring information about innovations might be beyond the resources of both suppliers and buyers. Institutional arrangements like those in the Third Italy can help to overcome the problem by creating *ad hoc* capabilities. Very few individual tile manufacturers have the resources to advertise their distinctive patterns worldwide, and very few tile distributors abroad have the time or money to visit the manufacturers to inform themselves on available styles. As the prosperity of the industry depends heavily on exports, one of the major functions of the producer cooperatives is to arrange with small

137

manufacturers to provide centralized exhibitions and organize participation in international trade fairs. As a result, quasi-horizontal integration – the producer cooperative – forms the basis of quasi-vertical integration, as the producers are able to add marketing expertise to their distinctive competences in design (Best 1990; Porter 1990).[141]

When an innovation has a wide scope of uses, small firms operating in established channels may be less successful at communicating their discoveries because the problem of gaining credibility expands as the developer needs to attract attention among firms in unfamiliar sectors. Potential users may also experience difficulties in locating innovations from diverse sources if the initial applications are in different industries. Thus there is likely to be a shortage of appropriate information-based capabilities on the part of both the source of an innovation and the potential users.

Major economy-wide changes like electrification or the use of semiconductors or railroads are extremely rare, but innovation across several industries occurs frequently. If discoveries are made by specialists, in line with the Smithian model, the developers may have neither knowledge of nor interest in applications in other industries. In other words, the very institutional framework that encourages the innovation in the first place can also retard its spread. Inventors with a wider perspective, however, who set out from the beginning to make discoveries with broad applicability, may not have the contacts with users required to gain adoption in any single industry, let alone in a variety of sectors.

These and similar institutional complications may account for the relatively slow spread of discoveries across industries. It took several decades, for example, for the diffusion of electricity for domestic, industrial, and traction purposes (Hughes 1983), and the spread of applications of electronic components is still gaining pace more than four decades after the invention of the transistor. The search for suitable institutions is again important because, the longer the time period involved in diffusion, the more difficult it becomes for the initial developers of an innovation to appropriate the gains.[142] As we discussed in Chapter 6, if the gains are uncertain, this may mean not only a disincentive to development in the first place, but also a loss to the country of development if the innovation is captured to a degree by foreign producers who recognize uses that were not apparent to potential users in the country of development. When the eventual adoption by foreigners is significantly greater than in the country of origin, even the original core industry may migrate internationally.

INNOVATION AND THE PRODUCT LIFE CYCLE

The choice of suitable forms of internal and external organization to promote innovation and capture the resultant gains depends as well on the product life cycles (PLCs) of industries that might adopt or be affected by the innovation. It is well known that uncertainty varies over the stages of the PLC, in general reducing as the product progresses from the introductory stage to maturity. Uncertainty can again increase in mature industries, however, if the impact of an innovation is so high that it greatly affects the nature of the product or the production process. The choice of an appropriate structure will therefore depend on which stages of the PLC the source and user industries are at.

When an innovation is adopted by an industry that is in the introductory and growth phases of the PLC, the degree of uncertainty in both the source and user industries is very high. There are unlikely to be established channels of communication that the firms in the source industry can tap because the nature of the user industry is amorphous, with a high turnover of firms and lack of knowledge as to the nature of the users' products until a standard variation is finally decided upon by users. In such cases, it is very difficult to economize on information costs for both the user and the source because the necessary information might be coming from many directions at once.

Coordination integration is unsuitable in such an environment because it increases "certainty" within an organization (a firm or closely articulated network) by artificially reducing the number of sources of information that are treated as credible. Innovations from external or non-accredited sources tend to be ignored or downgraded when there is coordination integration. When the flow of innovative ideas is high and the form of the user product in flux, it is crucial to be able to tap as many options as possible.

This implies the use of an Innovative Network, or "network of networks," that allows rapid exchanges in which both the source and user firms draw on the widest range of information available, consistent with a reasonable cost of collection and processing. A major characteristic of Innovative Networks is that they have both well-developed information capabilities and low transaction costs. The performance of such Innovative Networks is enhanced if they can draw on various types of clearing-house activities provided by trade associations and similar groups. Government organizations such as MITI in Japan can also perform generalized information services.

When the user industry is mature and the innovation is largely autonomous in that it does not require drastic changes to the product or the production process, then a Marshallian or Third-Italian type of network would be most appropriate. These minor, or parametric, changes do not justify the cost involved in establishing elaborate information capabilities, and coordination integration is also unnecessary because the cost to the would-be users is very low if they are not among the first to learn about a particular innovation.

Change along the product life cycle, however, is not necessarily unidirectional (Moenaert, *et al.* 1990). The most interesting case in many ways (and one that receives much attention from Lazonick, Florida and Kenney, and Porter) occurs when an innovation has a systemic impact on a mature product that, as a consequence, requires substantial revamping of other aspects of that product or its manufacturing process. When this occurs, as we saw in Chapter 5 (Figure 5.6), the path of the user industry is deflected from the usual S-curve of the PLC into either Mature Uncertainty or Mature Growth. In both cases, the mature user is returned to a stage of higher uncertainty similar to that in the growth stage of the PLC.[143]

Examples of these structural or strategic changes range from the incorporation of microcomponents into existing types of machinery to the adoption of just-in-time manufacturing methods. Because such an innovation requires a total rethinking of the nature of the product and/or the manufacturing process, users must have a detailed knowledge of the technology of the innovation and of the varieties available. This can best be achieved through substantial coordination integration that allows for synergy as provided by a vertically integrated Chandlerian firm or a Japanese network, because these are the forms of organization that (for a price) give users access to detailed information *that they can blend with their existing capabilities* at levels commensurate with the high importance of their requirements.

The choice between Chandlerian or Japanese network organizations will, in turn, be a function of the degree of maturity and hence of the extent of uncertainty prevailing in the industry supplying the innovation. If the supplying industry is in the early growth stage of the PLC and uncertainty concerning the nature of the innovation itself is high, the Japanese network solution is probably more appropriate because it permits the user of the innovation to collect information on a broader range of options. But when the innovation is near the end of the growth phase and the number of viable options has been narrowed, the Chandlerian solution is more suitable because the user firm does not need to spread its information net as widely and can therefore put more emphasis on coordination integration to make sure that the innovation is incorporated efficiently into the user product.

In either the Japanese network or Chandlerian case, however, the benefits of the innovation, as employed in that user industry, are likely to be appropriated by the user. This is because the other capabilities associated with the product are going to be held closely by the user firms which are already established. These user capabilities are particularly important in established oligopolies and include patents relevant to other aspects of the product or process, marketing skills, and the production of complementary products (Mitchell 1989 and 1991).[144]

The distinction between mature and innovative user industries is illustrated by the effects of the adoption of semiconductors on the consumer appliance and computer industries. Recent major changes in refrigerator technology, for example, have significantly increased the reliance of manufacturers on external capabilities. Whereas refrigerator firms previously had internal knowledge of all important aspects of their product, they must now conduct outside searches to obtain information on essential new technologies (Granstrand *et al.*, 1992). Similarly, Florida and Kenney (1990a) cite the decay of the mature consumer electronics industry as a major problem for American semiconductor manufacturers. In Japan, semiconductor researchers can work together with producers of washing machines and other white goods in environments with a high degree of coordination integration to find new uses for chips, as well as ways of introducing improvements into the appliances. In the U.S., however, opportunities are lost for semiconductor applications because developers and users are separated, resulting in lost efficiency to both groups.[145] Note that the problem for U.S. white goods firms in this case is not necessarily an *absence* of networks of external capabilities, but rather institutional difficulties in tapping into networks that are oriented in other directions.

By contrast, there have been significant reciprocal advantages for parts of the U.S. semiconductor industry, particularly microprocessors, and producers in such areas as microcomputers, work stations, and other computer-based systems (Langlois *et al.* 1988). In the latter case, both the source and user industries are growing rapidly and face considerable uncertainty. Thus the Innovative Network in Silicon Valley is well adapted to their needs (Saxenian 1991). Conversely, the more centralized organizational arrangements in Japan have contributed to the relative lack of success by Japanese firms in microprocessors and computers (*The Economist* 1992; Zachary and Yoder 1993).

CONCLUSION

The primary message that flows from our analysis is that the context of innovation is complex and varied. This may seem a mundane assertion – until one notices that many if not most of the leading theorists and commentators on industrial competitiveness have implied otherwise.

When there is innovation, firms may choose either to develop new capabilities internally or to purchase them on the market. This depends in turn on a firm's internal capabilities, the range and quality of capabilities available through purchase, and the relative production and transaction costs of the various options. The most efficient relationship between source and user firms also depends on, *inter alia*, the prior existence of information networks, the scope of the innovation, its impact on various user industries, the presence or absence of economies of scale, and the stages of the product life cycle reached by both the innovating product and any product into which it might be incorporated. It seems, therefore, that no single government policy designed to facilitate change in one or another of these environments will be suitable for all. In fact, the number of permutations and combinations of efficient relationships is so large that it is improbable that any policy, or even group of policies, would be suitable for more than a small fraction of a nation's industries. Attempts to implement broadbrush policies may therefore be destructive because they can upset useful forms of organization in industries that are relatively unaffected by a particular innovation. For example, even if one accepts the contention of Piore and Sabel and Best that small firms operating in networks are more likely than other types of firms to be innovative and conducive to flexible specialization in the future, most modern industrial economies are still highly dependent on industries with significant economies of scale whose existing capabilities, and therefore their ability to serve the public, would be severely damaged if they were to be broken up in a search for faster rates of change.

On the other hand, the wide assortment of useful forms of organization that we have discussed also casts doubt on the wisdom of antitrust laws and other broad policies that prohibit firms from freely entering into relationships that allow them to operate more efficiently and effectively. If coordinated networks like those in the Third Italy or Japan are needed to encourage and diffuse innovation, attempts to ban them can cause significant harm (Bower and Rhenman 1985; *Business Week International* 1992).

Overall, then, the most acceptable view of those surveyed here is Porter's. Government policy should be facilitating rather than narrow and prescriptive in that it should offer scope for firms to develop the organizational forms that are best adapted to their particular environments. This requires the provision of infrastructure and whatever institutions are needed to prevent anti-social activities and to channel rent-seeking behavior in productive directions; but it also entails self-discipline on the part of legislators and bureaucrats to resist the temptation to second guess firms and enforce overarching strategies.

8

CONCLUSION

In this book, we have concentrated on the ways in which two important sets of institutions – firms and markets – affect and are affected by economic change. Our primary concern has been to show how the boundary between firms and markets shifts over time depending on changes in their respective environments. Of particular importance in locating this boundary are relative production and transaction costs, which in turn are largely functions of knowledge. Firms possess groups of capabilities, which allow them to undertake activities efficiently. In many cases, capabilities that are bound together institutionally, as in a firm, are synergistic in the sense that they can accomplish more when combined than the individual capabilities can when used separately. Moreover, some capabilities are imitable while others are not, and some capabilities are contestable while others are idiosyncratic.

Firms are composed of an intrinsic core of idiosyncratic and synergistic capabilities that by definition cannot be duplicated, together with such ancillary capabilities as can be supplied more cheaply internally than they can be purchased externally through market transactions. But, since both idiosyncratic capabilities and transaction costs are often based on localized knowledge, we can expect that both may become less relevant as time passes and other institutions have opportunities to acquire the necessary learning. As this occurs, the boundary between firm and market may change as ancillary functions that were internalized are either spun off into separate firms or discontinued because it is now cheaper to buy them from external suppliers. But supply-side factors are not the only important element; on the demand side consumers also help to determine boundaries by expressing their preferences as to the nature of the product. Especially when there are differential rates of change among components or a wide variety of consumer tastes, goods may be produced as modules rather than as entities to allow consumers to obtain the individual bundles of characteristics that they desire most.

Finally, because capabilities and their associated routines generate institutional rigidities, it is possible that existing institutions – including market-based relationships as well as firms – may not be able to adjust satisfactorily to significant environmental shifts such as technological change. As a result, important changes in the environment can lead to shifts in the dominant institutions in particular industries or in the economy as a whole as firms or buyer–supplier relationships based on outdated capabilities are overtaken by other institutional arrangements whose deployment of capabilities is better suited to the changed conditions.

We have emphasized ownership and coordination as the two dimensions of control that best illustrate the effects of different distributions of capabilities in the economy on firm–market relationships. Ownership control allows a firm to appropriate the benefits arising from a particular set of capabilities, but this may not require the exercise of coordination control. Similarly, coordination of assets, and of capabilities, must be based on cooperation, but this does not imply common ownership.

The model that we have generated from these principles is deliberately pluralistic. Our contention, which accords with observed reality, is that many different ways of combining capabilities may be appropriate depending on the environment under consideration. This does not suggest randomness, however, since the choice of relevant institutions depends on the prevailing patterns of knowledge and cost. Moreover, path dependency narrows the range of institutions available in given circumstances. Thus as circumstances evolve, we can expect that the institutional framework will also change, but in ways that are responsive to the needs of the new environment[146] and that derive from existing institutional arrangements of capabilities.

THE ROLE OF LARGE FIRMS IN ECONOMIC GROWTH

Another way of explaining our position is by comparing it with those of Alfred D. Chandler, Jr. and William Lazonick, two recent writers whose ideas we have already met and which are in many respects similar to our own.

Chandler's analyses of corporate development in the United States, Britain, and Germany (1962, 1977, 1990) stress the importance of coordination control.[147] In the U.S., ownership control did not lead to greater efficiency until coordination control was implemented, while in Germany a high degree of coordination control within individual firms was combined with cartelization to bring efficiency. In Britain, however, ownership control in the absence of managerial coordination was insufficient to realize the full potential of modern technology.

The development of industry in the United States between 1870 and 1930 provides the exemplar of Chandler's argument (1977, 1990). Before the Civil War, markets in the U.S. were localized because the vastness of the country imposed high transport costs. As a consequence, manufacturing firms were small and not in a position to take full advantage of possible economies of scale. By the 1870s, however, the spread of the telegraph and railroads improved communications and lowered transport costs greatly. In the same period, improved technologies in many industries led to significant increases in economies of scale. Initially, firms merged into holding companies, but these often did not allow them to benefit from scale economies because production remained fragmented in outdated factories and the firms lacked strong central control. It was only when the "visible hand" of managers, many of whom were salaried experts, was imposed that the consolidation of businesses through horizontal integration resulted in modernization and rationalization.

In many respects, the new organizations resembled the bureaucracies described by Max Weber (1948, 1971). Traditional family leaders, whose positions were based on ownership, were increasingly replaced by salaried experts who managed "rationally," *i.e.*, by administering set rules designed to cover common situations and reduce risk. Although Chandler attributes success to investment in "manufacturing, marketing, and management," it is clear that the last is at the heart of his analysis. "At the core of this dynamic [of economic growth]," he writes, "were the organizational capabilities of the enterprise as a unified whole."

> [O]nly if these facilities and skills [of manufacturing and research] were carefully coordinated and integrated could the enterprise achieve the economies of scale and scope that were needed to compete in national and international markets and continue to grow. Thus even more important to the maintenance of market share than the capabilities of the lower-level managers in charge of the operating units were those of the middle managers responsible for the performance of the lower-level executives. These middle managers not only had to develop and apply functional-specific and product-specific managerial skills, but they also had to train and motivate lower-level managers and to coordinate, integrate, and evaluate their work. And most critical to the long-term health and growth of the industrial enterprise were the abilities of the senior executives – the top operating managers and those in the corporate office – who recruited and motivated the middle managers, defined and allocated their responsibilities, and monitored and coordinated their activities, and who, in addition, planned and allocated the resources for the enterprise as a whole.
>
> (Chandler 1990, p. 594)

Rationalization and risk aversion took other forms as well, including the reduction of excess capacity through the closing of obsolete factories. Most important was the vertical integration that large firms undertook to guarantee flows of inputs and the efficient marketing of outputs. As large investments in fixed capital called for insurance against unreliable suppliers and fickle merchants and customers, firms frequently found it desirable to reduce risk by generating their own inputs and providing for the whole-saling, and even retailing, of their production. Chandler believes that, in contrast to horizontal integration, which was undertaken for offensive purposes, most vertical integration was defensive. Both types were needed, however, to create an environment in which managers could make efficient use of the new and expensive technologies of mass production.

Chandler's argument is explicitly historical. Although he maintains that developments between the end of the Second World War and the 1970s confirm the important role played by management in the success of large firms, he makes only tentative attempts to project his model into the future (1990, pp. 605–628). Furthermore, Chandler recognizes that only some industries were affected by giantism and that small firms continued to operate efficiently in many sectors of the economy (1977, pp. 372–376).[148] But the most significant aspect of Chandler's empirical work is that it is based very heavily on the histories of firms that were operating in sectors that had already matured to a substantial degree and in which further change was incremental rather than fundamental or systemic. For example, *Scale and Scope* (1990) describes the development of the 200 largest firms in the United States, the United Kingdom, and Germany. For the most part, these firms dominated industries in which the basic patterns of product and process technology were already settled and the task of management was to foster and nurture capabilities that were consistent with mass production. When firms in newer industries such as Xerox enter the discussion after 1945, they had already joined the top 200 in their respective countries and made the necessary investments in manufacturing, marketing, and management. Chandler's work has little if anything to say about the environment of innovative firms at the technological frontier because they are beyond the scope of his analysis. Therefore, although he provides a shrewd and balanced account of the behavior of large mature firms, there is no way in which Chandler's work can be regarded as an analysis of the dynamics of industrial capitalism as a whole.

William Lazonick (1990, 1991a),[149] however, has used Chandler as one of the main props for his contention that technological change in general is most likely to be fostered and implemented by very large, centrally managed firms. As a believer in growth and innovation as the keys to economic development, Lazonick has accepted Schumpeter's contention that a positive, indeed a central, role is played by those who disturb equilibria by introducing important technological or organizational changes that upset existing economic practices. But such innovations do not take full effect instantaneously. They take time to mature for various reasons that include the need for learning on the part of innovating organizations, difficulties in convincing people of the value of new arrangements, and resistance from entrenched interests that could be adversely affected by

146

change and therefore feel threatened by the prospect of a Schumpeterian "gale of creative destruction."

The sort of ideal firm that Lazonick envisages is far from a textbook capitalist enterprise even though it operates for profit, buys at least some of its inputs in factor markets, and sells at least part of its output in goods markets. What Lazonick does in effect is to turn some of the characteristics that John Kenneth Galbraith deplores in *The New Industrial State* (1972) into virtues. Large capitalist firms do not have to cultivate a disregard for the public interest, as Galbraith would have it, if they are to defend their enormous investments in plant and equipment. For Lazonick, such firms are (or at least ought to be) public trusts, run by professional managers whose purpose is to represent the interests of all the stakeholders by supplying efficient coordination. If this is done properly, then it is possible to divide the firm's surplus among workers, owners, investment in innovative products, and the managers themselves. All groups benefit because proper management of the workforce elicits enough effort to permit innovation and growth to proceed within individual firms and across the economy as a whole. Lazonick is therefore highly critical of practices such as management buy-outs[150] because he sees owner/managers as potential disasters who will distribute an unsatisfactorily high share of a firm's surplus to their private purses at the expense of workers, capital investment and, ultimately, the economy in general (1992a).

CONVERGENCE AND DIVERGENCE IN ECONOMIC DEVELOPMENT

Lazonick's argument offers a clear scenario that complements Chandler's analysis and is plausible in many respects. Whereas the Chandlerian manager is primarily responsible for controlling assets, in Lazonick's work there is more emphasis on labor management and shop floor practices. Moreover, in contrast to Chandler, Lazonick constructs a more detailed case for the importance of large firms in promoting change. Lazonick's target is not small firms as such, but the efficiency of market transactions in general.

Lazonick's reasons for believing that organizations are superior to markets are cognitive and behavioral as well as economic. In a cognitive sense, organizations are superior to markets because organizations devoted to specific purposes can more easily direct information where it is needed than can firms operating blindly in response to market signals that they may or may not receive or be in a position to interpret correctly. Thus vertical integration can reduce search costs for information on innovations and increase the chance that messages will be delivered where needed. Behaviorally, organizations are also better than markets because they can order people to do whatever is necessary to implement innovation – assuming, of course, that the organization also takes the steps necessary to elicit

147

sufficient effort from the workforce. "The superior development and utilization of productive resources," he writes early on, "increasingly requires that business organizations have privileged access to productive resources. Inherent in such privileged access is the supersession of market coordination to some degree. The shift from market coordination to planned coordination within business organizations has become an increasingly central characteristic of a successful capitalist economy" (1991a, p. 8). The larger and more varied an organization is, the better the chance it will have of being in a position to coordinate diverse information and other resources.

In many respects, Lazonick offers a process-based account of innovation and firm development that is similar to the story that we are telling. The crucial difference, however, is that Lazonick (like Chandler and the neo-classicists) has constructed a system that emphasizes *convergence* (Figure 8.1). For him, uncertainty is capable of being tamed, or at least subdued, and one of the roles of firms as organizations is to control all aspects of innovation – including research and development – from the outset in order to acquire "privileged access" to knowledge that allows a firm to gain a competitive edge over others. As a result, any contest is likely to be won by firms that from the beginning are able to bring together the resources necessary to exploit an innovation. As this often requires the collation of a wide variety of types of knowledge and other inputs, the Lazonian firm is not only vertically integrated but diversified, and economic development leads to dominance by a small number of conglomerates that are self-perpetuating

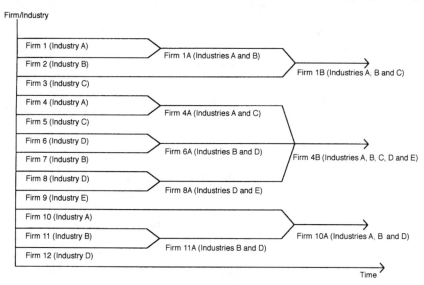

Figure 8.1 The evolution of converging firms

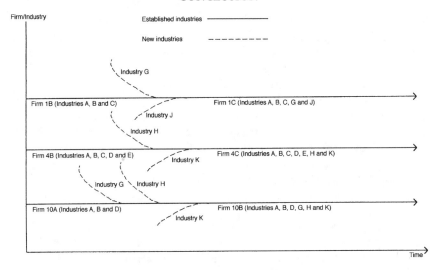

Figure 8.2 Innovation and the diversification of converging firms

because their very diversity gives them a better chance than smaller firms of being able to master future innovations (Figure 8.2).

We, however, believe not only that uncertainty is inevitable in innovative environments but that it may frequently be harmful to the economy to attempt to control uncertainty by encouraging firms to internalize change and thereby prematurely forestall the choice of variants in the early stages of product and process life cycles. The actual generation of innovative concepts under conditions of extreme uncertainty, in which product and process technologies are still evolving and the nature and size of markets have yet to be determined, may well be conducted most efficiently by large numbers of teams working independently and producing a rapid stream of ideas for the market to test. Independence does not mean isolation, however, and development may be enhanced by geographic concentrations of firms working on similar problems as in Silicon Valley. These variations on Marshallian industrial districts[151] can duplicate many of the advantages arising from more formal types of cooperation, including the provision of advanced training networks, while still retaining multiple channels of inspiration.

Our story, therefore, is one of alternating divergence and convergence (Figure 3.8).[152] An initial idea may be elaborated upon by numerous competitors, all of which are vying for public favor. Furthermore, knowledge and capabilities are unevenly spread throughout the economy. Depending on its own capabilities relative to those of others, a particular firm may decide that combined production and transaction costs for any given input justify either internalization or outsourcing. The supremacy of

Chandlerian firms in a given industry only comes after the rate of innovation has slowed significantly and a dominant variation of a product has been given the imprimatur of the public. But as time passes, capabilities may be expected to spread and transaction costs to decrease. In addition, innovation from outside an industry may lead to the generation of new capabilities that are more efficient than those of established firms. As a result, Chandlerian firms may experience a degree of vertical disintegration and, in extreme cases, particular firms may even become extinct as leadership passes to new firms with superior capabilities. For the economy as a whole, development proceeds not within an existing organizational mold, but by periodically shattering that mold as innovation generates new capabilities possessed by different organizations and breaks down relative cost relationships among firms (Figure 3.9).

Our story is therefore more general than Lazonick's because it incorporates the Chandlerian firm but in a framework that explicitly allows for more variation and is more true to the Schumpeterian vision of innovation and creative destruction.

This does not mean, of course, that large, centralized firms might not offer some advantages, especially in the implementation of new technologies. Large firms have a better chance than smaller ones of appropriating the benefits arising from innovation because they can often supply internally the complementary inputs required to produce and market new products successfully. Furthermore, systemic change tends to proceed by analogy. After having been developed for one purpose, innovations may then be applied to a very wide range of uses that were never envisaged, let alone intended, by their originators. This has occurred with steam power, electrification, and more recently with semiconductors (David, 1991b). Large and diverse organizations may be able to accelerate the spread of change by making faster connections between an innovation and its various uses than would occur in a network of smaller, less diversified firms that pick up their information through undirected market channels.

But as we have made clear, large and centralized firms are only one of several forms of organization that may speed innovation and growth. Depending on the nature of the problem under consideration, the stage of the product life cycle, the availability of external information channels and many other factors, small, independent firms operating in industrial districts, more formal networks as in the "Third Italy," joint ventures, or other organizational arrangements may also be the most efficient ways of generating innovation and growth. This is a message that is as important to governments when formulating industry policies as it is to individual private-sector producers.

NOTES

1 INTRODUCTION

1 Williamson (1975, p. xi) has long maintained that he takes the transaction as the fundamental unit of analysis. At the most abstract level, however, the New Institutional Economics takes rules and conventions as its building blocks. Thus, to develop a theory of business institutions based on the idea of productive routines is more in keeping with the larger New Institutional edifice.

2 Nicolai Juul Foss (1994) has recently described our work as representative of the "post-Marshallian" tradition typified by Richardson. We gladly accept this categorization. On the other hand, the term "neo-Schumpeterian," as used, for example, by Magnusson (1994), might be just as appropriate.

3 On the functionalist character of this kind of explanation, see Langlois (1984, 1986b).

4 For an argument that Schumpeter was attacking the neoclassical conception of competition rather than defending "monopoly" in the neoclassical sense, see Langlois (1987).

5 This usage follows Teece (1986b). The opposite of a systemic innovation is an *autonomous* one, in which change can proceed in one stage of production without requiring coordination with other stages.

6 More generally, dynamic transaction costs – or, more generally still, dynamic *governance* costs – are the costs of not having the capabilities you need when you need them (see Chapter 3).

7 In many of these cases, the non-price attributes of the products may initially have deteriorated in consumer eyes as mass-produced items were substituted for particularized or hand-made ones. But any such disadvantage was, of course, rapidly outweighed by reductions in product price.

8 To borrow a phrase from Schumpeter (1950, p. 83).

2 CAPABILITIES, STRATEGY AND THE FIRM

9 See especially Kirzner (1976).

10 Most practitioners of the specialty called Industrial Organization would no doubt bristle at the suggestion that their theory is inappropriate for the study of the relationship between firms and markets. And it is certainly true that the "appreciative" theories (Nelson and Winter 1982, p. 46) that many IO economists embrace have been far more flexible and adaptable to the concerns of

firms in practice than has the underlying formal theory. Nonetheless, it is the formal theory that is our concern here.

11 We borrow this phrase from Alfred Chandler (1992). Chandler uses this phrase to distinguish his approach from that of Williamson (1985), who takes the "transaction" as the unit of analysis. What Chandler really seems to mean is that the firm is his object of analysis – his ending point rather than his starting point. But he also seems to mean by it that he studies the operation of firms rather than the operation of transactions. Of course, to take the "firm as unit of analysis" in the methodological sense would make it impossible to study the issue of the boundaries of the firm, since it would require one to explain what are one's premises. This is a problem for neoclassical theory, but not, we think, for Chandler.

12 As is now well understood, however, the conception of the firm in the modern neoclassical literature of industrial organization is not Marshall's (Loasby 1976; Moss 1984). Marshall did not *start* with a "representative firm" and then aggregate to the industry. Rather, he started with the industry, which he conceived of in terms of population ecology. He then worked down to the level of the firm by constructing a pseudo-firm (the true "representative firm") that corresponds to no actual firm but that reflects the average characteristics of the population. Had followers of Marshall like Sraffa, Pigou, Robinson, and Chamberlin understood (or, at any rate, adopted) Marshall's conception, the entire controversy over monopoly and increasing returns (Sraffa 1926) might have been avoided. Modern IO theory takes its lead not from Marshall but from the gang of four just mentioned, whose conception of the firm also nicely dovetails with that of Cournot (1838), moving the late G. L. S. Shackle (1967, p. 70) to remark on the "sense in which [competition] theory during a precise century from 1838 had been traveling in a circle."

13 For a survey of various theories of "firm coherence," see Teece, Rumelt, Dosi, and Winter (1994).

14 For example, Williamson (1985).

15 Powell (1990, pp. 296–300) suggests that the notion that there is a "continuum" of organizational forms ranging from markets through networks to vertically integrated firms is both inaccurate and analytically unhelpful. We feel that there are systematic relationships between organizational forms and various exogenous and endogenous conditions that one can usefully represent as spectra. We do concede, however, that the order in which the organizational forms appear along a given spectrum may vary depending on which other factors are under consideration.

16 For a similar, but not identical, distinction, see Chi (1994).

17 Gilson and Roe (1993) apply a similar perspective to Japanese firms by arguing that the *keiretsu* form has been chosen as an efficient way of producing goods and services as well as being an efficient form of corporate governance.

18 Mahoney and Pandian actually refer to "idiosyncratic bilateral synergy," which they define as "the enhanced value that is idiosyncratic to the combined resources of the acquiring and target firms" (1992, p. 368). It is consistent with the remainder of their discussion, however, to alter the term to refer to the combination of any number of resources that are already under common ownership.

19 Teece (1986b) discusses "cospecialized" assets, which are the same as assets bound by contestable synergy. To use his example, the innovation of containerized cargo required the coordination of both containerized ships and specialized equipment. However, cospecialization (which resembles Richardson's

(1972) concept of "close complementarity") does not require idiosyncrasy, and cospecialized assets may therefore belong to separate organizations and be obtained on the market. Indeed, if individual container ships and port facilities were idiosyncratically related to each other, both would lose their value. Similarly, "core competences" (Prahalad and Hamel 1990) belong to a firm's core in the sense that they provide a competitive advantage because the firm performs these activities better than other firms do, but they may be contestable and therefore not part of the core as we define it here.

20 Recent important contributions on resource-based strategy include Barney (1991), Conner (1991), and Peteraf (1993).

21 Thus John Kay's (1993) attempt to mix capabilities and simple game theory in analyzing strategy is misleading since his games presuppose that the players possess identical capabilities, while he encourages firms to differentiate themselves by developing idiosyncratic capabilities or distinctive competences.

22 See Chapter 3 for examples of firm behavior when the market cannot or will not supply items that one could normally purchase.

23 For a discussion of these terms, see Langlois (1984). The choice of terminology is roughly comparable to the familiar terms Knightian (or "genuine") uncertainty and risk. But the rampant confusion about the meaning of these terms in Knight (on which see Langlois and Cosgel 1993) justifies the neologism.

3 A DYNAMIC THEORY OF THE BOUNDARIES OF THE FIRM

24 Actually, he proposes *two* hypotheses in this article. The second – perhaps equally well-known – hypothesis is that taxes and other government-induced distortions of market prices account for much vertical integration.

25 Babbage (1963) considerably extended Smith's observations on the division of labor. In particular, he noted that by dividing tasks minutely, employers could more easily match skill levels to the difficulty of particular tasks and thereby avoid having to use highly paid persons to perform simple jobs.

26 David Teece (1986a) defines an innovation as *autonomous* if it affects only one stage in a chain of production and *systemic* if the innovation requires the coordination of production across more than one stage.

27 A complicating issue, of course, is the existence of cospecialized activities elsewhere in the system that militate in favor of standardization: the need for replacement parts, for example, or for irreversible human-capital investments by users. This will be covered in more detail further on in our story.

28 As the tasks undertaken by a single laborer become increasingly narrow and specialized, the term artisan may no longer be merited.

29 For more on the inertia that may impede innovation, see Chapter 6 below.

30 For an example of extreme industrial diversity, see T. S. Ashton's classic study, *An Eighteenth-Century Industrialist: Peter Stubs of Warrington, 1756–1806* (1939).

31 And, as Nathan Rosenberg (1976, p. 125) has argued, such bottleneck stages are the most likely targets for innovation. See also Thomas P. Hughes (1992).

32 The methodological issues surrounding this assertion are in fact somewhat complex. For an introduction, see Langlois (1984, 1986b).

33 The phrase "real time" is inspired by O'Driscoll and Rizzo (1985).

34 This conception of the long run is similar to what Schumpeter (1934) called "the circular flow of economic life."

35 A point Barzel notes (1987, p. 105n).

36 For another version of this argument, see Langlois (1984). That article argues that transaction costs are ultimately the product of radical or "structural" uncertainty. We will deal with related ideas below.

37 A term due to Alchian and Woodward (1988).

38 This figure is inspired by, but modified from, Silver (1984, p. 44).

39 Such a diagram captures what Coase meant when he wrote that "a firm will tend to expand until the costs of organizing an extra transaction within the firm become equal to the costs of carrying out the same transaction by means of an exchange in the open market or the costs of organizing in another firm" (Coase 1937, p. 395).

40 This is not to say, of course, that the long run favors internal organization. Since, as we will see, the benefits of internal management lie largely in the superior flexibility (of a specific kind) such management offers, we might well expect the *benefits* of internal management to decline faster than the costs in the long run, since flexibility becomes less important in a world of routine.

41 For a discussion of the cost of licensing that is somewhat in the spirit of the present essay, see Caves, Crookell, and Killing (1983).

42 Nevertheless, this is a proposition that is by no means true in all cases. As we will see in Chapter 5, there are circumstances in which vertical disintegration is superior in the face of certain kinds of economic change. In this chapter we concentrate on the circumstances that make vertical integration a less costly institutional structure.

43 We might trace this observation back as far as Frank Knight (1921, p. 268).

44 For example, Fenoaltea (1976, pp. 147–148) and Dahlman (1980, pp. 175, 178) have suggested that the flexibility of unified ownership explains the transition to enclosures from the open-field system in England. Since they did not require a community consensus to experiment with new agricultural forms, enclosed farms gained favor when growth in the extent of the market made such experimentation desirable.

45 For an argument that this was ultimately Frank Knight's theory of the firm, see Langlois and Cosgel (1993). One could also make an argument that this was in the end Coase's theory as well. Consider the following passage.

It may be desired to make a long-term contract for the supply of some article or service . . . Now, owing to the difficulty of forecasting, the longer the period of the contract is for the supply of the commodity or service, the less possible, and indeed, the less desirable it is for the person purchasing to specify what the other contracting party is expected to do. It may well be a matter of indifference to the person supplying the service or commodity which of several courses of action is taken, but not to the purchaser of that commodity or service. But the purchaser will not know which of these several courses he will want the supplier to take. Therefore, the service which is being provided is expressed in general terms, the exact details being left until a later date. . . . The detail of what the supplier is expected to do is not stated in the contract but is decided later by the purchaser. When the direction of resources (within the limits of the contract) becomes dependent on the buyer in this way, that relationship which I term a 'firm' may be obtained.

(Coase 1937, pp. 391–392).

46 Brian Loasby (1976, 1991) has also suggested that the rationale of the firm lies in its ability to deal with structural, rather than merely parametric, uncertainty.

Like the institution of money, the institution of the firm can provide a "reserve" against unforeseen contingencies.

47 In fact, however, Smith also saw the division of labor as leading to systemic innovations:

All the improvements in machinery, however, have by no means been the inventions of those who had occasion to use the machines. Many improvements have been made by the ingenuity of the makers of the machines, when to make them became the business of a peculiar trade; and some by that of those who are called philosophers or men of speculation, whose trade it is, not to do any thing, but to observe every thing; and who, upon that account, are often capable of combining together the powers of the most distant and dissimilar objects.

(I.i.9, p. 21)

More on this below.

48 An early version of the argument is by Marvin Frankel (1955). (See also Gordon (1956) and Frankel (1956).) The idea has more recently found a champion in William Lazonick (1981: Elbaum and Lazonick 1986). Such notables as Sir Arthur Lewis (1957, pp. 583–584) and Charles Kindleberger (1969, pp. 146–147) have also pointed to vertical fragmentation as a cause of British industrial decline.

49 On this point, see Hirshleifer (1971) and Casson (1982, pp. 206–208).

50 The observation that problems associated with appropriability could affect innovation is, of course, not new. Patenting, in particular, has long received attention, but writers as early as Babbage, in 1835, noted difficulties in dividing the proceeds from an innovation (Babbage 1963, pp. 256–257, 360–361). See also, Rosenberg (1994, p. 36).

51 The notion of bottlenecks as a motive for vertical integration was first suggested by Adelman (1955). In a rapidly growing industry, he argued, suppliers of intermediate goods may not be able to expand quickly enough to meet the needs of the producer of final goods, thus motivating that producer to integrate backwards. Adelman also hinted at many of the effects we will discuss presently, including informational difficulties and potential hold-up problems.

52 Of course, it is also possible that the outcome may be the development of two vertically integrated firms if the second firm to use the capability decides to develop its own internal capacity because the transaction costs of purchasing from outsiders outweigh the costs of duplicating the capability.

53 The effects of technological change on an existing environment are discussed in Saviotti and Metcalfe (1991) and Dosi and Metcalfe (1991).

4 VERTICAL INTEGRATION IN THE EARLY AMERICAN AUTOMOBILE INDUSTRY

54 Among the authors we might cite are Klein, Crawford, and Alchian (1978); Abernathy (1978); Monteverde and Teece (1982a, 1982b); Klein (1988).

55 One typical account that underscores this point is Alfred P. Sloan's experience with the Hyatt Roller Bearing Company. See Sloan (1941).

56 Studebaker, for example, closed its Detroit factories and concentrated its operations in South Bend.

57 "Ford Must Distribute $19,000,000, but May Build Smelting Plant," *Automotive Industries*, February 13, 1919, p. 391.

58 Hence the use of "fordism" as a generic term for assembly line production.

59 Faurote (1915, p. 184) tells the same story, portraying it as apocryphal but nonetheless illustrative of Ford's capabilities.

60 In the sense of Williamson (1985), pp. 119–120.

61 Consider Ford's motives for acquiring the Detroit, Toledo, and Ironton railroad. "We bought the railway because its right of way interfered with some of our improvements on the River Rouge. We did not buy it as an investment, or as an adjunct to our industries, or because of its strategic position. The extraordinarily good situation of the railroad seems to have been apparent only since we bought it. That, however, is beside the point. We bought the railway because it interfered with our plans. Then we had to do something with it" (Ford with Crowther 1923, p. 224). Internalization seems a rather draconian solution to a land-use conflict of this sort, suggesting that this acquisition cannot be explained on grounds of cost-minimization. On the other hand, Ford clearly saw strategic value in the railroad from the outset, and his infusion of capital – and Ford management techniques – quickly turned a bankrupt line into a money-maker (Nevins and Hill 1957, pp. 220–225).

62 Indeed, it was during the changeover from the Model T to the Model A that the Detroit, Toledo, and Ironton began to lose money. And Ford quickly sold it to the Pennsylvania Railroad in 1928 (Nevins and Hill 1957, p. 225).

63 Crandall's measure is the ratio of internal value-added to sales.

64 Hence the comment reported by David Halberstam (1986, p. 81) that Eiji Toyoda of Toyota made to the chairman of Ford in 1982: "There is no secret to how we learned to do what we do, Mr. Caldwell. We learned it at the Rouge."

65 By all accounts, hand-to-mouth buying was the result of a combination of factors: (1) the development of excess capacity in parts manufacture as the growth rate of automobile demand abated; (2) the steady decline in commodity prices over this period, which made the holding of inventories unprofitable; and (3) the increased reliability of the transportation system – especially the railroads – which made prompt delivery routine. But contemporary accounts also note that the hand-to-mouth system had positive side-effects, including increased competition among parts suppliers and closer cooperation between buyer and seller. It is this last upon which present-day accounts of just-in-time delivery focus (see McGill (1927) and Stillman (1927)). In one sense, hand-to-mouth buying is by itself an instance of vertical disintegration, for it decoupled the function of speculation in inventories from the manufacturing function (Stillman 1927, p. 3).

66 For a contemporary account of innovations by parts suppliers, see Heldt (1933, pp. 546–548, 554).

67 Ford did, however, produce internally a new standard transmission that replaced the Model T's planetary gearbox.

68 By the mid-1920s, Fisher Body actually lagged behind some other firms in body technology by continuing to produce "composite bodies" (which had steel panels fixed to a wooden frame) after other firms had adopted all-steel bodies. It was not until 1937, for example, that Chevrolet eliminated wood – and in the process reduced the weight of its cars by 150 to 230 pounds as compared with 1936 models (Dammann 1972, p. 86; Langworth and Norbye 1984, p. 93).

69 In 1926, 75 per cent of all cars made had closed bodies (*Automotive Industries*,

August 6, 1927, p. 181). By 1931, that proportion had risen to 92 per cent (*Automotive Industries*, January 9, 1932, p. 40).

70 As we saw, Abernathy argues persuasively that product innovation favors disintegration. He is less clear on whether reduced – or institutionalized – product innovation will lead to reintegration, although he implies that it will. Silver (1984, p. 48), by contrast, argues that a slower pace of change should lead to less integration on balance.

71 Actually, the manufacturers could have reaped the same quasirents by passing along as "authorized" parts made on contract by outside suppliers. But the transaction costs of such arrangements were probably high.

5 EXTERNAL CAPABILITIES AND MODULAR SYSTEMS

72 For an interesting exception, see Clark and Fujimoto (1991), esp. pp. 1–3. Recently, formal price theory has also turned its attention to some of the demand-side aspects of modular systems. But this literature does not simultaneously address the supply-side issues of technology, innovation, and firm boundaries. The work most relevant to our concerns is that of Matutes and Regibeau (1988), who cast the problem of "mix and match" in the form of a game. In this model, two firms who produce a two-component system must each decide whether to make parts compatible or incompatible with those of the competitor. Apart from being rather stylized, however, this model does not look at the issue of vertical integration, assuming instead that both firms produce both components. The model also does not examine the effect of the compatibility decision on innovation or production costs.

73 In the sense of Lancaster (1971).

74 Even in the case of prepackaged entities, however, one often sees manufacturers attempting to take advantage of a modular system inhouse. For example, the prewar "flexible specialization" that allowed GM to manufacture a wide variety of models economically (Chapter 4 *infra*; Raff 1991) represented a kind of proprietary modular system. Also, jet engine manufacturers have discovered that modularization allows them to reduce lead times in design and therefore to gain competitive advantage.

As of July 1989, 63 percent of commercial airliners used engines manufactured by Pratt and Whitney (P&W). The main strength of the long-time leader in jet engines for commercial aircraft lay in better fuel economy. But for engines under construction and in backlog, the picture changes completely: General Electric engines are outselling P&W engines by a margin of 51 percent to 31 percent. Many industry observers ascribe this turnaround to efficient product development; GE responded flexibly to the recent needs of airline and aircraft companies for product variety (e.g., engines for long-body and wide-body craft) by introducing a series of modular engines that shared a basic design, so that a variety of engines with very different thrusts could be created with dramatically shorter lead time and at less cost.

(Clark and Fujimoto 1991, p. 5)

75 For a straightforward introduction, see Waterson (1984, chapter 6).

76 Although price factors can be important, we must be careful not to place too much emphasis on them. Poor or unsophisticated consumers will be much more susceptible to low-cost products (have lower budget constraints); but, as incomes and sophistication increase, a higher proportion of buyers will seek a better selection of attributes. A sufficient number of people were able to afford

better bundles of attributes that, even at the peak of its popularity, the Model T did not force Cadillac, Lincoln, or Packard from the market. And, as incomes rose generally in the 1920s, the Model T itself succumbed as a higher proportion of consumers had the means to purchase superior selections of non-price features.

77 Although the barriers between the two types of communication now appear to be diminishing as a result of technological convergence.

78 On which see Rosenberg (1976, chapter 1).

79 For example, the relationship between the manufacturers of subassembly B and those of component C in Figure 5.5.

80 A phonograph included all the equipment necessary for reproduction. With the advent of electric models in the late 1920s, this meant a speaker and an amplifier as well as the turntable. A record player was only a turntable and had to be plugged into a radio. Finally, a "combination" included both a radio and a phonograph in a single unit.

81 In practice, "fidelity" is a concept with several meanings. When pioneers like Edison sought fidelity, they wanted their recordings to sound exactly like the original performances. This warts-and-all approach has subsequently been adopted by some acoustic puritans including Read and Welch and also Maxfield, one of the pioneers of electrical recording techniques at Western Electric. Among other things, these observers decry the ability of recording engineers to produce musical painted ladies by using techniques developed since the 1920s to alter the nature of the product by compensating for expected distortion, splicing together portions of different performances, etc. (Read and Welch 1976, chapter 17). With the growing sophistication of recording equipment, this tendency to meddle with performances has increased in recent years. In the absence of any "real" standard of how a recording should sound, the quality of recordings has become a subjective matter to be decided by recording engineers and consumers who can choose from a range of sound mixtures according to personal preferences.

82 Which markets its records on the London label in the United States.

83 The problem was apparently caused by phase distortion, which leads to "listener fatigue." It can be eliminated by using amplifiers with ranges that greatly exceed the actual hearing range.

84 According to *Fortune*, a "golden ear" like Kennedy is "a purist [who] insists that the tones be noise-free and undistorted, sharp, clear, and full from treble to bass." Their opponents were "tin ears," who, like the listeners surveyed by CBS, were so accustomed to distortion that they preferred it to high fidelity. "Some people don't even like what they hear in a concert hall. The real thing, they say, is too bright and loud" (October 1946, pp. 160–161).

85 Columbia offered a 33-rpm attachment in 1948, and RCA placed its 45-rpm rapid-drop changer on the market in the following year.

86 Garrard, for instance, used different-sized flywheels for the American and European markets to allow for local differences in the number of cycles per second in electricity transmission. Otherwise, the same record changers were compatible with other components everywhere.

87 The first great recording star was Enrico Caruso, who earned royalties of more than $3 million (*Fortune*, September 1939, p. 73).

88 There was considerable rivalry between Wallerstein and Peter Goldmark over the respective roles that each had played in the commercial development of LP records (Goldmark 1973). Our concern here, however, is with the

general path of development and not with precedence within the Columbia organization.

89 Much of the material on FM reception is derived from Inglis (1990).

90 At present, the AM (medium wave) band extends from 550 to 1600 kHz and the FM band from 88 to 108 MHz.

91 The fidelity advantages of FM were also largely ignored in Britain. When the British Broadcasting Corporation began VHF/FM transmission in 1955, it was for local stations rather than the Third Programme (Briggs 1979, p. 562).

92 An integrated amplifier includes both a preamplifier, which "takes an audio signal from a phono cartridge, tuner, tape deck, or CD player, boosts the gain, or volume, and sends the signal to a power amplifier for further amplification," and the power amplifier that drives the speakers. Receivers add a tuner to the integrated amplifier (Gillett 1988, p. 74).

93 Although these systems are sold as integrated appliances, most are in fact composed of separate components manufactured by a single firm. When they do not include the full range of options such as CD players, they usually offer provisions for plug-in sets for buyers who wish to diversify later.

94 For a much longer and better-documented history of the microcomputer, see Langlois (1992a), on which this section draws. A condensed version of this case study also appears in Langlois (1990).

95 Data from Apple Computer, cited in "John Sculley at Apple Computer (B)," Harvard Business School Case no. 9–486–002, revised May 1987, p. 26.

96 Although touted as a 16-bit chip – and thus an advance over the 8-bit 8080 and 6502 – the 8088 processed data internally in 16-bit words but used 8-bit external buses.

97 Zenith has since been acquired by Groupe Bull of France, though its operations continue to be based in Illinois.

98 The successes were the PC XT in 1983 and the PC AT in 1984. The failures include the infamous PC Jr., an attempt at the home computer market; the PC portable in 1984; a workstation called the RT PC in 1986; and the PC convertible, a laptop, also in 1986. For a chronology of IBM product introductions, see Chposky and Leonsis (1988, pp. 220–222).

99 Paul B. Carroll, "How an IBM Attempt to Regain PC Lead Has Slid into Trouble," *The Wall Street Journal*, December 2, 1991, p. A1.

100 The proprietory attitude lasted well into the Sculley era at Apple. Indeed, Sculley has recently described as his biggest regret his failure to open up the Apple standard and allow clones (*Fortune*, July 26, 1993, p. 119).

101 The microcomputer as a modular system had also partaken of certain types of integrative innovations, that is, innovations that allow a single device to perform functions that had previously required several devices. A good example of this would be a chip set designed by Chips and Technologies to integrate into a few ICs 63 of the 94 circuits on the original IBM AT, thus greatly facilitating the making of clones.

102 Indeed, in the long run, audio and computers will arguably become part of the same set of systems: audio is but one of the media in multimedia computer systems. And audio will be part of the "software" that will travel along the much-ballyhooed information superhighway of the near future.

103 RISC stands for Reduced Instruction Set Computing, and refers to a technique for simplifying the design of, and therefore for speeding up, a microprocessor.

104 See, for example, *Business Week International*, November 1, 1993, p. 74.

105 Unix is an operating system developed by AT&T Bell Labs and used

extensively in minicomputers and workstations. Versions of Unix are in the public domain, but Sun Microsystems has bought the rights to the AT&T versions.

106 Ferguson and Morris (1993, pp. 119–124) argue that, in a world of open systems, competitive advantage comes from somehow "capturing" important architectures, as Microsoft and Intel have done. The case of Sun (Garud and Kumaraswamy 1993), however, suggests that one can acquire and maintain competitive advantage with a strategy of aggressively opening up the system one is selling, and living well on the quasi-rents of the short-run technological leads that strategy creates.

6 INERTIA AND INDUSTRIAL CHANGE

107 By organization, we mean both internal firm organization and market-based relationships between producers and their suppliers and customers.

108 Recently, several writers, of whom the most prolific is William Lazonick, have argued that the tendency of British producers to adapt existing technologies rather than adopt new ones has been one of the principal causes of Britain's relatively poor economic record since the 1870s (Lazonick, 1990 and 1991a; Elbaum and Lazonick, 1986).

109 The literature on this subject has become enormous in recent years. For a comprehensive treatment of the issues, see Dertouzos, Lester, and Solow (1989).

110 Although general cultural variables such as "national character" are also institutions in the sense meant here, they are not considered in this chapter because of the difficulties in establishing criteria and finding usable data.

111 What we term semi-endogenous institutions are "endogenous" in much the same way that the evolution of government institutions is endogenous to the market in the Theory of Public Choice (Olson, 1982).

112 This notion of routines is developed presently. But on the affinity between social institutions (such as norms) and organizational routines, see Langlois (1986a) and the other essays in the same volume.

113 Although Michelin was an established tire manufacturer in Europe, it had an insignificant share of the U.S. market and, like a new entrant to the field in general, had litttle to lose if the innovation were rejected in America but a great deal to gain if it were successful.

114 From our standpoint, Stiglitz seems to reverse the time dimension involved in change. He writes, for example, that "the basic concept of 'weaving' is involved in virtually all textile production, but much of the technical knowledge associated with modern automated factory production is inapplicable to hand-loom weaving" (1987, p. 127). It seems far more relevant, however, that the knowledge of the hand-loom weavers was not readily transferable to later technologies.

115 This is particularly true of tacit knowledge since proprietary knowledge may be obtained through industrial espionage or other surreptitious methods.

116 Although somewhat exaggerated, this is a fair description of Britain's position following the Napoleonic Wars (Landes, 1969, ch. 3).

117 Cooper and Schendel (1976), Foster (1986), and Tushman and Anderson (1986) all indicate that the ability of existing firms to adjust to radical product or process innovation is highly limited.

118 Tariffs are only one means that a late mover can use to assist its firms in achieving control over a major innovation. Other tools include regulations

that make it difficult for foreign firms to become established in the follower nation, as is alleged to happen in Japan, the use of "safety" regulations to discriminate against imports, and campaigns to encourage local customers, especially governments, to buy locally produced goods.

119 DC power was still supplied in sections of major cities at least as late as the 1960s.

120 In fact, an alternative definition of a major innovation is one that requires a shift to a different experience curve since minor innovations are among the factors that contribute to a movement down a particular curve.

121 In the initial stages, before the necessary capabilities to deal with the innovation have been developed and total costs are higher for innovators than for users of the older technology, preferential government policies would probably not be available for innovators in the same economy as the current leaders under the earlier technological regime. Other devices to "protect" the innovators would be possible, however, such as the cross-subsidization of innovating divisions by other parts of diversified firms.

122 For alternative views, see Sandberg (1974) and, in particular, Saxonhouse and Wright (1984, 1987).

7 INNOVATION, NETWORKS AND VERTICAL INTEGRATION

123 The "Third Italy" is the area of northeast Italy centering on the regions of Emilia-Romagna and Tuscany. Although a number of substantial cities – such as Bologna, Modena, Florence, and Reggio-Emilia – are in the area, much of the industry is located in smaller towns that specialize in the production of various items including ceramic tiles, textiles, and machine tools. These local industries are frequently organized in government-sponsored cooperatives that provide access to cheap capital and to services in marketing, accounting, etc. Initiative in design and other fields, however, is retained by the member firms, which are commonly family owned and have twenty or fewer employees. See also, Lazerson (1988), Brusco (1982), and Hatch (1987).

124 The historical material in chapter 2 of Piore and Sabel (1984) is a reworking of an article by Sabel and Zeitlin (1985). See also Sabel (1989) and Sabel et al. (1987). The latter article contrasts the recent decline of large textile machinery firms based in Massachusetts and the prosperity of similar but much smaller firms in Baden-Württemberg.

125 Chandler (1990), p. 236. Chandler explains the three prongs in more detail on p. 8.

126 This chapter is reproduced in Florida and Kenney (1990b). See also, Lazonick (1991b).

127 Except, of course, for a few specialist firms such as Rolls Royce that could produce in small volumes because customers were willing to pay premium prices for high quality or distinctive features.

128 Lazonick, Piore and Sabel, Best, and Florida and Kenney are also explicitly interested in finding ways of providing more interesting work, greater job stability, and better wages for the industrial labor force than currently prevails in the United States. In general, they recommend that this can be accomplished by increasing the intellectual content of factory employment and the scope for decision-making available to individual workers. Florida and

161

Kenney, for example, "see the Japanese model as a successor to fordism that uses new organizational forms to harness the intellectual as well as the physical capabilities of works" (1991, p. 383). Here, however, we concentrate on the authors' proposals concerning firm and industrial organization.

129 For a summary of the literature surrounding networks, see Bureau of Industry Economics (1991).

130 This is consistent with the analysis that Bettis, Bradley, and Hamel (1992, pp. 18–20) present of outsourcing by Western firms, in which they indicate that firms should protect their core competences by producing them internally and that they should restrict outsourcing to peripheral activities. Sabel *et al.* (1987) describe similar conditions in Baden-Württemberg. Sabel (1989, p. 53) also discusses the role of distinctive competences in networking situations.

131 Good descriptions of the operation of Italian industrial districts are given in Best (1990) and Lazerson (1988). Similar arrangements prevail in certain American agricultural cooperatives such as Land-o-Lakes or Ocean Spray that provide infrastructure and processing and marketing facilities for members.

132 According to Saxenian (1991), however, in Silicon Valley there is now considerable cooperation among vertically specialized firms in the computer systems industry.

133 Although Florida and Kenney are moderately well disposed towards venture capitalists in their article, they are far most negative in chapter 4 of their 1990 book *The Breakthrough Illusion.*

134 However, this is not universal. For example, Fruin (1992, p. 20) estimates that perhaps slightly more than one-half of Toshiba's factories are focal factories.

135 On networks in Japan from a native's perspective, see Imai and Itami (1984) and Imai (1989).

136 Williamson (1985) discusses this decentralization in cybernetic terms: that it permits a separation of control over disturbances in degree (day-to-day management) from control disturbances in kind (strategic management).

137 For example, Womack, Jones, and Roos (1990), p. 143.

138 Although, even in nineteenth-century Britain certain kinds of collective action were common, especially employers' associations to combat unions.

139 The distinction between parametric and structural follows Langlois (1984).

140 Contrary to widespread prediction, however, the personal computer industry has not matured in such a way that advantage has fallen to large vertically integrated concerns. Rather, the industry has arguably matured into a high-volume mass-production network akin to nineteenth-century Lancashire in cotton textiles. Large firms continue to be singularly unsuccessful, and those large firms that do play in the market do so by emulating their vertically decentralized competitors. The Japanese and Koreans have made few inroads despite dominance in certain high-tech components like flat-panel displays and CD drives. The most successful firms in the industry are Intel and Microsoft, both of whom essentially limit their integration to some strategic alliances. Overall, unit costs and industrial concentration continue to fall hand in hand (Langlois 1992a).

141 These arrangements result in important two-way channels of information because they reduce the cost to producers of collecting information on customers' preferences as well as spreading information on the producers' wares.

142 The need for (vertical) ownership integration may be strengthened by the

limited time period allowed to holders of patents. If potential users of an innovation cannot be recruited quickly, the effective life of patents, as measured by the profits to their holders, is shortened significantly.

143 The major difference between Mature Uncertainty and Mature Rebirth centers on the elasticity of demand for the product. When elasticity is high, a systemic innovation in a mature product may result in a renewed acceleration of growth, or "rebirth," but if demand is inelastic the innovation will result only in greater uncertainty. See Cheah and Robertson (1992).

144 If the innovation is truly revolutionary, however, existing firms may not possess sufficient capabilities to absorb it. Indeed, other firms, with different capabilities, may be better equipped than established firms to adopt the innovation and thus win a niche in the industry or even come to dominate it. See Chapter 6.

145 This is, in fact, the anticipated outcome for a mature industry that undergoes vertical disintegration and comes to rely so heavily on outside suppliers that it suffers degradation of its basic competences and can no longer respond adequately to changes in its environment (Bettis, Bradley, and Hamel 1992).

8 CONCLUSION

146 This, of course, does not mean that there will necessarily be "progress." Appropriate capabilities may not be available initially, or perhaps ever, to cope as efficiently with a new environment as the prior set of capabilities had coped with the earlier environment.

147 For a detailed discussion of Chandler's position, see Langlois (1991).

148 Although he contends that large firms dominated the most modern sectors of the economy and were the most important source of growth.

149 Further discussion of Lazonick's work can be found in Robertson (1993) and Langlois (1994).

150 Lazonick is reacting against attitudes such as those of Michael C. Jensen (1988, 1989).

151 As Lazonick, himself, has pointed out (1993).

152 The sequence that we outline is similar in many respects to punctuated equilibrium as discussed by Gersick (1991) and Gould (1989).

BIBLIOGRAPHY

Abell, D. F. and Hammond, J. S. (1979) *Strategic Market Planning*, Englewood Cliffs, N.J.: Prentice Hall.

Abernathy, W. J. (1978) *The Productivity Dilemma: Roadblock to Innovation in the Automobile Industry*, Baltimore: Johns Hopkins University Press.

Abernathy, W. J. and Clark, K. B. (1985) "Innovation: Mapping the Winds of Creative Destruction," *Research Policy* 14: 3–22.

Abramovitz, M. (1986) "Catching Up, Forging Ahead, and Falling Behind," *Journal of Economic History* 46: 385–406.

Adelman, Morris (1955) "Concept and Statistical Measurement of Vertical Integration," in *Business Concentration and Price Policy*, Princeton: Princeton University Press: 318–320.

Alchian, A. and Demsetz, H. (1972) "Production, Information Costs, and Economic Organization," *American Economic Review* 62, 5: 772–795.

Alchian, A. and Woodward, S. (1988) "The Firm Is Dead; Long Live the Firm: A Review of Oliver E. Williamson's *The Economic Institutions of Capitalism*," *Journal of Economic Literature* 26, 1: 65–79.

Aldcroft, D. H. and Richardson, H. W. (1969) *The British Economy 1870–1939*, London: Macmillan.

Ansoff, H. I. (1965) *Corporate Strategy*, Harmondsworth: Penguin.

Ashton, T. S. (1939) *An Eighteenth-Century Industrialist: Peter Stubs of Warrington, 1756–1806*, Manchester: Manchester University Press.

Axelrod, R. (1984) *The Evolution of Cooperation*, New York: Basic Books.

Babbage, C. (1963) *On the Economy of Machinery and Manufactures*, New York: Augustus M. Kelley (reprint of the 4th edn, enlarged, 1835).

Barney, J. (1991) "Firm Resources and Sustained Competitive Advantage," *Journal of Management* 17: 99–120.

Barzel, Y. (1982) "Measurement Costs and the Organization of Markets," *Journal of Law and Economics* 25: 27–48.

—— (1987) "The Entrepreneur's Reward for Self-Policing," *Economic Inquiry* 25: 103–116.

Ben-Porath, Y. (1980) "The F-Connection: Families, Friends, and Firms in the Organization of Exchange," *Population and Development Review* 6, 1: 1–30.

Berg, M. and Hudson, P. (1992) "Rehabilitating the Industrial Revolution," *Economic History Review* 45, 1: 24–50.

Best, M. (1990) *The New Competition: Institutions of Industrial Restructuring*, Cambridge, Mass.: Harvard University Press.

Bettis, R. A., Bradley, S. P. and Hamel, G. (1992) "Outsourcing and Industrial Decline," *Academy of Management Executive* 6, 1: 7–22.

Blaug, M. (1987) *Economic Theory in Retrospect*, 4th edn, Cambridge: Cambridge University Press.

Bower, J. L. and Rhenman, E. A. (1985) "Benevolent Cartels," *Harvard Business Review* 63: 124–132.

Briggs, A. (1979) "Sound and Vision," vol. IV of *The History of Broadcasting in the United Kingdom*, Oxford: Oxford University Press.

Brusco, S. (1982) "The Emilian Model: Productive Decentralisation and Social Integration," *Cambridge Journal of Economics* 6: 167–184.

Brusco, S. and Righi, E. (1987) "The Loan Guarantee Consortia," *Entrepreneurial Economy* 6, 1: 11–13.

Bureau of Industry Economics (1991) "Networks: A Third Form of Organisation," Discussion Paper 14, Canberra: Australian Government Publishing Service.

Business Week International (1992) "Learning from Japan," January 27: 38–44.

Butcher, L. (1988) *Accidental Millionaire: The Rise and Fall of Steve Jobs at Apple Computer*, New York: Paragon House.

Byatt, I. C. R. (1968) "Electrical Products," in D. H. Aldcroft (ed.) *The Development of British Industry and Foreign Competition 1875–1914*, London: Allen & Unwin: 238–273.

—— (1979) *The British Electrical Industry 1875–1914*, Oxford: Clarendon Press.

Camerer, C. and Vepsalainen, A. (1988) "The Economic Efficiency of Corporate Culture," *Strategic Management Journal* 9, special issue: 115–126.

Cameron, Rondo (1995) "Misunderstanding the Industrial Revolution," in R. Cameron and L. F. Schnore (eds), *Cities and Markets*, Lanham, Md.: University Press of America.

Carroll, P. B. (1993) *Big Blues: The Unmaking of IBM*, New York: Crown Publishers.

Casson, M. (1982) *The Entrepreneur: An Economic Theory*, Towota, N.J.: Barnes and Noble.

Caves, R., Crookell, H. and Killing P. J. (1983) "The Imperfect Market for Technology Licenses," *Oxford Bulletin of Economic Statistics* 45, 3: 249–267.

Chandler, A. D., Jr. (1962) *Strategy and Structure: Chapters in the History of Industrial Enterprise*, Cambridge, Mass.: MIT Press.

—— (1964) *Giant Enterprise: Ford, General Motors, and the Automobile Industry*, New York: Harcourt, Brace, and World.

—— (1977) *The Visible Hand: the Managerial Revolution in American Business*, Cambridge, Mass.: The Belknap Press of Harvard University Press.

—— (1990) *Scale and Scope: the Dynamics of Industrial Capitalism*, Cambridge, Mass.: The Belknap Press of Harvard University Press.

—— (1992) "Organizational Capabilities and the Theory of the Firm," *Journal of Economic Perspectives* 6, 3: 79–100.

Cheah, H. B. and Robertson, P. L. (1992). "The Entrepreneurial Process and Innovation in the Product Life Cycle," Economics and Management Working Paper No. 4/1992, Department of Economics and Management, University College, University of New South Wales.

Cheung, S. N. S. (1983) "The Contractual Nature of the Firm," *Journal of Law and Economics* 26: 386–405.

Chi, T. (1994) "Trading in Strategic Resources: Necessary Conditions, Transaction Cost Problems, and Choice of Exchange Structure," *Strategic Management Journal* 15: 271–290.

Chposky, J. and Leonsis, T. (1988) *Blue Magic: The People, Power and Politics Behind the IBM Personal Computer*, New York: Facts on File.

Clark, K. B. and Fujimoto, T. (1991) *Product Development Performance: Strategy,*

Organization, and Management in the World Auto Industry, Boston, Mass.: Harvard Business School Press.

Coase, R. H. (1937) "The Nature of the Firm," *Economica* (N.S.) 4: 386–405.

—— (1972) "Industrial Organization: A Proposal for Research," in V. R. Fuchs (ed.) *Policy Issues and Research Opportunities in Industrial Organization*, New York: National Bureau of Economic Research.

Cohen, W. M. and Levinthal, D. A. (1989) "Innovation and Learning: The Two Faces of R&D," *Economic Journal* 99: 569–596.

—— (1990) "Absorptive Capacity: A New Perspective on Learning and Innovation," *Administrative Science Quarterly* 35: 128–152.

Conner, K. R. (1991) "A Historical Comparison of Resource-Based Theory and Five Schools of Thought within Industrial Organization Economics," *Journal of Management* 17: 121–154.

Cooper, A. C. and Schendel, D. (1976) Strategic Responses to Technological Threats," *Business Horizons* 61–69, reprinted in M. L. Tushman and W. L. Moore (eds.) *Readings in the Management of Innovation*, 2nd edn, Cambridge, Mass.: Ballinger, 1988, 249–258.

Cournot, A. A. (1838) *Recherches sur les Principes Mathématiques de la Théorie des Richesses*, Paris: Hachette.

Crandall, R. W. (1968) "Vertical Integration in the American Automobile Industry," unpublished Ph.D. dissertation, Northwestern University.

Currie, M. and Steedman, I. (1990) *Wrestling with Time: Problems in Economic Theory*, Ann Arbor: University of Michigan Press.

Dahlman, C. (1979) "The Problem of Externality," *Journal of Law and Economics* 22: 141–162.

—— (1980) *The Open Field System and Beyond*, New York: Cambridge University Press.

Dammann, G. H. (1972) *Sixty Years of Chevrolet*, Glen Ellyn, Ill.: Crestline Publishing.

David, P. A. (1985) "Clio and the Economics of QWERTY," *American Economic Review* 75, 2: 332–337.

—— (1991a) "The Hero and the Herd in Technological History: Reflections on Thomas Edison and the Battle of the Systems," in P. Higonnet, D. S. Landes and H. Rosovsky (eds) *Favorites of Fortune: Technology, Growth and Economic Development since the Industrial Revolution*, Cambridge, Mass.: Harvard University Press, 72–119.

—— (1991b) "Computer and Dynamo. The Modern Productivity Paradox in a Not-Too-Distant Mirror," *Technology and Productivity: The Challenge for Economic Policy*, Paris: OECD, 315–347.

David, P. A. and Bunn, J. A. (1990) "Gateway Technologies and Network Industries," in A. Heertje and M. Perlman (eds) *Evolving Technology and Market Structure*, Ann Arbor: University of Michigan Press, 121–156.

Demsetz, H. (1988) "The Theory of the Firm Revisited," *Journal of Law, Economics, and Organization* 4, 1: 141–161.

Denison, E. F. (1967) *Why Growth Rates Differ*, Washington, D.C.: The Brookings Institution.

Dertouzos, M., Lester, R. and Solow, R. (1989) *Made in America: Regaining the Productivity Edge*, Cambridge, Mass.: MIT Press.

Dorfman, N. (1983) "Route 128: The Development of a Regional High Technology Economy," *Research Policy* 12: 299–316.

Dosi, G. and Metcalfe, J. S. (1991) "On Some Notions of Irreversibility in Economics," in P. P. Saviotti and J. S. Metcalfe (eds) *Evolutionary Theories of Economic and Technological Change: Present Status and Future Prospects*, Chur: Harwood Academic Publishers, 133–159.

Economist (1992) "Japan's Less-than invincible Computer Makers," January 11, 59–60.

Eisenberg, N. (1976) "High Fidelity Pathfinders: The Men Who Made an Industry," *High Fidelity Magazine*, April.

Elbaum, B. (1986) "The Steel Industry before World War I," in B. Elbaum and W. Lazonick (eds) *The Decline of the British Economy*, Oxford: Clarendon Press, 51–81.

Elbaum, B. and Lazonick W. (eds) (1986) *The Decline of the British Economy*, Oxford: Clarendon Press.

Epstein, R. C. (1928) *The Automobile Industry: Its Economic and Commercial Development*, Chicago: A. W. Shaw.

Faurote, F. L. (1915) "Ford Methods and the Ford Shops, XIV, Special Ford Machines and Ford Fixtures," *The Engineering Magazine* 49, May 2.

Federal Trade Commission (1939) *Report on the Motor Vehicle Industry*, House Document No. 468, 76th Congress, 1st session, Washington, D.C.

Fenoaltea, S. (1976) "Risk, Transaction Costs, and the Organization of Medieval Agriculture," *Explorations in Economic History* 13, 2: 129–151.

Ferguson, C. H. and Morris, C. R. (1993) *Computer Wars: How the West Can Win in a Post-IBM World*, New York: Times Books.

Florida, R. and Kenney, M. (1988) "Venture Capital-Financed Innovation and Technological Change in the USA," *Research Policy* 17: 119–137.

—— (1990a) *The Breakthrough Illusion: Corporate America's Failure to Move from Innovation to Mass Production*, New York: Basic Books.

—— (1990b) "Silicon Valley and Route 128 Won't Save Us," *California Management Review*, 33, Fall: 68–88.

—— (1991) "Transplanted Organizations: The Transfer of Japanese Industrial Organization to the U.S.," *American Sociological Review*, 56: 381–398.

Flugge, E. (1929) "Possibilities and Problems of Integration in the Automobile Industry," *Journal of Political Economy* 37: 150–174.

Ford, H. with Crowther, S. (1923) *My Life and Work*, Garden City: Doubleday.

—— (1926) *Today and Tomorrow*, Garden City: Garden City Publishing.

Foss, N. J. (1994) "G. B. Richardson, Austrian Economics, and the Post-Marshallians," Working Paper 94-3, Institute of Industrial Economics and Strategy, Copenhagen Business School.

Foss, N. J., Knudsen C. and Montgomery, C. A. (1995) "An Exploration of Common Ground: Integrating Evolutionary and Resource-based Views of the Firm," in C. A. Montgomery (ed.) *Resources in an Evolutionary Perspective: A Synthesis of Evolutionary and Resource-based Approaches to Strategy*, Dordrecht: Kluwer Academic Publishers.

Foster, R. N. (1986) "Timing Technological Transitions," in M. Horwitch (ed.) *Technology in the Modern Corporation: a Strategic Perspective*, New York: Pergamon, reprinted in M. L. Tushman and W. L. Moore (eds) *Readings in the Management of Innovation*, Cambridge, Mass.: Ballinger, 1988: 215–228.

Frankel, M. (1955) "Obsolescence and Technological Change in a Maturing Economy," *American Economic Review* 45: 295–319.

—— (1956) Obsolescence and Technological Change in a Maturing Economy: Reply," *American Economic Review* 46: 652–656.

Fruin, W. M. (1992) *The Japanese Enterprise System: Competitive Strategies and Cooperative Structures*, Oxford: Clarendon Press.

Galbraith, J. K. (1972) *The New Industrial State*, 2nd edn, Harmondsworth: Penguin.

Garud, R. and Kumaraswamy, A. (1993) "Changing Competitive Dynamics in Network Industries: An Exploration of Sun Microsystems' Open Systems Strategy," *Strategic Management Journal* 14: 351–369.

Gersick, C. J. G. (1991) "Revolutionary Change Theories: A Multilevel Exploration of the Punctuated Change Paradigm," *Academy of Management Review* 16: 10–36.

Gillett, T. R. (1988) "Separates," *Stereo Review*, November.

Gilson, R. J. and Roe, M. J. (1993) "Understanding the Japanese Keiretsu: Overlaps Between Corporate Governance and Industrial Organization," *Yale Law Journal* 102: 871–906.

Goldmark, P. (1973) *Maverick Inventor*, New York: Saturday Review Press.

Gordon, D. F. (1956) "Obsolescence and Technological Change: Comment," *American Economic Review* 46: 646–652.

Gould, S. J. (1989) "Punctuated Equilibrium in Fact and Theory," *Journal of Social Biological Structure* 12: 117–136.

Graham, M. B. W. (1986) *The Business of Research: RCA and the VideoDisk*, New York: Cambridge University Press.

Granstrand, O., Bohlin E., Oskarsson, C. and Sjoberg N. (1992) "External Technology Acquisition in Large Multi-technology Corporations," *R&D Management* 22, 2: 111–133.

Greenleaf, W. (1961) *Monopoly on Wheels: Henry Ford and the Selden Automobile Patent*, Detroit: Wayne State University Press.

Grossman, S. and Hart, O. (1986) "The Costs and Benefits of Ownership: A Theory of Vertical Integration," *Journal of Political Economy* 94: 691–719.

Gustafsson, B. (1991) "The Rise and Economic Behaviour of Medieval Craft Guilds," in B. Gustafsson (ed.) *Power and Economic Institutions: Reinterpretations in Economic History*, Aldershot: Edward Elgar: 69–106.

Halberstam, D. (1986) *The Reckoning*, New York: Avon Books.

Hallwood, C. P. (1994) "An Observation on the Transaction Cost Theory of the (Multinational) Firm," *Journal of Institutional and Theoretical Economics* 150, 2: 351–361.

Hannan, M. T. and Freeman, J. (1989) *Organizational Ecology*, Cambridge, Mass.: Harvard University Press.

Harrigan, K. R. (1983) "A Framework for Looking at Vertical Integration," *Journal of Business Strategy*, 3, 3: 30–37.

Harrison, A. E. (1969) "The Competitiveness of the British Cycle Industry," *Economic History Review* 22: 287–303.

Hart, O. D. (1988) "Incomplete Contracts and the Theory of the Firm," *Journal of Law, Economics, and Organization* 4, 1: 119–140.

—— (1989) "An Economist's Perspective on the Theory of the Firm," *Columbia Law Review* 89, 7: 1757–1774.

Hatch, C. R. (1987) "Learning from Italy's Industrial Renaissance," *Entrepreneurial Economy* 6, 1: 4–11.

Hayek, F. A. (1945) "The Use of Knowledge in Society," *American Economic Review* 35, 4: 519–530.

—— (1967) *Studies in Philosophy, Politics, and Economics*, Chicago: University of Chicago Press.

Heldt, P. M. (1933) "Parts Makers' Role Gets Bigger as Automotive History Unfolds," *Automotive Industries*, May 6.

Helper, S. (1991) "Strategy and Irreversibility in Supplier Relations: The Case of the U.S. Automobile Industry," *Business History Review* 65: 781–824.

Helper, S. and Levine, D. I. (1992) "Long-Term Supplier Relations and Product Market Structure: An Exit-Voice Approach," *Journal of Law, Economics, and Organization* 8: 561–581.

Henderson, R. M. and Clark, K. B. (1990) "Architectural Innovation: the Recon-

168

figuration of Existing Product Technologies and the Failure of Established Firms," *Administrative Science Quarterly* 35: 9–30.

Hirschleifer, J. (1971) "The Private and Social Value of Information and the Reward to Inventive Activity," *American Economic Review* 61: 561–574.

Holmstrom, B. R. and Tirole, J. (1989) "The Theory of the Firm," in R. Schmalensee and R. D. Willig (eds) *Handbook of Industrial Organization*, vol. 1, Amsterdam: North Holland: 61–133.

Hounshell, D. A. (1984) *From the American System to Mass Production, 1800–1932: The Development of Manufacturing Technology in the United States*, Baltimore: Johns Hopkins University Press.

Hudson, P. (1992) *The Industrial Revolution*, London: Edward Arnold.

Hughes, T. P. (1983) *Networks of Power: Electrification in Western Society, 1880–1930*, Baltimore: Johns Hopkins University Press.

——— (1992) "The Dynamics of Technological Change: Salients, Critical Problems, and Industrial Revolutions," in G. Dosi, R. Giannetti and P. A. Toninelli (eds) *Technology and Enterprise in a Historical Perspective*, Oxford: Clarendon Press, 97–118.

Hurley, N. P. (1959) "The Automotive Industry: A Study in Industrial Location," *Land Economics* 35: 1–14.

Imai, K.-i. (1989) "Network Industrial Organization in Japan," in B. Carlsson (ed.) *Industrial Dynamics: Technological, Organizational, and Structural Changes in Industries and Firms*, Dordrecht: Kluwer Academic Publishers: 123–155.

Imai, K.-i. and Itami, H. (1984) "Interpenetration of Organization and Market: Japan's Firm and Market in Comparison with the U.S.," *International Journal of Industrial Organization* 2: 285–310.

Inglis, A. F. (1990) *Behind the Tube: A History of Broadcasting Technology and Business*, Boston, Mass.: Focal Press.

Jaffé, W. (1976) "Menger, Jevons, and Walras De-homogenized," *Economic Inquiry* 14: 511–524.

Jensen, M. C. (1988) "Takeovers: Their Causes and Consequences," *Journal of Economic Perspectives* 2: 29–48.

——— (1989) "Eclipse of the Public Corporation," *Harvard Business Review* 67, 5: 61–74.

Jensen, M. C. and Meckling, W. H. (1976) "Theory of the Firm: Managerial Behavior, Agency Costs and Ownership Structure," *Journal of Financial Economics* 3: 305–360.

Jevons, W. S. (1911) *The Theory of Political Economy*, 4th edn, London: Macmillan.

Jones, R. (1993) "Collaborative Mindsets in Declining and Expanding Industrial Sectors: The Case of the NSW and Queensland Boat Building Sectors," paper presented to the Australia–New Zealand Academy of Management Conference, Geelong, Victoria, December 6.

Katz, H. (1977) *The Decline of Competition in the Automobile Industry, 1920–1940*, New York: Arno Press.

Kay, J. (1993) *Foundations of Corporate Success: How Business Strategies Add Value*, Oxford: Oxford University Press.

Kelly, D. and Amburgey, T. L. (1991) "Organizational Inertia and Momentum: A Dynamic Model of Strategic Change," *Academy of Management Journal* 34: 591–612.

Kennedy, E. D. (1972) *The Automobile Industry: the Coming of Age of Capitalism's Favorite Child*, Clifton, N.J.: Augustus M. Kelley.

Kindleberger, C. P. (1969) *Economic Growth in France and Britain, 1851–1950*, New York: Simon and Schuster.

Kirzner, I. (1976) *The Economic Point of View*, 2nd edn, Kansas City: Sheed and Ward.

Klein, B. (1988) "Vertical Integration as Organizational Ownership: The Fisher Body–General Motors Relationship Revisited," *Journal of Law, Economics, and Organization* 4, 1: 199–213.

Klein, B., Crawford, R. G. and Alchian, A. (1978) "Vertical Integration, Appropriable Rents, and the Competitive Contracting Process," *Journal of Law and Economics* 21, 2: 297–326.

Knight, F. H. (1921) *Risk, Uncertainty, and Profit*, Boston, Mass.: Houghton Mifflin.

Kotter, J. P. and Heskett, J. L. (1992) *Corporate Culture and Performance*, New York: The Free Press.

Lancaster, K. (1971) *Consumer Demand: A New Approach*, New York: Columbia University Press.

Landes, D. S. (1969) *The Unbound Prometheus: Technological Change and Industrial Development in Western Europe from 1750 to the Present*, Cambridge: Cambridge University Press.

—— (1991) "Introduction: On Technology and Growth," in P. Higonnet, D. S. Landes and H. Rosovsky (eds) *Favorites of Fortune: Technology, Growth and Economic Development since the Industrial Revolution*, Cambridge, Mass.: Harvard University Press: 1–29.

Langlois, R. N. (1984) "Internal Organization in a Dynamic Context: Some Theoretical Considerations," in M. Jussawalla and H. Ebenfield (eds) *Communication and Information Economics: New Perspectives*, Amsterdam: North-Holland: 23–49.

—— (1986a) "The New Institutional Economics: An Introductory Essay," in R. N. Langlois (ed.) *Economics as a Process: Essays in the New Institutional Economics*, New York: Cambridge University Press: 1–25.

—— (1986b) "Rationality, Institutions, and Explanation," in R. N. Langlois (ed.) *Economics as a Process: Essays in the New Institutional Economics*, New York: Cambridge University Press: 225–255.

—— (1987) "Schumpeter and the Obsolescence of the Entrepreneur," paper presented at the History of Economics Society annual meeting, June 21, Boston (circulating as Working Paper 91-1503, Department of Economics, University of Connecticut, November 1991).

—— (1988) "Economic Change and the Boundaries of the Firm," *Journal of Institutional and Theoretical Economics* 144, 4: 635–657, reprinted in B. Carlsson (ed.) *Industrial Dynamics: Technological, Organizational, and Structural Changes in Industries and Firms*, Dordrecht: Kluwer Academic Publishers, 1989, 85–107.

—— (1990) "Creating External Capabilities: Innovation and Vertical Disintegration in the Microcomputer Industry," *Business and Economic History*, 2nd Series 19: 93–102.

—— (1991) "The Capabilities of Industrial Capitalism," *Critical Review* 5, 4: 513–530.

—— (1992a) "External Economies and Economic Progress: The Case of the Microcomputer Industry," *Business History Review* 66, 1: 1–52.

—— (1992b) "Transaction-cost Economics in Real Time," *Industrial and Corporate Change* 1, 1: 99–127.

—— (1992c) "Capabilities and Vertical Disintegration in Process Technology: The Case of Semiconductor Fabrication Equipment," Working Paper 92–10, Consortium on Competitiveness and Cooperation, University of California, Berkeley, November.

—— (1993) "Orders and Organizations: Toward an Austrian Theory of Social

Institutions," in B. C. and S. Böhm (eds) *Austrian Economics: Tensions and Directions*, Dordrecht: Kluwer Academic Publishers.

—— (1994) Book review of *Business Organization and the Myth of the Market Economy* by William Lazonick, *Journal of Economic Behavior and Organization* 23, 2: 244–250.

Langlois, R. N. and Cosgel, M. M. (1993) "Frank Knight on Risk, Uncertainty, and the Firm: A New Interpretation," *Economic Inquiry* 31: 456–465.

Langlois, R. N. and Everett, M. J. (1992) "Complexity, Genuine Uncertainty, and the Theory of Organization," *Human Systems Management* 11: 67–75.

Langlois, R. N. and Koppl, R. G. (1991) "Fritz Machlup and Marginalism: A Reevaluation," *Methodus* 3, 2: 86–102.

Langlois, R. N. and Robertson, P. L. (1989) "Explaining Vertical Integration: Lessons from the American Automobile Industry," *Journal of Economic History* 49: 361–375.

—— (1992). "Networks and Innovation in a Modular System: Lessons from the Microcomputer and Stereo Component Industries," *Research Policy* 21, 4: 297–313.

Langlois, R. N., Pugel, T. A., Haklisch, C. S., Nelson, R. R. and Egelhoff, W. G. (1988) *Microelectronics: An Industry in Transition*, London: Unwin Hyman.

Langworth, R. M. and Norbye J. P. (1984) *Chevrolet, 1911–1985*, Skokie, Ill.: Publications International.

Lazerson, M. H. (1988) "Organizational Growth of Small Firms: An Outcome of Markets and Hierarchies?," *American Sociological Review* 53: 330–342.

Lazonick, W. (1981) "Competition, Specialization, and Industrial Decline," *Journal of Economic History* 41: 31–38.

—— (1990) *Competitive Advantage on the Shop Floor*, Cambridge, Mass.: Harvard University Press.

—— (1991a) *Business Organization and the Myth of the Market Economy*, New York: Cambridge University Press.

—— (1991b) "The Enterprise, the Community, and the Nation: Social Organization as a Source of Global Competitive Advantage," paper presented at the Business History Seminar, Harvard Business School, November 25.

—— (1992a) *Organization and Technology in Capitalist Development*, Aldershot: Edward Elgar.

—— (1992b) "Controlling the Market for Corporate Control: The Historical Significance of Managerial Capitalism," *Industrial and Corporate Change* 1, 3: 445–488.

—— (1993) "Industry Clusters versus Global Webs: Organizational Capabilities in the American Economy," *Industrial and Corporate Change* 2, 1: 1–24.

Leijonhufvud, A. (1986) "Capitalism and the Factory System," in R. N. Langlois (ed.) *Economics as a Process: Essays in the New Institutional Economics*, New York: Cambridge University Press: 203–223.

Levering, R., Katz, M. and Moskowitz, M. (1984) *The Computer Entrepreneurs*, New York: New American Library.

Levin, R. C., Klevorick, A., Nelson, R. R. and Winter, S. G. (1987) "Appropriating the Returns from Industrial R&D," *Brookings Papers on Economic Activity* 3: 783–831.

Lewis, W. A. (1957) "International Competition in Manufactures," *American Economic Review* 47 (Supplement): 578–587.

Lieberman, M. B. and Montgomery, D. B. (1988) "First-mover Advantages," *Strategic Management Journal* 9 (supplement): 41–58.

Loasby, B. J. (1976) *Choice, Complexity, and Ignorance*, Cambridge: Cambridge University Press.

—— (1989) "Knowledge and Organization: Marshall's Theory of Economic Progress and Coordination," in B. J. Loasby, *The Mind and Method of the Economist*, Aldershot: Edward Elgar.

—— (1990) "Firms, Markets, and the Principle of Continuity," in J. K. Whitaker (ed.) *Centenary Essays on Alfred Marshall*, Cambridge: Cambridge University Press.

—— (1991) *Equilibrium and Evolution: An Exploration of Connecting Principles in Economics*, Manchester: Manchester University Press.

Lundgren, K. (1990) "Vertical Integration, Transaction Costs and 'Learning by Using,'" in M. Aoki, B. Gustafsson and O. Williamson, *The Firm as a Nexus of Treaties*, London: Sage: 112–132.

McCloskey, D. (1981) "The Industrial Revolution 1780–1860: A Survey," in R. Floud and D. McCloskey (eds) *The Economic History of Britain since 1700*, vol. 1. Cambridge: Cambridge University Press: 103–127.

McGill, H. N. (1927) "Hand-to-Mouth Buying and Its Effect on Business," *Industrial Management*, June, 344–347.

Machlup, F. (1967) "Theories of the Firm: Marginalist, Behavioral, Managerial," *American Economic Review* 57: 1–33.

Magee, S. P. (1981) "The Appropriability Theory of the Multinational Corporation," *Annals of the American Academy of Political and Social Science*: 328–335.

Magnusson, L. (ed.) (1994) *Evolutionary and Neo-Schumpeterian Approaches to Economics*, Dordrecht: Kluwer Academic Publishing.

Mahoney, J. T. and Pandian, J. R. (1992) "The Resource-Based View Within the Conversation of Strategic Management," *Strategic Management Journal* 13, 5: 363–380.

Malerba, F. (1993) "The National System of Innovation: Italy," in R. Nelson, ed., *National Innovation Systems: A Comparative Analysis*, New York: Oxford University Press.

Marshall, A. (1961) *Principles of Economics*, 9th (variorum) edn, vol. I, London: Macmillan.

Mass, W. and Lazonick, W. (1990) "The British Cotton Industry and International Competitive Advantage: the State of the Debates," *Business History* 32: 9–65.

Matutes, C. and Regibeau, P. (1988) "'Mix and Match': Product Compatibility without Network Externalities," *RAND Journal of Economics* 19: 221–234.

Miller, R. and Côté, M. (1985) "Growing the Next Silicon Valley," *Harvard Business Review* 63: 114–123.

Mitchell, W. (1989) "Whether and When? Probability and Timing of Incumbents' Entry into Emerging Industrial Subfields," *Administrative Science Quarterly* 34: 208–230.

—— (1991) "Dual Clocks: Entry Order Influences on Incumbent and Newcomer Market Share and Survival when Specialized Assets Retain their Value," *Strategic Management Journal* 12: 85–100.

Moenaert, R., Barbé, J., Deschoolmeester, D. and De Meyer, A. (1990) "Turnaround Strategies for Strategic Business Units with an Ageing Technology," in R. Loveridge and M. Pitt (eds) *The Strategic Management of Technological Innovation*, New York: John Wiley: 39–61.

Monteverde, K. and Teece, D. (1982) "Appropriable Rents and Quasi-vertical Integration," *Journal of Law and Economics* 25, 2: 321–328 (October).

Moore, J. (1992) "The Firm as a Collection of Assets," *European Economic Review* 36: 493–507.

Moritz, M. (1984) *The Little Kingdom: The Private Story of Apple Computer*, New York: William Morrow.

Moss, S. (1984) "The History of the Theory of the Firm from Marshall to Robinson and Chamberlin: The Source of Positivism in Economics," *Economica* 51: 307–318.

Mowery, D. (1989) "Collaborative Ventures Between U.S. and Foreign Manufacturing Firms," *Research Policy* 18: 19–32.

Mullin, J. (1976) "Creating the Craft of Tape Recording," *High Fidelity Magazine*, April.

Musson, A. E. (1976) "Industrial Motive Power in the United Kingdom, 1800–1870," *Economic History Review* 29, 3: 415–439.

Mytelka, L. K. (1992) "Dancing with Wolves: Global Oligopolies and Strategic Partnerships," paper presented to the Conference on "Convergence and Divergence in Economic Growth and Technical Change: Maastricht Revisited," December 10–12.

Nelson, R. R. (1991) "Why Firms Differ, and How Does It Matter?" *Strategic Management Journal* 12: 61–74.

Nelson, R. R. and Winter, S. G. (1977) "In Search of More Useful Theory of Innovation," *Research Policy* 5: 36–76.

—— (1982) *An Evolutionary Theory of Economic Change*, Cambridge, Mass.: Harvard University Press.

Nelson, R. and Wright, G. (1992) "The Rise and Fall of American Technological Leadership," *Journal of Economic Literature* 30, 4: 1931–1964.

Nevins, A. with Hill, F. E. (1954) *Ford: The Times, the Man, the Company*, New York: Charles Scribner's Sons.

Nevins, A. and Hill, F. E. (1957) *Ford: Expansion and Challenge, 1915–1933*, New York: Charles Scribner's Sons.

O'Driscoll, G. P. and Rizzo, M. J. (1985) *The Economics of Time and Ignorance*, Oxford: Basil Blackwell.

Odaka, K., Ono, K. and Adachi, F. (1988) *The Automobile Industry in Japan: A Study in Ancillary Firm Development*, Oxford: Oxford University Press.

Olson, M. (1982) *The Rise and Decline of Nations: Economic Growth, Stagflation, and Social Rigidities*, New Haven: Yale University Press.

Osborne, A. and Dvorak, J. (1984) *Hypergrowth: the Rise and fall of Osborne Computer Corporation*, Berkeley, Calif.: Idthekkethan Publishing Corporation.

Panzar, J. C. and Willig, R. D. (1981) "Economies of Scope," *American Economic Review* 71: 268–272.

Penrose, E. T. (1959) *The Theory of the Growth of the Firm*, Oxford: Basil Blackwell.

Peteraf, M. A. (1993) "The Cornerstones of Competitive Advantage: A Resource-Based View within the Conversation of Strategic Management," *Strategic Management Journal* 14: 179–191.

Piore, M. J. and Sabel, C. F. (1984) *The Second Industrial Divide*, New York: Basic Books.

Polanyi, M. (1958) *Personal Knowledge*, Chicago: University of Chicago Press.

Pollard, S. and Robertson, P. (1979) *The British Shipbuilding Industry, 1870–1914*, Cambridge, Mass.: Harvard University Press.

Porter, M. E. (1980) *Competitive Strategy*, New York: The Free Press.

—— (1990) *The Competitive Advantage of Nations*, New York: The Free Press.

Pound, A. (1934) *The Turning Wheel: The Story of General Motors through Twenty-five Years, 1908–1933*, Garden City: Doubleday, Doran.

Powell, W. W. (1990) "Neither Market nor Hierarchy: Network Forms of Organization," *Research in Organizational Behavior* 12: 295–336.

Prahalad, C. K. and Hamel, G. (1990) "The Core Competence of the Corporation," *Harvard Business Review*, 68, 3: 79–91.

Prescott, E. and Visscher, M. (1980) "Organizational Capital," *Journal of Political Economy* 88: 446–461.

Rae, J. B. (1984) *The American Automobile Industry*, Boston, Mass.: Twayne Publishers.

Raff, D. (1991) "Making Cars and Making Money in the Interwar Automobile Industry: Economies of Scale and Scope and the Manufacturing behind the Marketing," *Business History Review* 65, 4: 721–753.

Read, O. and Welch, W. L. (1976) *From Tin Foil to Stereo: Evolution of the Phonograph*, Indianapolis: Howard W. Sams and Bobbs-Merrill.

Richardson, G. B. (1972) "The Organisation of Industry," *Economic Journal* 82: 883–896.

Richardson, J. (1993) "Parallel Sourcing and Supplier Performance in the Japanese Automobile Industry," *Strategic Management Journal* 14: 339–350.

Rifkin, G. and Harrar, G. (1988) *The Ultimate Entrepreneur: The Story of Ken Olsen and Digital Equipment Corporation*, Chicago: Contemporary Books.

Robertson, P. L. (1981) "Employers and Engineering Education in Britain and the United States, 1890–1914," *Business History* 23: 42–58.

—— (1987) "The Strategic Development of Repco and National Consolidated Limited, 1945–83," *Australian Economic History Review*, 27: 3–36.

—— (1990) "Economies of Scope, Organizational Culture, and the Choice of Diversification Strategies," Economics and Management Working Paper No. 2/1990, Department of Economics and Management, University College, University of New South Wales.

—— (1993) "Innovation, Corporate Organisation and Policy: William Lazonick on the Firm and Economic Growth," *Prometheus* 11, 2: 271–287.

Robertson, P. L. and Alston, L. J. (1992) "Technological Choice and the Organization of Work in Capitalist Firms," *Economic History Review* 45, 2: 330–349.

Robertson, P. L. and Langlois, R. N. (1992) "Modularity, Innovation, and the Firm: the Case of Audio Components," in F. M. Scherer and M. Perlman (eds) *Entrepreneurship, Technological Innovation, and Economic Growth: International Perspectives*, Ann Arbor: University of Michigan Press, 321–342.

Robinson, E. A. G. (1934). "The Problem of Management and the Size of Firms," *Economic Journal* 44: 242–257.

—— (1935) *The Structure of Competitive Industry*, revised edn, Cambridge: Cambridge University Press.

Romanelli, E. and Tushman, M. L. (1986) "Inertia, Environments, and Strategic Choice: A Quasi-Experimental Design for Comparative-Longitudinal Research," *Management Science* 32: 608–621.

Rosenberg, N. (1963) "Technological Change in the Machine Tool Industry, 1840–1910," *Journal of Economic History* 23, 2: 414–443.

—— (1976) *Perspectives on Technology*, New York: Cambridge University Press.

—— (1994) "Charles Babbage: Pioneer Economist," in N. Rosenberg *Exploring the Black Box: Technology, Economics, and History*, Cambridge: Cambridge University Press.

Rosenberg, N. and Birdzell, L. E., Jr. (1986) *How the West Grew Rich: the Economic Transformation of the Industrial World*, New York: Basic Books.

Rumelt, R. P. (1974) *Strategy, Structure, and Economic Performance*, Boston, Mass.: Harvard Business School Press.

Sabel, C. F. (1989) "Flexible Specialization and the Re-emergence of Regional Economies," in P. Hirst and J. Zeitlin (eds) *Reversing Industrial Decline? Industrial Structure and Policy in Britain and Her Competitors*, Oxford: Berg, 17–70.

Sabel, C. F. and Zeitlin, J. (1985) "Historical Alternatives to Mass Production: Politics, Markets, and Technology in Nineteenth-Century Industrialization," *Past and Present* 108: 133–176.

Sabel, C. F., Herrigel, G., Kazis, R. and Deeg, R. (1987) "How to Keep Mature Industries Innovative," *Technology Review* 90: 26–35.

Sahal, D. (1981) *Patterns of Technological Innovation*, Reading, Mass.: Addison-Wesley.

Sandberg, L. G. (1974) *Lancashire in Decline*, Columbus: Ohio State University Press.

Saul, S. B. (1968) "The Engineering Industry," in D. H. Aldcroft (ed.) *The Development of British Industry and Foreign Competition 1875–1914*, London: Allen & Unwin, 186–237.

Saviotti, P. P. and Metcalfe, J. S. (1991) "Present Development and Trends in Evolutionary Economics," in P. P. Saviotti and J. S. Metcalfe (eds) *Evolutionary Theories of Economic and Technological Change: Present Status and Future Prospects*, Chur: Harwood Academic Publishers, 1–30.

Saxenian, A. (1990) "Regional Networks and the Resurgence of Silicon Valley," *California Management Review* 33: 89–112.

—— (1991) "The Origins and Dynamics of Production Networks in Silicon Valley," *Research Policy* 20: 423–437.

Saxonhouse, G. R. and Wright, G. (1984) "New Evidence on the Stubborn English Mule and the Cotton Industry, 1878–1920," *Economic History Review* 37: 507–519.

—— (1987) "Stubborn Mules and Vertical Integration: the Disappearing Constraint," *Economic History Review* 40: 87–94.

Schumpeter, J. A. (1934) *The Theory of Economic Development*, Cambridge, Mass.: Harvard University Press.

—— (1950) *Capitalism, Socialism, and Democracy*, 2nd edn, New York: Harper and Brothers.

Scott, B. R. (1973) "The Industrial State: Old Myths and New Realities," *Harvard Business Review* 51: 133–148.

Sculley, J. with Byrne, J. A. (1987) *Odyssey: Pepsi to Apple . . . the Journey of a Marketing Impresario*, New York: Harper and Row.

Seltzer, L. E. (1928) *A Financial History of the American Automobile Industry*, Boston, Mass.: Houghton-Mifflin.

Shackle, G. L. S. (1967) *The Years of High Theory*, Cambridge: Cambridge University Press.

Shidle, N. G. (1927) "Trend Toward More Car Models Helping Outside Suppliers," *Automotive Industries*, July 30.

Silver, M. (1984) *Enterprise and the Scope of the Firm*, London: Martin Robertson.

Silverberg, G., Dosi, G. and Orsenigo, L. (1988) "Innovation, Diversity and Diffusion: a Self-organisation Model" *Economic Journal* 98: 1032–1054.

Sloan, A. P. (1941) *Adventures of a White-Collar Man*, New York: Doubleday, Doran.

—— (1965) *My Years with General Motors*, New York: McFadden-Bartel.

Smith, A. (1976) *The Wealth of Nations*, Glasgow edition, Oxford: Clarendon Press.

Smitka, M. J. (1991) *Competitive Ties: Subcontracting in the Japanese Automotive Industry*, New York: Columbia University Press.

Spence, A. M. (1981) "The Learning Curve and Competition," *Bell Journal of Economics* 12: 49–70.

Sraffa, P. (1926) "The Laws of Returns Under Competitive Conditions," *Economic Journal* 36: 536.

Sterling, C. H. (1968) "WTMJ-FM: A Case Study in the Development of Broadcasting," *Journal of Broadcasting* 12, 4: 341–352, reprinted in L. W. Lichty and M. C. Topping (eds) *American Broadcasting: A Source Book on the History of Radio and Television*, New York: Hastings House.

Stigler, G. J. (1951) "The Division of Labor is Limited by the Extent of the Market," *Journal of Political Economy* 59, 3: 185–193.

Stiglitz, J. E. (1987) "Learning to Learn, Localized Learning and Technological

Progress," in P. Dasgupta and P. Stoneman (eds) *Economic Policy and Technological Performance*, Cambridge: Cambridge University Press, 125–153.

Stillman, K. W. (1927) "Hand-to-Mouth Buying: What Has It Done – and What Will It Do?" *Automotive Industries*, July 2, 1–4.

Sugden, R. (1986) *The Economics of Rights, Cooperation, and Welfare*, Oxford: Basil Blackwell.

Supple, B. (1991) "Scale and Scope: Alfred Chandler and the Dynamics of Industrial Capitalism," *Economic History Review* 44: 500–514.

Tang, M.-J. (1988) "An Economic Perspective on Escalating Commitment," *Strategic Management Journal* 9 (supplement): 79–92.

Teece, D. J. (1976) *Vertical Integration and Vertical Divestiture in the U.S. Oil Industry: Analysis and Policy Implications*, Stanford: Stanford University Institute for Energy Studies.

—— (1980) "Economies of Scope and the Scope of the Enterprise," *Journal of Economic Behavior and Organization* 1, 3: 223–247.

—— (1982) "Towards an Economic Theory of the Multiproduct Firm," *Journal of Economic Behavior and Organization* 3: 39–63.

—— (1986a) "Firm Boundaries, Technological Innovation, and Strategic Management," in L. G. Thomas (ed.) *The Economics of Strategic Planning,* Lexington, Mass.: D. C. Heath, 187–199.

—— (1986b) "Profiting from Technological Innovation: Implications for Integration, Collaboration, Licensing, and Public Policy," *Research Policy* 15: 285–305.

Teece, D. J., Rumelt, R. P., Dosi, G. and Winter, S. G. (1994) "Understanding Corporate Coherence: Theory and Evidence," *Journal of Economic Behavior and Organization* 23, 1: 1–30.

Thomas, R. P. (1973) "Style Change and the Automobile Industry During the Roaring Twenties," in L. P. Cain and P. J. Uselding (eds) *Business Enterprise and Economic Change*, Kent: Kent State University Press.

—— (1977) *An Analysis of the Pattern of Growth of the Automobile Industry, 1895–1929*, New York: Arno Press.

Thompson, G. V. (1954) "Intercompany Technical Standardization in the Early American Automobile Industry," *Journal of Economic History* 14, 1: 1–20.

Tushman, M. L. and Romanelli, E. (1985) "Organizational Evolution: A Metamorphosis Model of Convergence and Reorientation," in L. L. Cummings and B. M. Staw (eds) *Research in Organizational Behavior* 7: 171–222.

Tushman, M. L. and Anderson, P. (1986) "Technological Discontinuities and Organizational Environments," *Administrative Science Quarterly* 31: 439–465.

Tyson, R. E. (1968) "The Cotton Industry," in D. H. Aldcroft (ed.) *The Development of British Industry and Foreign Competition 1875–1914*, London: Allen & Unwin: 100–127.

Veblen, T. (1915) *Imperial Germany and the Industrial Revolution*, New York: Macmillan.

von Hippel, E. (1976) "The Dominant Role of Users in the Scientific Instrument Innovation Process," *Research Policy* 5: 212–239.

—— (1987) "Cooperation Between Rivals: Informal Know-how Trading," *Research Policy* 16: 291–302, reprinted in B. Carlsson (ed.) *Industrial Dynamics: Technological, Organizational, and Structural Changes in Industries and Firms*, Dordrecht: Kluwer Academic Publishers, 1989.

Wallerstein, E., as told to W. Botsford (1976) "Creating the LP Record," *High Fidelity Magazine*, April.

Waterson, M. (1984) *Economic Theory of the Industry*, Cambridge: Cambridge University Press.

Webb, S. B. (1980) "Tariffs, Cartels, Technology and Growth in the German Steel Industry, 1879 to 1914," *Journal of Economic History* 40: 309–329.

Weber, M. (1948) "Bureaucracy," in H. H. Gerth and C. W. Mills (eds) *From Max Weber: Essays in Sociology*, London: Routledge and Kegan Paul: 196–244.

———— (1971) "Legitimate Authority and Bureaucracy," in D. S. Pugh (ed.) *Organization Theory: Selected Readings*, London: Penguin: 15–27.

Whale, P. B. (1930) *Joint Stock Banking in Germany*, London.

Wiener, M. J. (1981) *English Culture and the Decline of the Industrial Spirit, 1850–1980*, Cambridge: Cambridge University Press.

Williams, G. and Moore, R. (1985). "The Apple Story. Part 2: More History and the Apple III," *Byte*, January: 167–180.

Williams, K., Haslam, C. and Williams, J., with Adcroft, A. and Johal, S. (1993) "The Myth of the Line: Ford's Producton of the Model T at Highland Park, 1909–16," *Business History*, 35, 3: 66–87.

Williamson, O. E. (1975) *Markets and Hierarchies: Analysis and Antitrust Implications*, New York: The Free Press.

———— (1985) *The Economic Institutions of Capitalism*, New York: The Free Press.

Winter, S. G. (1988) "On Coase, Competence, and the Corporation," *Journal of Law, Economics, and Organization* 4, 1: 163–180.

Womack, J. P., Jones, D. T. and Roos, D. (1990) *The Machine that Changed the World*, New York: Rawson Associates.

Young. A. A. (1928) "Increasing Returns and Economic Progress," *Economic Journal* 38: 523–542.

Zachary, G. P. and Yoder, S. K. (1993) "Order from Chaos: Computer Industry Divides into Camps of Winners and Losers," *The Wall Street Journal*, January 27.

INDEX

Heldt, P. M. 156
Helper, Susan 127–128
Hewlett-Packard 94, 115
Hill, Frank Ernest 47, 50, 51, 52–53, 54, 55, 64, 156
Hirshleifer, Jack 155
hold up 18, 28–29, 35–36, 39–40, 42, 65–66, 155
Holmstrom, Bengt 7
Homebrew Computer Club 88
Hong Kong 93
Houndsfield, Godfrey 117
Hounshell, David 51, 52, 53, 54, 56, 64
Hudson Motor Car Company 49, 63; Hudson Essex 63
Hudson, Pat 101
Hughes, Thomas P. 75, 113, 138, 153
Hurley, Neil P. 49
Hyatt Roller Bearing 57, 155
Hyundai 92

IBM 5, 90–96, 114–115, 135, 159; AS400 minicomputer 115; clones 91–94; Corporate Management Committee 90–91; Micro Channel Architecture 93; RT PC 159; personal computer 91–94, 98; PC AT 92, 159; PC Jr. 159; PC portable 159; PC Convertible 159; PC XT 159; PowerPC 99; PS/2 93; RS6000 workstation 115; System 370 115
Imai, Ken-ichi 162
IMSAI (computer manufacturer) 88
incomplete contracts 28–29, 37
industrial districts 123–127, 132, 136–137; see also networks
industrial policy 2, 6, 120, 123, 141–142, 150
industrial revolution 101
Industry Standard Architecture (ISA) 93
inertia 5, 6, 101–119, 153
Inglis, Andrew F. 78, 158
inimitability 13
innovation 19, 30, 38–41, 54–55, 56, 57, 60, 65-67, 71, 98, 103–109, 111, 116–121, 124, 131–134, 136–142, 150, 156–157, 161, 163; autonomous 5, 22–23, 37, 69, 75–76, 81, 98, 132, 135, 139, 151, 153; competence-destroying 106, 108, 116; competence-enhancing 106, 108,

116; differentiating 37; integrating 37; organizational 62, 66, 131; process 51, 58, 63, 160; product 51, 58, 63, 64, 76, 157, 160; radical 135, 160; systemic 3, 5, 22–23, 43, 53, 55, 68–69, 75–76, 81–82, 132–133, 135, 140, 146, 150, 151, 153
institutions: endogenous 103–104, 160; exogenous 103–104, 114
integrated circuits 15: DEC Alpha 99; DRAM 136; Intel: 8080 87–88, 91, 159; Intel 8088 91, 98, 159; Intel 80286 92; Intel 80386 93; Intel 80486 93; Intel Pentium 93; Motorola 6800 88; MOS technology 6502 88, 159; PowerPC 99; RISC chips 99; Sun SPARC 99
Intel 92, 98, 99, 160, 162 (see also integrated circuits)
Italy 92, 121; "Third Italy" 120–121, 125–126, 132, 136–137, 139, 142, 150, 161
Itami, Hiroyuki 162

Jaffé, William 8
Japan 2, 73, 92–93, 102, 114–116, 120, 122, 127–130, 132, 134, 136, 139–142, 152, 160–163
Jeffery (car company) 48
Jensen, Michael C. 28, 163
Jevons, William Stanley 8
Jobs, Steven 89, 95–96
John R. Keim Mills 53–54
Jones, Daniel T. 116, 129, 162
Jones, Robert 126
just-in-time purchasing 62, 130, 140, 156; see also hand-to-mouth buying

Katz, Harold 47, 48, 59, 60, 64, 65
Kay, Alan 96
Kay, Andrew 90
Kay, John 153
Kaypro computer 89–90, 91
keiretsu 134, 152
Kelly, Dawn 106
Kennedy, E. D. 60
Kennedy, T. R., Jr. 80, 158
Kenney, Martin 122, 124, 128, 140–141, 161–162
Killing, Peter J. 154
Kindleberger, Charles P. 155
Kirzner, Israel M. 151

rent-seeking behavior 142
Reo (car company) 57
resources 14, 131, 152
Rhenman, Eric A. 142
Richardson, George B. 2, 14–15, 40,
    151–152
Richardson, Harry W. 102
Richardson, James 130
Righi, Ezio 125
Rizzo, Mario J. 153
Roberts, Ed 87–88, 89
Robertson, Paul L. 11, 16, 18, 37, 66,
    117–118, 127, 163
Robinson, E. A. G. 15, 99
Robinson, Joan 152
Roe, Mark J. 152
Rolls Royce 161
Romanelli, Elaine 106
Roos, Daniel 116, 129, 162
Rosenberg, Nathan 24, 55, 75, 153,
    155, 158
Route 128 (Massachusetts) 99, 126–127
routines 1, 3, 5, 16–17, 22–23, 29, 35,
    38, 41, 104–105, 108, 112, 119, 143,
    151, 154, 160
Rubinstein, Artur 83
Rumelt, Richard P. 105, 152

S-100 bus (microcomputer
    architecture) 88, 90
Sabel, Charles F. 120–123, 127, 142,
    161–162
Sahal, Devendra 106
Sandberg, Lars 161
Saul, S. B. 116
Saviotti, P. Paolo 155
Saxenian, AnnaLee 127, 141, 162
Saxonhouse, Gary 116, 161
scale economies: see economies of scale
Schendel, Dan 76, 160
Schnberg, Arnold 83
Schumpeter, Joseph A. 2, 3, 4, 38,
    146–147, 150–151, 153
Scott 79
Scott, Bruce R. 105
Sculley, John 96, 159
Selden patent 49
Seltzer, Lawrence E. 49, 55, 60, 62, 63
Shackle, G. L. S. 152
Shidle, Norman G. 60
shipbuilding industry 49, 101, 117, 124
Siemens-Martin steel process 119

Silicon Valley 98–99, 122, 126–127,
    149, 162
Silver, Morris 2, 4, 32, 38-40, 47, 53, 58,
    134, 154, 157
Silverberg, Gerald 107
Sloan, Alfred P. 57, 59, 63, 155
Smith, Adam 2, 8, 14, 20–22, 25, 30,
    33, 37, 68, 132–133, 138, 153, 155
Smitka, Michael J. 116, 129–130
Society of Automotive Engineers 49, 99
Solow, Robert M. 160
Sorensen, Charles 53
Spence, A. Michael 107
Sraffa, Piero 152
Steedman, Ian 26
Stereo Review 86
stereo systems 5, 6, 77-87, 99
Sterling, Christopher H. 85
Stigler, George 20–21, 24–25, 29, 33,
    43, 47
Stiglitz, Joseph 106, 160
Stillman, K. W. 156
Storrow, James J. 57
strategy 17–19, 67, 162; proprietary 75,
    84, 88; non-proprietary 99, 160;
    resource-based 153
Studebaker 48, 49, 59, 155
Sugden, Robert 29
Sun Microsystems 99, 115, 159–160
Supple, Barry 123
Sweden 135
Swift, Gustavus 4
Switzerland 118

tacit knowledge 1, 4, 7, 16, 23, 34, 40,
    41, 43, 107, 125
Taiwan 92–92
Taligent 99
Tandy Corporation 89, 90, 91
Tang, Ming-je 108
taper integration 131
tariffs 103, 109, 160
Taylor, Frederick W. 115
technical education 103–104, 109, 118
Technicare 117
technology transfer 34
technological convergence 71, 97, 158
Teece, David J. 2, 14, 16, 36–37, 39–40,
    57, 58, 105, 117, 133, 152–153, 155
Texas Instruments 94
Thailand 93
Thomas (car company) 48

Thomas, Robert Paul 47, 48, 50, 51, 52,
56, 58, 63, 65
Thompson, George V. 49
Thorn Electrical Industries, Ltd. 117
tire manufacture 76
Tirole, Jean 7
Toscanini, Arturo 83
Toshiba 129, 162
Toyoda, Eiji 156
Toyota Motor Corporation 156
transaction costs, dynamic: see dynamic
transaction costs
Tushman, Michael L. 106, 160
Tyson, R. E. 116

uncertainty 36, 75, 98, 121, 140,
148–149, 153; parametric 18, 136,
154, 162; structural 18, 136, 154, 162;
strategic 136
Uniroyal 116
United States 4, 47–48, 77. 79, 81, 84–
85, 92–93, 101–102, 113, 116, 119,
120, 122, 127–130, 132, 136, 140,
144, 158, 160–161
Unix operating system 99, 159
upgradability 72, 99

Veblen, Thorstein 112
venture capital 91, 126–127
Vepsalainen, Ari 16
Victor (division of RCA) 78, 82
VisiCalc 89
Visscher, Michael 13
Volvo A. B. 135
von Hippel, Eric 31, 134

Wacker Chemie
Wall Street Journal, The 159
Wallerstein, Edward 78, 82–84, 158
Walrasian system 8

"war of the speeds" 80, 84
Waterson, Michael 157
Webb, Steven B. 119
Weber, Max 145
Welch, Walter L. 78–84, 158
Western Electric 158; see also Bell
Telephone Laboratories
Weston-Mott 57
Whale, P. Barrett 119
Wiener, M. J. 102
Wilkinson Sword 104
Williams, Greg 96
Williams, Karel 52
Williamson, Oliver E. 1, 2, 12, 28, 30.
38, 42, 67, 71, 131, 151–152, 156,
162
Willig, Robert D. 15
Willys, John N. 48
Willys-Overland 49
Winter, Sidney G. 1, 2, 14, 16, 75, 105,
131, 151
Winton (car company) 47, 48, 51
Womack, James P. 116, 129, 162
Woodward, Susan 27, 154
WordStar 89
Wozniak, Stephen 89, 95–96, 98
Wright, Gavin 102, 116, 161
Wrigley, Leonard 105
WTMJ-FM 85

Xerox Corporation 94, 146

Yoder, Stephen Kreider 141
Young, Allyn A. 20, 29, 33, 47

Zachary, G. Pascal 141
Zeitlin, Jonathan 120–121, 161
Zenith Data Systems 92, 159
Zeos International Ltd. 93